The Black O

Racism and Redemption

in an American

Corporate

Empire

The Black O

STEVE

WATKINS

The University of Georgia Press

Athens and London

Published by the University of Georgia Press
Athens, Georgia 30602
Designed by Erin Kirk New
Set in 10 on 14 Trump Mediaeval by G & S Typesetters
Printed and bound by Maple-Vail Book Manufacturing Group
The paper in this book meets the guidelines for permanence and
durability of the Committee on Production Guidelines for Book
Longevity of the Council on Library Resources.
Printed in the United States of America

01 00 99 98 97 C 5 4 3 2 1

Library of Congress Cataloging in Publication Data
    Watkins, Steve.
    The black O : racism and redemption in an American corporate
empire / Steve Watkins.
        p. cm.
    Includes bibliographical references (p.   ) and index.
    ISBN 0-8203-1916-3 (alk. paper)
    1. Shoney's Inc.—Personnel management.   2. Discrimination in
restaurants—United States—Case studies.   3. Discrimination in
employment—United States—Case studies.   4. Race discrimination—
United States—Case studies.   5. Afro-Americans—Employment—
United States—Case studies.   I. Title.
HD8081.A65W38   1997
338.7′616479573—dc21   97-11783

British Library Cataloging in Publication Data available

for Laurie

66 One wonders whether

the majority still believes

that race discrimination—

or, more accurately,

race discrimination against

non-whites—is a problem

in our society, or even

remembers that it was. 99

U.S. SUPREME COURT JUSTICE

HARRY BLACKMUN

CONTENTS

ACKNOWLEDGMENTS

The research for this account of *Haynes v. Shoney's* began in May 1990 when I first visited attorney Tommy Warren's gray-walled office in Tallahassee, Florida. Since that time I have conducted more than a hundred interviews, studied thousands of pages of court documents and hearing transcripts, and supplemented those sources with dozens of newspaper and magazine articles, books, and government reports.

A great many people helped me write this book, but none more than my friend Leo Rigsby and my wife Laurie Watkins, who in their generosity have edited, supported, challenged, tolerated, and inspired. I offer my deepest thanks to them and to many others: Jerome Stern, Susan Ramer, Pete Ripley, Lynn Harvey, Steve Farmer, Clyde and Norie Watkins, Eleanor Wilson, John and Marilyn Bryant, Johanna Branch, Wayne Watkins, Dan and Mary Abel, Shah and Martha Mehrabi, Joe Straub and Joni Branch, Bucky McMahon, Mark Hinson, Drew Gallagher, Mike Fuhrman, Ellen Rigsby, Bob Gettlin, and my colleagues at Mary Washington College, especially Mary Rigsby, Taddesse Adera, Dick Hansen, and Susan Hanna. Thanks also to my daughters Maggie and Eva; they, too, have great heart.

The Black O

ONE

" Shit Rolls Downhill.
This Starts at the Top "

Ray Danner, the 266th richest man in America, chairman, CEO, and principal shareholder of the country's second-largest family restaurant chain, a diminutive man whom *Time* magazine once described as "a thin, brown-haired version of Mickey Rooney," held a cut of frozen flounder in the back of a quick-serve seafood restaurant in Murfreesboro, Tennessee, run by Ron Murphy, the only black manager out of dozens of Captain D's in the Nashville area. The fish was underweight, one and one-half ounces instead of two, and Danner wasn't happy.

Danner stuck the flounder in an Igloo cooler and finished his surprise inspection of Murphy's store. Then the man corporate officials once hailed as "our great leader" went back to his car, back to Nashville, back to the corporate headquarters of Shoney's, Inc., whose fifteen hundred restaurants in thirty states were cranking out more than a billion dollars worth of coffee shop, seafood, and fried chicken business by the end of the 1980s.

In a sworn statement given in 1989, several years after the incident, and again in a deposition taken under oath a few years after that, a company official named Jerry Garner testified about what he said happened next: "On Monday morning after this weekend inspection, approximately twelve or thirteen of the highest level supervisors in that area, including a group vice president, gathered for a meeting in the Central Office in Nashville. These Monday morning conferences were regular occurrences.

"At the meeting, Danner put the Igloo cooler on the conference table, reached into it and picked out the fish he had brought back from Ron Murphy's restaurant, which was thawed out by that time, and threw it against the wall where it stuck."

Garner, who was one of those present, said Danner then addressed the conferees.

"That," Danner is purported to have said, "is a prime example of black management in our company."

Everyone in service industry has a Ray Danner story, though it's often hard to tell which are real and which are apocryphal, products of a restaurant lore designed to keep nervous managers on edge, ever vigilant for fear that the "great leader" or one of his "mystery squealers" would slide into a Naugahyde booth and hang around just long enough to make life hell, the silverware spotless, the floors scrubbed, and the cigarette butts gone from the flower pots. That hard-nosed commitment to detail, and the pit-bull ferocity to see that everything was done right, for more than three decades they called "the Danner Way." Every Shoney's, Captain D's, and Lee's Famous Recipe Chicken employee was expected to know it inside and out when they took the floor at a Ray Danner shop.

In the past it spawned tales like the one the *New York Times* wrote about then-Shoney's president Gary Spoleta rolling up his sleeves to help wait tables when a Kansas City restaurant was suddenly flooded with hungry visitors from a nearby convention center. Hands on, that was the Danner Way. And there's the story a Nashville friend of Danner's, Bobby Garrison, tells about the time he and Danner dropped into a Shoney's in Donaldson, Tennessee, for lunch. Danner, says Garrison, suddenly became upset and called the manager over: "He asked the manager to look around

and tell him ten things that were wrong in the restaurant. The
manager said he noticed cobwebs in the light fixtures, cigarette
butts in the floral arrangements, dirty ketchup bottles, and some
other things. Danner told the manager to rope off the restaurant
and close it until everything was clean, and tell any customer stop-
ping by that the restaurant was not fit to eat in, and why."

The most famous Danner story, first told twenty years ago in a
short article in *Business Week* and repeated often since, was supposedly witnessed by a former Shoney's supplier: "The scene
would have warmed the heart of Captain Bligh. An angry Ray
Danner, forty-six-year-old president of Nashville-based Shoney
Big Boy Enterprises, stormed into the kitchen of one of his Shoney's Big Boy hamburger restaurants. 'There's a woman out there
who says her soup is cold,' he snapped at the cook. 'No, no,' the
frightened cook argued, 'it's hot enough'—and he waved a restraining hand at the executive. With a quick move, Danner
grabbed [the cook's] hand and plunged it into the soup kettle.
'Now how damn hot is the soup?' he shouted. 'Not even hot
enough to burn.'"

For years Wall Street analysts called Shoney's the best-managed
restaurant company in the business, and for proof pointed to the
fact that the corporation reported increases in sales, net income,
and earnings per share every single quarter for the first thirty years
it was in operation. Danner reaped a few profits himself along the
way, too, claiming a net worth of $310 million in 1985, good
enough for a spot on *Forbes*'s list of the nation's four hundred
wealthiest. And when he cashed in on more than $140 million in
stock benefits as part of a 1988 corporate recapitalization, he further secured his position among the very rich.

The son of an immigrant German paperhanger in Depression-
era Louisville, a man who never went to college and who once aspired to be a jazz saxophone player, Danner was the classic American success story, recognized in 1985 by the New York-based
Horatio Alger Association, which inducted him that year into the
company of other rags-to-riches phenomena like Bob Hope, Ed
McMahon, Mary Kay Ash, and Ronald Reagan.

And there were other awards as well during the mid-1980s, including the *Wall Street Transcript*'s Gold Award for best restaurant CEO in the country. To get that one Danner had to beat out

the chief executives of McDonald's and Wendy's, but with Shoney's unbroken string of record profits, Wall Street analysts fell all
over themselves with compliments. "I don't know who does what
at Shoney's," one told the *Transcript* in 1985, "but you can't do
what they've done over a long period of time without some awfully capable people. The restaurant business is a matter of exe-
cution minute by minute, day by day, and they seem to have done
that a good many years." Said another, "He *is* the company. He's
dynamic, and a very forceful type person. He's tops at motivating
people. The people he has surrounding him are strong, very aggressive, hard working, and he is able to keep those people motivated
on a day to day basis." A Danner associate said one of the keys
was Danner's penchant for hiring college dropouts and promoting
them up from store-level positions to management, since he believed dropouts tended to be more success-oriented to compensate
for earlier failures. They work harder, the associate said, because
they're hungrier: "No MBAs around here."

In the long lineup of testimonials in that 1985 *Wall Street Transcript* article, however, stuck at the end of the long back-patting
parade there was a curious quote from an unidentified analyst,
though one that must have seemed harmless enough at the time.
"Actually I think he does a lot of things wrong," this analyst said.
"I think some of his personnel policies are not good."

Those comments have had a suggestive ring to them, a haunt-
ing echo since April 4, 1989, when a former college quarterback-
turned-lawyer named Tommy Warren and nine named plaintiffs,
all former Shoney's and Captain D's employees or job applicants,
served Ray Danner and Shoney's, Inc. with what the *National Law
Journal* said was the largest racial discrimination class-action suit
against a private employer in the history of civil rights law. The
plaintiffs in *Haynes et al. v. Shoney's, Inc.* sought more than half
a billion dollars in back pay and punitive damages, plus an aggressive, court-ordered affirmative action plan to counteract what
witnesses swore in deposition after deposition was years of racist
company policy based on Danner's belief that "too many blacks"
weren't good for business.

The putative class, which Warren and his eventual cocounsel,
civil rights attorney Barry Goldstein, fought to have certified by

the conservative federal judge assigned to the case, included tens of thousands of workers, former workers, and frustrated job applicants, many of whom claimed they were denied opportunities for even the lowest-paying jobs because they were black. It also included others, mostly low-level white managers, who testified that they were fired because they wouldn't follow company orders to reduce the number of blacks or, in what they said was Shoney's vernacular, "lighten up" their stores. Many said they were instructed to carry out a corporate strategy not found in any Shoney's procedure manuals: color-coding minority job applications by blackening in the "O" in Shoney's, making sure they were passed over for jobs.

Suddenly a whole new set of Ray Danner stories started making the rounds, allegations made under oath and entered into the court record that Danner would spend the next several years denying, like the frozen fish incident, and Danner's supposed threats to run over blacks loitering in Shoney's parking lots, and the charge, made by a former Shoney's CEO, that Danner once privately discussed putting up money to match contributions senior executives might be willing to make to the Ku Klux Klan.

One restaurant manager testified that when he complained about the discriminatory practices to a Shoney's regional vice president, the company official just laughed. "Shit runs downhill," the manager said he was told. "This starts at the top." And a long-time vice president testified that everyone in the corporation knew what this official said were Ray Danner's laws: "Blacks were not qualified to run a store. Blacks were not qualified to run a kitchen of a store. Blacks should not be employed in any position where they would be seen by customers."

Bringing an end to what the plaintiffs dubbed "the Danner Way" would prove to be a brutal undertaking, claiming five years of Tommy Warren's life, plunging him into a vicious and protracted litigation that grew "bloodier and bloodier and bloodier" in the words of one Shoney's executive, and raising a number of deeply troubling questions along the way. How was it possible that allegations of deliberate corporate racism were still being made decades after passage of the Civil Rights Act of 1964? And where had the federal Equal Employment Opportunity Commission been? Hundreds of complaints were filed against Shoney's and its various divisions over the years, but according to records provided by the company itself, the agency charged with enforcing employment discrimination laws did little besides negotiate small settlements in some cases.

And where was the civil rights leadership? The NAACP Legal Defense and Educational Fund supported the case, but the Southern Christian Leadership Conference provided Shoney's with a public relations boost shortly after the suit was filed when it signed a nonbinding "covenant" with the corporation targeting business for minority-owned companies, a covenant that the plaintiffs' attorneys said Shoney's avoided fulfilling in key areas until that failure was exposed in the litigation.

The case against Ray Danner and Shoney's cuts to the heart of the nation's civil rights legacy through the 1980s and now into the 1990s, with charges of the kinds of systemic and specific prejudice that many say no longer exists in America, but that others believe continues to divide the country along race and class lines. The case is important for another reason as well, as part of the debate in the legal community going on even now after passage of the Civil Rights Act of 1991, a debate that tends to focus on the costs of enforcement rather than on the continuing reasons behind the need for employment discrimination laws.

The tone of that legal debate has been lively, academic, and divorced from the realities of the workplace. Certainly there is nothing academic or abstract about workers like Josephine Haynes, Denise Riley, Buddy Bonsall, Lester Thomas, Leonard Charles Williams, Billie and Henry Elliott, and the thousands of others who said they lost jobs, were denied jobs, or were cut out of opportunities at Shoney's, a company, they charged, where racist attitudes and discriminatory policies were woven into the fabric of the corporate culture.

This is their story.

TWO

66 Billie, You Got to See What's Happening. You Got to See What's Happening 99

Tommy Warren wasn't looking for work. The forty-year-old lawyer was renting a room for his part-time solo practice in the back of a rambling, two-story house that held the offices of another firm, Patterson and Traynham. His landlords were old friends of Warren in the Florida capital of Tallahassee, a city of a hundred thousand that in May 1988 still clung to its small-town roots despite the seasonal tide of legislators and lobbyists, and the forty thousand college students at two local universities, predominantly white Florida State and historically black Florida A&M. A pair of giant matriarch oaks, staples of the north Florida landscape, shaded the Patterson and Traynham offices overlooking traffic heading north of town on the recently widened Thomasville Road, which shot up into Georgia and was lined with its own spreading live oaks. Before the widening, other trees had formed a canopy out over the road with their gray moss and their arching branches, but now the sun cut cleanly through.

The clients Warren had scheduled that afternoon, May 2, 1988, were a referral from an attorney, Frank Baker, whom Warren had argued against on a couple of employment discrimination cases in rural, landlocked Jackson County, an hour west of Tallahassee in the Florida Panhandle, an area once considered the heart of cotton country but now better known for its peanut production, limestone caverns, and state-of-the-art maximum security federal prison. The prospective clients, a white couple named Billie and Henry Elliott, had just been fired from their jobs as managers of a Captain D's quick-serve seafood restaurant in the county seat of Marianna, and according to Baker, they had "a pretty amazing story" to tell. The only problem was they needed a civil rights lawyer to tell it to, and Baker didn't know any attorneys in Marianna, or Jackson County, or indeed in that whole piece of the Panhandle, who practiced civil rights law.

So Warren, an athletically handsome man with chiseled features, still as lean and hard as he'd been eighteen years earlier when he had quarterbacked the Florida State Seminoles football team, agreed, if somewhat reluctantly, to meet with the Elliotts. After all, he had just quit a demanding partnership six months earlier to spend more time at home raising his two children, Gabe, then four, and Aileen, eighteen months, as part of an agreement with his wife, who had left her own law partnership to have the children but was ready to return to her career handling utilities cases before the Florida Public Service Commission. Warren had a few things still on his plate—a couple of small discrimination cases, a copyright infringement action—but he liked the part-time work just fine.

He had to admit, though, that he'd been struck, intrigued, by what the Elliotts had already told him over the phone, and what they would later repeat for the court record in sworn statements and depositions: that the reason they'd been fired was for refusing to carry out company orders to reduce the number of African Americans working at their Captain D's and because Henry Elliott had promoted an African American to assistant store manager and then wouldn't follow orders to remove him from the position. Warren, who is white, had heard a lot of discrimination claims since he'd been practicing law—he dealt with those claims literally every day—and he'd seen enough to convince him that racial

bias still permeated the workplace, if only in more subtle forms,
even in 1988, twenty-four years after passage of the landmark
Civil Rights Act of 1964. The Elliotts' charges, however, were of
another order of magnitude.

"The biggest thing that struck me at the time was how blatant
and egregious the actions were—that white managers were retaliated against," Warren said later. "*That* you don't hear all the time.
Usually the people making complaints are minorities who subjec-
tively view themselves as having been victimized, and the evidence is usually circumstantial: 'I got fired and I think it's because
of my race.' Those cases become statistical ones, primarily. The
Elliotts, though, were there as managers. They saw it all. And they
were telling me they got fired themselves because they wouldn't
go along."

Of course Warren had worked on more than his share of race
discrimination cases over the years, most of them in his now-
defunct law partnership with attorney Kent Spriggs, a civil rights
activist since the early days of the movement who had gone on to
build a reputation as one of the top employment discrimination
lawyers in the country. He was also known as one of the most intense and demanding attorneys around, and had gone through a
number of partners and associates over the years; Warren's own
enduring "marriage" to Spriggs was considered a record of note in
the local legal community. The two had gotten along well enough
since the older lawyer gave the younger one a chance to cut his
legal teeth as a law clerk ten years before in a large and complicated class action against the Monsanto Corporation, which ran
an Astroturf manufacturing facility in Pensacola, at the western-
most tip of Florida.

By his own account Warren had gone on to do good work with
Spriggs in dozens of class actions and individual discrimination
claims, first as a clerk, then as an associate, and for the past six
years as partner. Practicing civil rights law was why Warren had
gotten into the profession in the first place, and Spriggs's office had
been the place to do it. But he'd been through a lot in those years
since coming off the bench during a football game back in 1970
and making a permanent name for himself around the state as
"Touchdown Tommy Warren." He was ready for a break.

What he couldn't have known that May afternoon in 1988,

waiting for the Elliotts to make the hour drive over from Marianna through the rolling Panhandle hills to Tallahassee, was that it would be another four and a half years before he got that break. He couldn't have known that the Elliotts' tale would plunge him into a case that would touch the lives of thousands of people and at times threaten to end his legal career, a career that had been derailed once before, only to be revived with the help of an intense lobbying effort by Warren's friends in the legal community. Maybe, one of those friends would say later, it had been resurrected for this.

The Elliotts were an odd couple, Billie small and talky, thirty-six years old, four times married, with two daughters and an infant grandson already, dyed-blonde pretty, Alabama twang rising in blunt anger; Henry the quiet one, eleven years younger, big, maybe six-two, with round, Asian features, black hair, thin black moustache, and an improbable Panhandle cowboy accent of his own. Her family was originally from Dothan, Alabama, but she'd grown up in Jackson County; he was a military brat—father career Air Force, mother Japanese—whose family had moved all over the world when he was little but who had lived in Panama City, the Gulf Coast vacation town that locals called the Redneck Riviera, since he was in seventh grade.

They had married in 1986, several months after Henry moved to Marianna to help with the rudderless Captain D's there, which had gone through an average of two managers a year since opening in 1982. Billie's third marriage had ended earlier in the spring of 1986 when her then-husband Kirby Lytle left suddenly and went to Wyoming. Kirby himself had briefly managed the Marianna D's, but after he took off Billie was left struggling alone to make ends meet and raise her two daughters on $280 a week from her dining-room supervisor's job there.

"I admit it," she said later. "I robbed the cradle with Henry." But he was kind to her in the crash of her life after Kirby left, she said, and he was sweet with the girls, and he was a hard worker who had been in fast-food restaurants since his high school days in Panama City at a hot dog place called Wiener World. In fact, the restaurant business was about all Henry knew. From Wiener World he'd taken a job after high school as a cook at a Captain D's in Panama City and worked his way up from there to store manager, where he regularly put in sixty-hour weeks. By all accounts Henry never stopped working those long hours throughout his eight years with the franchise company, right up to the end.

In a 1989 deposition, he indicated how heavy the workload was when he ran through a list of the jobs that had to be taken care of every morning before the store's 10:30 opening: "Cutting fish, making hushpuppy mixes, cole slaw, breading shrimp, peeling shrimp for the next day, bagging and boiling shrimp, doing up tartar sauce, doing up cocktail sauce, sweet and sour; making tossed salads, making sure the flounder is weighed out to proper weight, making up green beans, making up white beans, checking bread, making sure it wasn't stale or left over—if it was, you throw it out; make sure there was enough food in the store to get by until you had another truck come in as far as produce; check the dining room overall, check the sign change, check the building. In general, make sure it was clean and ready to go." After that, Henry would spend hours standing over the fryers, "dropping fish" and filling orders for Billie and the dining room workers up front in their navy slacks, white blouses, striped company vests, and Captain D's baseball caps, which everyone in the restaurant preferred to the peaked paper crowns they had worn in the past. And of course everyone wore rubber-sole shoes whether they worked the front of the house or the kitchen because no matter how well they cleaned, walking the slick floors in their seafood restaurant was always a treacherous business.

For the first hour that the Elliotts met with Tommy Warren they sat together; Billie did most of the talking while Henry kept his own counsel and Warren took notes on a yellow pad. After that, Warren asked first one then the other to step out of the room so he could interview them separately to see if the details matched up. Billie would later remember the entire first meeting lasting a single hour, but Warren said it took three hours that day for the Elliotts to lay out their stories—which did indeed match, he said—and then for him to write it up for them to swear to and sign: the first in a stream of sworn statements, charges, and depositions

through which they would repeat that story again and again over
the next four years.

There had always been a constant, low-grade pressure to hire
more whites, both told Warren, and later repeated in their depositions, but the harassment had gotten harsher and more systematic
since the previous November, in 1987, when the store's advertising budget was cut to zero. They said they were told the move was
necessary to save money, but sales subsequently dropped off dramatically, although Henry Elliott assured Warren that the Marianna store was still the most profitable of the four operated by
Robertson Investment Company, and had been since he'd come up
from Panama City, where the other three stores in the franchise
group were located.

The Elliotts would testify in their depositions that the company's area supervisors, another work-team couple named Paul
and Jan Suggs, blamed the drop in sales on too many blacks in the
store and said that Marianna whites didn't want to eat at such a
place. The Suggses, whom Henry had worked for as a high school
kid at the Wiener World, and who Billie said at one time treated
him as if he were their adopted son, said there had been complaints, the Elliotts claimed. (The Suggses, who in affidavits formally denied ever giving discriminatory orders, declined to discuss any of the charges against them for this account.)

On the day of that first meeting, and a year later in depositions,
Warren asked the Elliotts if they had ever actually fired any black
workers or refused to hire them because of their race. Billie said
that she hadn't; she said it had been like a family at their Captain D's, that the counter workers even took up a collection once
to buy her a microwave for Christmas. Henry, though, said that
yes, there had been one occasion when Paul Suggs ordered him
directly to fire a black cook named Jerome Robinson. "He said that
he didn't want no nigger faggot back there in the kitchen and that
he was supposed to have been fired already," Henry said in his
deposition.

Warren later found another witness, a former black counter
worker named Julia Hunter, who in her own deposition contra-
dicted Billie and said that Billie had in fact turned down a qualified
black applicant once to hire a white girl who ended up only work-

ing a few days before she quit. Hunter said Billie, who had con-
fided that she was under pressure from the Suggses to hire more
whites, was upset about what she had done. "Billie put her head
down," Hunter testified. "She was almost about to cry."

All along, according to Billie, the orders from the Suggses and
from the franchise owner, a Panama City businessman named
Charlie Robertson, were to hire "attractive white girls" to run the
counter and serve the sit-down customers. "There would be a lot
of little statements made, such as 'The counter is getting too dark;
you need to have more white girls in here. We need more attractive, good-looking girls, like you,'" Billie said in her deposition. So
she culled through applications for whites who wanted to work.
Robertson, a tall, heavy man with short gray hair, urged her to put
her own daughters on the serving line, she said.

Another black witness, a former counter worker named Deborah Bell, later confirmed Billie's account. Bell said she had been
having difficulty with Jan Suggs whenever Suggs visited the store,
and so she went to Billie Elliott to find out why. "I asked her why
was Ms. Suggs harassing me and all," Bell recalled in her deposition. "[Billie] just broke down, and she started crying. She said,
'Deborah, they have been telling us for some time we have to get
rid of some of the blacks in here because we have too many blacks
employed.'

"And I told her, I said, 'Why, you are hiring who will work,'"
Bell said. "I said if they will come up here and see that you do hire
whites and they don't last for about a week, they will understand
that you are not being prejudiced against whites or you are not
prejudiced against blacks. You are just hiring who will work.'"
Bell testified that she was later forced to quit when her hours were
reduced from twenty-five or thirty a week down to as few as ten.
She said she never knew who was directly responsible, but she
blamed the Suggses.

In the months before the Elliotts were fired from the Marianna
store, Henry was working an impossible eighty to ninety hours a
week as they tried to find good help who met the Suggses' criteria
and who would stick around. It was a bad staffing situation anyway, they said in their depositions, exacerbated by the racial orders. As the Elliotts saw it, the reason most of their workers were

black, maybe 90 percent of the twenty-six or so they employed at any given time, was because a disproportionate number of the blacks around Marianna didn't have the skills or education to get better-paying jobs and because few whites were willing to apply for minimum-wage restaurant work. And the whites who did take the jobs didn't stay long.

Another former dining room supervisor, Kim Gilmore, when later contacted by Warren, characterized hiring at the Marianna Captain D's in much the same way: "Generally from my observations the black applicants were more in need of the positions," she said. "You know, most of my black applicants were ladies that had children, had families, and just really needed jobs. And they would come in, you know, ready to work, wanting to work any shift, it didn't matter, whatever I wanted to do with them I could do. Most of my white applicants were young girls in either high school or college or had other jobs that just needed some part-time work and could not work the hours that I would need them to work. Most of the white applicants had specifications: 'I can work five to nine or I can work on Monday, Wednesday, and Friday but I can't work on Tuesday and Thursday' and so forth. The blacks weren't that way. They would just work."

The Elliotts claimed that they told all that to the Suggses, making the argument that even if terminating black workers wasn't illegal it was still impractical, but the order stayed the same: hire more whites, get rid of the blacks.

The Suggses, meanwhile, were calling the Marianna Captain D's every day from Panama City for the "two-o'clocks," the gross receipts from each day's lunch sales. At the same time, the Elliotts said in their depositions, the Suggses regularly asked what Billie and Henry were doing to get more white workers. It quickly became apparent that they weren't doing enough, both testified, and they said that in January 1988, after they were caught in a surprise inspection by Charlie Robertson, Paul Suggs drove up from Panama City to confront them about it directly. According to Henry, what Suggs said was, "You know, Charlie drove up here and there was nothing but black people working yesterday, and he got mad as hell. He called me from Marianna and said that we was going to have a meeting." Out of that meeting with Charlie Robertson came an explicit directive from the Suggses, the Elliotts both said:

70 percent whites in the store, and no more than 30 percent
blacks.

Paul Suggs instructed Henry on how to get rid of the black workers to make room for more whites so he could achieve that 70:30
ratio, Henry claimed. Those instructions, he said in his deposition, were to force the blacks to quit rather than fire them out-
right: "Cut their pay on their paychecks with the hours and things,
to where they couldn't afford to live, to pay their bills with the
hours they were getting from Captain D's." Suggs repeated the instructions to Billie by the back door during that same visit, she
also testified, apparently oblivious to the presence of James Stephens, a black kitchen worker who was cleaning vent filters in the
galvanized sinks close by. Henry said Stephens asked him about it
in front of the rest of the kitchen workers: Barry Perry, James
Woodham, Troy Holmes, Randy McMillan, and Dennis Toombs.

"Henry," James Stephens purportedly asked, "am I—are you going to fire me because I am black?"

Henry said he assured them he wouldn't: "No," he said. "I am
not going to fire anyone just because they are black. I will probably
lose my job over it, but I am not going to fire anyone just because
they are black. As long as you do your job, and you do it right, you
will have a job. If you don't do your job right, you are not going to
have a job."

What Henry remembered was "shock and disbelief" among the
black workers, but he testified that he believed the threat from the
Suggses was real because he'd heard stories, when he managed one
of the Panama City D's, how Jan Suggs, newly appointed at the
time as area dining-room supervisor, had taken on the task of
"cleaning up" the restaurant on 15th Street. "The store up front
had gone all black," Henry said in his deposition. "And right after
that she had gone in and cleaned them all out. Whether they had
gotten fired or quit, or whatever, she made the comment that 'I am
glad that—I am going to have to go in there and clean them all
out,' or she made a comment to that effect, that she had gone in
and cleaned out all the blacks and hired whites back in."

At the time Henry was shuttling back and forth between the
Captain D's in the Panama City suburb of Parker, which he was

managing, and the one on 15th where he often went to pick up supplies. He testified that he witnessed the racial transformation firsthand: "From what I seen the counter was black, and the next thing you knew, it was white. She had gotten all the 'niggers' out of the 15th Street store."

Billie, too, said that she believed the orders were for real, and that another employee had tried to warn her about the discriminatory practices when she had first been hired back in 1985. The previous store manager and dining-room supervisor, Glen Mc-Clain and Kim Gilmore, both white, had been abruptly fired when Billie came on. After they left, Billie said, Gilmore's friend Donna Mongoven, who also worked at the Marianna D's, tried to convince Billie that the reason was because they had too many blacks in the store. Charlie Robertson and the Suggses, Mongoven purportedly said, expected Billie to do something about it. Mongoven, in her own deposition, confirmed Billie's account.

In her deposition, Billie said that she remembered Mongoven's warnings: "She was just telling me that they didn't like black people, that's what I was there for. They didn't want them in the store. That's why Kim was fired. Then why Glen left. She kept saying that's why Glen was fired. She said, 'Billie, you got to see what's happening. You got to see what's happening.' And I said, 'I don't believe you, Donna.'"

Shortly after that, Donna Mongoven was fired, too.

From November 1987 to March 1988, the Elliotts testified, the pressure mounted for them to get rid of their black workers and hire whites instead, and their relations with the Suggses grew steadily more tense. When Henry promoted a young black man, Lester Thomas, to assistant store manager, he said he was ordered to replace Lester with someone else. Henry protested that he couldn't, that there wasn't anyone else available. In his deposition he said the white assistant they had had before Lester, Billie's own nephew Mike Groover, wasn't reliable so they'd had to let him go. Henry also argued that he'd been working at least eighty hours a week himself for a couple of months to fill the management void. Lester, he said, had already been running the store on some nights without Henry, so he had earned the chance to learn the assistant manager's job. And Henry had to have *somebody*.

Things continued to slide downhill rapidly. First the Marianna Captain D's was hit by a surprise inspection in March and a much
more detailed inspection form than Henry had ever seen. They did
fine up front, in Billie's section of the store, but poorly in the
kitchen. Henry didn't worry about it initially because he said his
shopper's reports, anonymous evaluations of the store's quality
and service, were still above average in most categories. On the
heels of the inspection, though, the Suggses and Charlie Robertson summoned the Elliotts to a meeting away from the store at
the Marianna Waffle House where they delivered a handful of ul-
timatums: fix everything the inspection report listed as wrong
with the store, within three weeks; replace Lester Thomas; and get
rid of Barry Perry, their morning prep worker. Billie later testified
that she tried to bring up the business about getting rid of the
blacks—that it was illegal, that it wasn't right—but the Suggses
and Robertson refused to discuss it with her. Henry was too tired
to argue about the bad franchise report, but he did tell them that
he wouldn't fire Lester.

Barry Perry (a white man, ironically) for months had been improperly breading trays of shrimp despite repeated warnings and
instructions on how to do the job right. So Billie went out and recruited a former coworker, an older black woman named Madeline
Herring whom Billie knew from the years she had worked as a
waitress at the Union 76 Truck Stop and Diner out by the
interstate.

A couple of days after that, Billie charged, Paul Suggs walked
into the store, took one look at Madeline Herring, and pulled Billie
off by the pie case. "Well, she is black as the Ace of Spades, isn't
she?" Billie said he told her. "She don't have any teeth. How old is
that woman anyway?"

"I don't know how old she is, Paul, but she does a good job,"
Billie said she responded. "I worked with her a long time. She can
do the job. She can get the kitchen cleaned up and the work will
be done."

Less than a week after that incident, Ray Danner came to town.

Raymond L. Danner, the Elliotts explained to Warren, was the
chairman of the board and longtime chief executive officer of Shoney's, Inc., which was the second-largest family restaurant chain

in the country. Only the Denny's chain had more stores. Half of the fifteen hundred restaurants in Shoney's three main divisions, the full-service Shoney's Restaurants and the fast-food Captain D's and Lee's Famous Recipe Chicken, were company-owned and half were run by franchisees like Charlie Robertson, but Danner had made it a point for thirty years to personally visit as many of both as he could every year. Sunday was usually "Danner Day" in the corporation, the easiest time for him to travel to distant stores on the company jet. One-time Shoney's president Gary Spoleta once bragged that he and Danner had spent 102 consecutive Sundays during the mid-1980s on the road inspecting restaurants.

Danner had special reason to tour the Marianna and Panama City stores, the Elliotts said, beyond just making sure everybody followed what they called the Danner Way, half of which seemed to be about keeping up high standards and the other half, according to the Elliotts, about keeping employees anxious, afraid of messing up and suddenly having Danner or one of his people march an offending store manager into the cooler for a dressing down—or drag the manager in by his tie. Several former company officials later testified that these encounters were known as Danner's "one-minute interviews"; Henry called them his "spells."

Henry said he'd never experienced one himself, though he'd heard of others who had, including Billie, who both Henry and Billie testified, was once berated by Danner in front of other employees for having the wrong size beer pitcher on the counter at the Marianna store. Billie said she tried to explain to Danner that the Suggses had told her to buy that particular style of pitcher for water, not beer, but her response apparently wasn't what he wanted to hear and he quickly became angry. Someone, either Charlie Robertson or Paul Suggs, interceded before Billie said anything else and risked making Danner even angrier, she said, and perhaps getting herself fired for insubordination.

The reason Danner visited the Panhandle Captain D's as much as he did, though, sometimes three or four times a year, was because his son Roger owned 49.75 percent of the franchise company, matching Charlie Robertson's 49.75 percent. (A third, silent partner, a Pensacola friend of Ray Danner's, owned the remaining one-half percent.) Roger, or "Baby Danner" as the plaintiffs' attorneys would later call him, always tagged along when his father flew in on the company plane from Shoney's headquarters in Nashville to inspect the Panhandle stores.

On the morning of Danner's March 1988 visit, the week after the Waffle House meeting, Jan Suggs called Henry Elliott early at the store. For months Henry had been showing up at 6:00 A.M. to help with the hours of prep work before they could open the restaurant for early lunch at 10:30, when Billie usually clocked in as dining-room supervisor. That morning, though, Jan Suggs asked who was working prep, and when Henry named the employees— James Stephens, Madeline Herring, Stephanie Cooper, all of whom were black—Henry said Jan insisted that he call Billie and have her come in early to be at the store when Ray Danner arrived with Roger and Charlie Robertson for his inspection. In his deposition, Henry said he suspected the reason, and so did Billie when he called to wake her up at their mobile home just south of town: managers were expected to staff as many whites as possible when Ray Danner came to town. Jan Suggs also told Henry that they would have a new white employee there, one the Suggses had found and hired earlier in the week, although the man hadn't worked yet and Henry didn't know what position he'd been hired to fill.

By 9:30, Billie was up front in the dining room with Stephanie Cooper, and Henry was cutting and weighing fish at the butcher block in the kitchen. Frustrated about having to come in early, Billie later testified that she was also angry that she was expected to be there just for the Danners. Before the visitors showed up, though, Billie said she took Cooper aside for a private conversation: she had a surprise in mind for when those boys showed up from Nashville and she needed the young black woman's help to pull it off. They might not be able to do much about the way the Suggses and Charlie Robertson and Mr. Danner wanted to run their business, but for that one day, at least, they were going to do *something*.

The Suggses, meanwhile, arrived before the other visitors and immediately told James Stephens to go outside to pick up any trash he could find at the edges of the parking lot. There was still a lot of prep work that needed to be done in the kitchen, but Henry later testified that he assumed the Suggses sent Stephens away for the same reason they'd called Billie in early. The Suggses also spirited in the new white employee, a pony-tailed man named Robert Wheeler, whom they said they intended to introduce to the Danners as the store's new "assistant manager trainee." This was the first time Henry had heard about the exact nature of Wheeler's job, he said, and it was also the first time he'd heard the title "assistant manager trainee." Lester Thomas was still the assistant manager in charge of the evening shift, as far as Henry knew. Robert Wheeler wasn't even in uniform.

Henry didn't have too long to think about it, though, because about that time Charlie Robertson's big boat of a car cruised into the parking lot and docked out back. In it were Robertson, Ray Danner, Danner's son Roger, and another man whom Henry had never seen before. In short order, all the men left the car together to walk around the parking lot, check out the landscaping, the building, the sign, the stuff Ray Danner usually did before coming inside as part of his set inspection routine. Once he did enter the restaurant, Danner was polite, almost deferential. He asked Henry about the flounder he was cutting, fish he'd recently started purchasing from a new supplier. Was it satisfactory? Did any customers complain about the brown spots? Danner was a small man, officially 5'7", but he appeared to be a couple of inches shorter than that, Henry said. He had a red face and a gin-blossom nose, and he wore a white, short-sleeve shirt and tie. He favored his right arm that day, Henry remembered, and when he shook anyone's hand he used his left instead of his right. Someone said that he had fallen out of a golf cart and hurt the arm, but Henry didn't ask about it. He was too busy getting ready for the lunch crowd.

Billie Elliott hadn't had much to do up front. Stephanie Cooper had taken care of almost everything before she came in, so they were just cutting the pastries, lemon, pecan, and apple pies, chocolate cake, cheesecake. She had seen Charlie Robertson's car pull in with Danner and the others, and she had seen them walking in a little parade of shirtsleeves and ties around the parking lot. When she heard them come in the back, she was nervous about what she had planned and wondered if Danner would separate from the others as he sometimes did and eventually come up front into the dining area by himself.

She didn't have to wait long. Danner was efficient, after all, he didn't dawdle on inspections, and before Billie could worry about it too much there he was, by himself, stepping through the swinging door out of the kitchen and behind the counter. He might have smiled at her. He was usually polite, except for that one time with the beer pitcher. He might have said something, but Billie couldn't remember later if he did. She was busy motioning Stephanie Cooper to come over.

"Mr. Danner," she said, "let me introduce you to my assistant, Stephanie Cooper."

Billie remembered the moment vividly, and when Warren later contacted Cooper she confirmed Billie's account in her own deposition. "His eyes got wide and he looked at me," Billie said in an interview, "like if he was going to say something it would be 'Lady, what do you think you're doing?'"

But he didn't speak, both women said. He grabbed Stephanie Cooper's outstretched right hand with his left, according to Billie, then he walked off.

One week later, on April 11 (Tommy Warren's fortieth birthday, as it happened), Henry Elliott was fired. The Suggses, he said, told him that Ray Danner had complained about the condition of the restaurant after his visit and that Charlie Robertson wanted Henry out. "You don't have a Captain D's kitchen," Paul Suggs purportedly said.

Henry had little to say in response. He had known for a while what was coming, and he left the store tired and depressed. Billie was out of town that day—her grandmother had died earlier in the week and she had gone to Georgia for the funeral—so it wasn't until she drove by the Captain D's to find Henry that she learned he'd been fired. She went home angry and immediately tried to contact Roger Danner in Nashville to tell him what Charlie Robertson and the Suggses were up to. But either he wasn't in or he wouldn't take her call. She later testified that she was transferred instead to Barry Abbott, the Captain D's division franchise director, and she registered her complaint with him: the real reason

Henry was fired had nothing to do with the way he kept up his kitchen, it was because he wouldn't follow orders to terminate their black employees. Barry Abbott said he'd look into it, Billie said. She threatened to take legal action if something wasn't done.

Three days later, on April 14, Paul Suggs called Billie into the store. Ray Danner, Barry Abbott, and Charlie Robertson didn't want anybody who was thinking about suing the company to work at Captain D's, she said he told her. Then Jan Suggs purportedly chimed in, saying, "I have tried to warn you that you can't fight this company. They have too many attorneys and too much money, and you don't have any."

"Yes ma'am," Billie testified that she answered. "But you have inserted your number tens in your mouth too many times, and you will be hearing further from me."

THREE

❝ I Went Directly from a Necktie to a Shovel ❞

Tommy Warren came away from his first meeting with the Elliotts with three things convincing him that their story was true: their willingness to sign sworn statements; a commitment to locate other witnesses from Marianna and Panama City who could corroborate their story; and their prediction that a number of the blacks working at the Marianna Captain D's would soon leave the store as the new manager, a young white woman named Debora Newton, took over to run the restaurant with the Suggses. That prediction proved accurate. Within a few weeks six black workers were either fired or forced to quit, including Lester Thomas, the assistant manager, Stephanie Cooper, who had shaken Danner's hand, and Madeline Herring, whom Paul Suggs had called "black as the Ace of Spades."

Gwendolyn Smith, Angela Sorey, and Madeline Herring told Warren they were forced to quit when Newton, under orders from

Jan Suggs, cut their hours so severely that they could no longer afford to work at Captain D's. Lester Thomas and Stephanie Cooper were both demoted, he from his job as assistant manager, she as assistant dining-room supervisor. Cooper said she refused to accept the demotion and quit; Thomas said he was fired shortly afterward for missing a day of work. Maxine White, who had just come back from maternity leave when the Elliotts were fired, said she was harassed by Newton and Jan Suggs about every aspect of her job—not handling orders fast enough, not smiling and talking enough, not wearing the proper makeup or uniform—until she finally quit "to get out of that situation." All the workers repeated their allegations under oath in depositions.

Tracie Holley, a twenty-year-old white woman who had been hired by Billie Elliott shortly before the firings, testified that Jan Suggs talked openly in the restaurant after the Elliotts were gone about the need to get rid of black employees and required prospective employees to include photographs with their applications. Holley said she witnessed the subsequent harassment and termination of a number of the black employees who had worked under the Elliotts. Most of those forced out were in "customer contact" positions, greeting customers, taking orders, serving food, and running the cash register, where the Elliotts alleged that the Suggses and Robertson had been most insistent that whites should work.

Warren was disturbed but, after what the Elliotts had already told him, he was not surprised. "You learn to evaluate stories pretty well in this business, and it's often the case that what people believe happened to them is in fact what happened," he said later. Proving it, though, would be another matter entirely, especially proving racist practices such as those the Elliotts claimed they had experienced, and doing so in a manner powerful enough for a Southern jury to recognize them, too. On top of that, two problems stood out right away in the counterclaims Warren knew the company would eventually make against Henry Elliott if the case was carried forward. One was a robbery that had taken place several months before the firing. Henry told Warren he had left the day's receipts locked in a cabinet rather than in the floor safe, and after the robbery he had agreed to sign a personal note to repay the money himself, despite evidence implicating a former employee in the theft. Then there was the substandard franchise report, criticizing the store's cleanliness and food preparation practices, and the company's charge that Henry "didn't run a Captain D's kitchen."

But because the Elliotts' predictions came true and because they were able to deliver other witnesses as promised, Warren wasn't overly troubled. "These were the normal things you get, the employer's reasons for getting rid of somebody. But there are always reasons and ways to make clients look bad," he said. To Warren, those blemishes on Henry's record were more than offset by the fact that other managers had been robbed and had received poor evaluations and not been fired from their jobs at Robertson Investment. They were also mitigated by Henry's longstanding employment with the franchise group, his steady movement up the managerial ladder, the significant profits he turned at the restaurants he had managed, and his past recognition and rewards by the company. Henry had been named store manager of the year in the franchise group before moving to Marianna.

Warren's first glimpse of the Elliotts' Captain D's came a few days after the Tallahassee meeting when he drove over to Marianna. He entered town on old Highway 90, at one time the principal route across the top of Florida from the Atlantic beaches to Pensacola, crossing over into the city limits where the highway was called Lafayette Street at the bridge over the Chipola River. A long, steep hill up from the river brought him to the heart of town at the intersection of Lafayette and Highway 73 by the Jackson County courthouse, and a half-mile later the Captain D's sign peeked out suddenly from the heavy-limbed oaks on the left-hand side of the road. Under the name on the sign was the Captain D's mascot, an orange-faced sea captain with his big whiskers and pipe. The chain had originally been called Mister D's, which was executive shorthand for "Ray Danner" at Shoney's headquarters, but when the fast-seafood concept caught hold and prospered, "Mister" was promoted to the more nautical-sounding "Captain." A black-top parking lot surrounded the restaurant, and heavy, arm-thick nautical rope was looped around the building through a series of knee-high posts meant to resemble a section of a dock or pier. The gray vinyl prefabricated faux-wood siding rose behind the rope like the hull of a sailing ship up to a blue, high-peaked roof, and the windows resembled a sailing ship's, too, with all their small square panes; the waitresses cleaned them with large paper coffee filters.

Over the next few months Warren would come to know the place well as he made frequent trips to talk to witnesses and corroborate the Elliotts' story. The other place he came to know well, what would become his Marianna base of operations, was the Elliotts' double-wide mobile home five miles south of town, tucked under a stand of water oaks down a dead-end dirt road that bottomed out a rock's throw away at the Chipola River. Nearby were some prefabs with brick siding and some other trailers, but mostly it was oak and pine trees and corn fields gone to weed. The cypress-lined Chipola snaked south out of Alabama and across Jackson County on its lazy way to the Gulf of Mexico; a couple of miles north of the Elliotts' trailer it marked the eastern city limits of Marianna. They said there were places all up and down the river where the Indians used to swim.

Billie and Henry had bought the trailer in 1986, shortly after they married, and had lived there ever since with Billie's younger daughter, Christy, and Christy's infant son. Before that, Billie and the girls had rented a house in town on Russ Street, a quarter-mile from Captain D's. That's where they had been living when Kirby Lytle left, and when he called from Wyoming for the last time back in 1986—he wanted Billie to send his clothes—she told him she'd burned them and to stay away because she was with somebody else.

"Who?" Billie said Kirby asked over the long distance line. "Who is it?"

"It's Henry," she told him. "And I guarantee, you don't want to be messing around with that big Japanese."

They hadn't seen or heard from Kirby since.

A block past Russ Street was Daniel Street, which ran by Marianna High School, where in 1988 Christy was in tenth grade and where Billie's older daughter Melissa had gone before her. When Billie was growing up, her family had lived in the country out by the Washington County line so she'd gone to school in the town of Chipley, at least until she dropped out to get married when she was sixteen to "a poor old country boy who worked at the peanut mill in Cottondale." His name was John Harris. That marriage had lasted twelve years, most of it living with his mother in a converted mill room. Billie stayed at home most of that time raising her daughters while John worked his mill job, but she said it was never a very good marriage and it finally collapsed. When it did, she returned to school for her GED and got a job selling Mary Kay cosmetics. "I might put up with a lot, and for a long time," she said later, "but there comes a time when you have to just say enough is enough and do something about it." That's the way it had been when she left home, she said, left her father, who once put a gun to her head in an alcoholic rage. And that's the way she said it was when she and Henry were fired from Captain D's.

The drive in to Marianna from the Elliotts' trailer was a subtle climb from the mossy oaks that shaded the river and the damp floodplain up to the open warmth of the green peanut fields and a series of long low hills on Highway 73 leading into town.

At the end of the 1980s the Marianna population hovered around six thousand, fifteen thousand counting the subdivisions in the Greater Marianna Area, with maybe forty thousand people in all of Jackson County, 40 percent of them black. At the southside city limits everyone slowed their cars to crawl over the tracks of the Louisville and Nashville Railroad in the shadow of giant twin grain silos that towered above the old depot. The area around the depot was a crowded basin of shotgun shacks, one of the predominantly black neighborhoods they called Jailhouse Bottom, or sometimes Babyland. The other black neighborhood, to the west of Highway 73, they just called the Quarters. It was bigger, a web of streets, many still unpaved, in a wedge of town cut off from the rest of Marianna by the Louisville and Nashville tracks. To get to work, a lot of the Captain D's employees had to cross those tracks, or duck under the low trestle at Cottondale Road, to come up behind the restaurant on Lafayette Street.

The face of Marianna had changed considerably since the early 1970s. Older residents complained how Marianna had lost its Old South charm. The courthouse had been rebuilt into what one called "a big ugly box of a thing." Lafayette Street had been widened in a failed attempt to keep cross-state traffic coming through town instead of out on Interstate 10, then all the old established businesses left downtown for the strip malls on the edge of town. The widening of Lafayette was the worst, they said, because it meant tearing down many of the old Georgian-style houses and mansions from cotton days and replacing them with insurance offices, gas stations, tire stores, and fast-food restaurants like Captain D's.

The dominant feature at Marianna's main intersection downtown, where Highway 73 ran into Lafayette, was the Hanging Oak in front of the courthouse, a symbol of law and order for some older white residents, but infamous in the black community, and nationally, as the site of one of the last public lynchings, in the 1930s, announced in newspapers around the country days in advance and attended by more than two thousand people. The victim, a young black farmworker, had been accused of raping and killing a white woman. By the time of the actual hanging, he was already dead, tortured, castrated, and mutilated. Anti-black rioting broke out afterward, and several blacks were reportedly killed before local authorities reluctantly called in the National Guard.

Locals blamed outside agitators for the violence, and many old-time Marianna families, those still willing to talk about the lynching, have incorporated stories into their family histories about ancestors sheltering helpless black servants and employees from the "foreign" mob. In a detailed history of the lynching written in the early 1980s by a historian from the University of West Florida, no whites would admit on the record that they or their family members had taken part in the killing, the lynching, or the riot. Racial conflicts continued in the decades that followed. Marianna had bitter race riots in the 1970s, too, when they integrated the schools.

Another prominent reminder of Marianna's racial past, one block west of the Hanging Oak and the new courthouse, was Confederate Park, with its granite obelisk and plaque dedicated to "The Cradle and the Grave," referring to the old men and boy volunteers who fought in Marianna's one Civil War battle, which they lost. Engraved on the obelisk was the partisan inscription: "Where overwhelming federal forces were stubbornly resisted by a home guard of old men and boys and a few sick and wounded

Confederates at home on furlough." The aspect of the battle most often dredged up in the highly mythologized local history, one still capable of provoking moral outrage, was the Union force's assault on the Episcopal church, where a number of Marianna citizens had supposedly sought refuge.

To that white, Chamber-of-Commerce perspective, a curious sort of martyrdom and denial figures in the historical incidents central to the story of Marianna and Jackson County since the time of the European settlers. The lynching of the 1930s, one of dozens carried out in the area, was considered the work of outsiders, who gave proper Marianna citizens a bad name. The Civil War assault on the town by Union troops was memorialized as a slaughter of the innocents, not as the armed resistance of a people intent on defending their slave-driven cotton economy. And in the local version of the settling of Jackson County, it was the Seminole attack on a boatload of white soldiers that was remembered, not the subsequent massacre of much greater numbers of Native Americans by the Indian fighter, former territorial governor, and U.S. president Andrew Jackson, who literally drove the Indians out of the Florida Panhandle and gave the county its modern name.

It didn't take Warren long to find out that the Elliotts hadn't been the first managers who claimed they had been pressured to get rid of their black workers. Twenty-seven-year-old Donna Mongoven, the former Captain D's employee who Billie said had warned her about the discriminatory practices, was one of the first to contact Warren and confirm Billie's story. Moreover, Mongoven said, when she was assistant dining-room supervisor to Kim Gilmore during the early 1980s, they were pressured by Mike Haisten, the area supervisor who preceded the Suggses, to reduce the number of black counter workers at the Marianna store. Mongoven repeated her charges in a later deposition, and in his own deposition testimony Mike Haisten said her charges were true.

At first, Mongoven testified, Haisten made a point of merely urging them to hire more whites. "Mike would come down to the store and he would say, 'Did you all get any white applicants? Did any white girls apply this week?'" Mongoven said in her deposition. "At first we would think, 'What's he talking about?' or whatever. And we would let him go back through the applications and say, 'This is what we got,' and they were all black. He throwed little hints here and there. I knew from day one that Ray Danner, Roger Danner, and Charlie Robertson was racists because I was told, 'If you know they are coming to the store, please don't have any blacks working.'"

The pressure changed dramatically at the end of December 1984, according to Mongoven, when Haisten gave her and Gilmore a note which he said was an order from Charlie Robertson. The note said "All blacks fired by January 1."

"I said, 'Mike, are you crazy?'" Mongoven testified. "Kim told Mike that she would not do this. And then she looked at me. She said, 'Donna, are you going to do this, something like this?' I said, 'No way. It was illegal. It was discrimination, and I will have no part because I could be sued if I carried out such illegal policies.'

"Mike said it was not him. He was being pressured by Charlie Robertson, Ray Danner, and Roger Danner to carry out this order. He did not agree with it. He also told us that either the blacks would go or he would go."

Shortly after, Mongoven and Gilmore decided to confront Robertson. Mongoven described that confrontation in her deposition: "Me and Kim, we took him in the store cooler and we said, 'Look, Charlie, what is going on? Don't tell me you didn't say it. Mike told me it came from you and Roger and Ray [Danner].' I said, 'So don't sit here and deny it and tell us it's not true, because I have the note.' I had the note in my possession for a long time after this. I kept it just to hold onto it. He said, 'Donna, it's not me. The order came from Mr. Danner.'"

In a meeting similar to the one Henry Elliott had with his kitchen employees, Mongoven claimed, Gilmore sat down with the counter workers after that to assure them that she wouldn't carry out the orders from Robertson and Haisten. At the time, half the workers were white and half were black.

But Mongoven said she and Gilmore didn't want it to end there, and they decided to confront Ray and Roger Danner the next time they came down from Nashville to visit the store. When that finally happened, early in the spring of 1985, it was Gilmore who approached them first. Gilmore addressed Ray Danner, according to Mongoven in her deposition, and she was blunt: "Mr. Danner,

we would like to know what's going on with this policy of firing 3 1
black employees for no reason."

Roger Danner, whom Mongoven described succinctly—"yellow
hair, little dude"—then "smirked and walked off," she testified, Black
but Ray Danner answered. "He gave us some mumbo-jumbo
about, 'Wait, I am not a discriminator. I have such and such number of blacks. I employ Orientals. I employ everything. I am not a
discriminator.'"

Not long after the Danners' visit, Mike Haisten was fired, and
Charlie Robertson brought in Paul and Jan Suggs as area supervisors. Mongoven claimed that the Suggses, who had previously
worked for Robertson Investment Company cleaning Captain D's
parking lots in Marianna and Panama City after their stint at Wiener World, began harassing Gilmore and writing up formal letters
of reprimand. A series of clashes followed, Mongoven said, esca-
lating until Gilmore "blew up" at Jan Suggs one day in late May or
early June 1985. Gilmore was fired. Then-store manager Glen
McClain, who later lost his own Captain D's job but went on to
serve in the Coast Guard, said in a deposition that the actual reason for Gilmore's termination was her refusal to comply with the
orders to reduce the number of her black employees. "[Paul Suggs]
told me that she was not getting rid of the black counter help like
he told her to, and I needed to fire her," he testified.

Mongoven lost her own job not long after that in the wake of an
armed robbery at the store. She said she asked the Suggses if that
was why she was fired, for giving up the money during the robbery,
but she said they told her they didn't have to give her a reason.
Mongoven worked briefly in the following months for Kim Gilmore at a convenience store outside Marianna, then was unemployed for a year as she shuttled back and forth between Marianna
and Dothan, Alabama, thirty miles north to the north. "I was nervous all the time," she later testified. "I couldn't sleep, worrying
about what would come next, and worrying about how could
somebody do this. This is the 1980s. How could something like
this happen?"

Kim Gilmore wouldn't talk to Warren at first. She had landed a job
working in the commissary at the federal prison, but only with
some difficulty, because she'd been arrested for trespassing at

Captain D's shortly after she was fired. She had also been accused of harassing Billie Elliott. She said she didn't want to complicate her life with anything more to do with Captain D's, and she denied having anything to do with the harassment, which had started when Billie was hired and ended after Gilmore's arrest.

That harassment, Billie Elliott alleged, consisted largely of prank calls to the store when Billie worked. The caller might ask if Captain D's sold eggs, for example, and when Billie said no, they didn't have any, the caller would tell her to look on the side of the building where someone would have smashed a dozen eggs. On other occasions people made threats over the drive-through intercom, and once Billie showed up at the store to find a dead possum on the doorstep.

When she finally did give Warren a sworn statement, Gilmore confirmed Mongoven's account, about the orders from Mike Haisten, about the note, about scheduling whites when Ray Danner visited, and about confronting Charlie Robertson and the Danners. She said she herself never discriminated against her black workers, although she wasn't unaffected by it in her hiring. "I guess unconsciously in the back of my mind, you know, everybody wants to please their boss," she testified. "I guess if I had a white girl here and a black girl here and both of them equally qualified I probably would have leaned towards the white girl to please Mr. Robertson and Mr. Haisten. Everybody wants to please the boss." Despite their willingness to confront Robertson and the Danners at their store, Gilmore and Mongoven both said they felt powerless to do anything about the racial policies once they were fired.

As Warren continued to press his investigation through May and into June 1988, other former restaurant managers began lining up to confirm the racial policies at the Panhandle Captain D's. (Their confirmations were all sworn, entered into the court record, and repeated later in depositions.) Mike Oglesby, the first manager at the Marianna Captain D's when it opened in 1982, testified that he got his racial marching orders from Charlie Robertson when he started the job. "During the course of the interviews when we first started doing it, Mr. Robertson instructed us to try to keep blacks down to a minimum, but there was a mess of black people that came in," said Oglesby, who had worked construction before taking a job in Robertson's Captain D's. "And I mean it got to the

point where I can't do that. There was more black applicants than there was white applicants.

"I think I basically hired every white person that came through the door, to be honest with you. I don't think we turned away any of them because we were trying to meet the guidelines that was set up for us."

John Corley, who managed Captain D's restaurants for Robertson for eight years, said the company's racial practices were well known by all the managers. Robertson himself, Corley testified, told him the orders came directly from Ray Danner. In his deposition, Corley listed what he indicated were the rules of operation:

"They had a three-to-one ratio discrimination. Three whites for every one black."

"Blacks were not in management."

"Sometimes when we would hire too many blacks they would want us to cut it back."

And managers, he said, were told not to schedule blacks when Ray Danner came to town.

Corley told Warren that he had terminated black workers and refused to hire prospective black employees at his Panama City stores, and later in Marianna, in order to meet the company's racial quotas. He described those actions in a sworn statement taken June 5, 1988: "There were approximately eight or nine blacks employed at the 15th Street store on the various shifts in the various jobs," he wrote. "All of them were doing their jobs satisfactorily. Notwithstanding this fact, I was forced to make up reasons to fire all but one of them. I did this in various ways. Sometimes I would cut back their hours so that they would quit, and while cutting back on their hours I would give these extra hours to white employees. Or I would make up reasons such as firing an employee for being five minutes late, which, of course, I had never done before, and I had never seen such a policy applied to white employees. . . . I then proceeded to the Marianna store, where I replaced the manager of the store at that time, Mr. Glen McClain, who had not implemented the policy of firing the black employees. I then began firing the blacks and replacing them with whites."

On one occasion, Corley said, Roger Danner paid a surprise visit to his Panama City store and got angry when he saw five blacks working the serving line. Corley had already gotten rid of a number of his black workers, but now, with Roger Danner standing beside them, Robertson purportedly told Corley that they wanted more of the blacks gone.

"I told [Robertson] at that time, you know, can we get in trouble for doing that, wasn't it illegal to do that," Corley said. "He said, 'No. That's why we have lawyers.'"

Roger Danner didn't say a word through the entire conversation, according to Corley, but he heard it all.

"Charlie said, 'Well, if you can't do it, we'll find somebody who can do it,'" Corley said. "So I went ahead and did it."

Corley had kept his job as a manager with the company even though he'd been arrested and convicted for possession of marijuana at one point and served time when he violated his probation, something he acknowledged in his deposition. It wasn't until a fall a few years later aggravated injuries from a motorcycle accident and prevented him from working that he left the Marianna store.

Another witness, the former area supervisor Mike Haisten, also testified about Roger Danner, saying Ray Danner's son often used racial slurs in conversation with him and Robertson about black employees, calling them "nigs" and "jungle monkeys." Once in the early 1980s, Haisten said, he suggested promoting a black worker in one of the Panama City stores, Leonard Charles Williams, to an assistant manager's position. Roger Danner adamantly opposed it, he claimed. "I remember bluntly a statement regarding the fact that we had never had a nigger in management, and we're not about to start now," Haisten testified. Although Williams was later given the promotion, he was allegedly fired soon after when he questioned why a number of black female counter workers, and no whites, were being terminated from one of the Panama City stores. (In his own deposition, Roger Danner denied giving any discriminatory orders, or knowing of anyone else who did at Robertson Investment. He also denied ever using racial slurs in his work.)

In addition to his testimony about Danner, Mike Haisten also confirmed Gilmore and Mongoven's story about the note ordering them to get rid of all their black employees. Haisten said that

Charlie Robertson had just visited the Marianna store that day in December 1984, and then gave him the note, "All blacks fired by January 1," which Haisten passed on to Gilmore.

"It was a list of several things, which is not uncommon of notes taken during the visit, and one of them was the two week statement as far as you've got two weeks to get rid of the blacks," Haisten said. "I showed [Gilmore] the memo, as I recall, and we were all just a little upset about it, and questioning what to do. . . . I didn't know what to do, and they didn't know what to do. Well, they refused to as I recall. They weren't going to. And I wasn't going to make them, so it was a standoff." A month later Haisten was fired. Personal and professional problems, which he acknowledged in his deposition, had something to do with his termination, he said, but his failure to carry out the racial policies of the company was also a factor.

Yet another witness, Kim Barbero, a single mother who worked for several years as a dining-room supervisor at one of the Panama City Captain D's, told Warren that she was given instructions when she was first hired on how to code applications so the store managers could weed out black applicants. She would color in the "O" or the "A" in the word "Application" (similar to the way others were instructed to blacken the "O" in Shoney's) to indicate that the applicant was African American so her store manager could skip it later when looking through the application files for new workers. Sometimes she drew flowers instead.

Charlie Robertson, she said, was explicit about the kind of women he wanted working at the counter of his Captain D's. Once, when a young Taiwanese woman was working the line, Barbero testified that Robertson pulled Barbero aside, pointed to the worker, and said, "Don't do that again." Then he added, "No niggers, no chinks, and nothing less than a ten."

"It kind of upset me," Barbero recalled in a deposition, "and I said, 'Well, I don't feel like I'm a ten.' And he goes, 'No. You're like an eight, but you try so hard.'"

Robertson was also adamant that she not schedule any blacks when Ray Danner visited the store, Barbero claimed. John Corley, who was her manager at the time, and Mike Haisten, who was then area supervisor, both knew about the racial policies, she said, which included cutting the hours of black workers when there were "too many" so they would quit and the company wouldn't have to pay unemployment compensation.

Only Leonard Charles Williams, a former semiprofessional football player who by 1985 was the only black worker in a management position at Robertson Investment, challenged Barbero about what was happening to the black women working at the Captain D's counter, she said. "By that point in time, Charles was making comments about how come, you know, like questioning me as to why the blacks didn't stay on the counter too long," Barbero said. "How come there was such a higher turnover in the blacks than there was the whites, or why didn't [I] have a black on the counter at all?"

Once Williams started questioning Barbero and other Captain D's managers about the disappearance of the black counter workers, which had happened suddenly after Paul and Jan Suggs took over as area supervisors, Barbero claimed she was told that the company planned to get rid of him once they could find a reasonable excuse. So Barbero said she tried to warn Williams. "I told him to cover his butt," she said. "And I did not go into anything with him, other than the fact I said, 'Watch every single thing you do, and just be careful—you know, make sure you're doing everything proper, make sure, you know, whatever it is, don't miss a step on anything.'"

Williams, who had worked his way up from kitchen worker to relief manager to assistant manager, confirmed Barbero's account when Warren tracked him down in Panama City. In his deposition he blamed Jan Suggs for firing many of the black counter workers, and for firing him. "She was the killer," Williams testified. "She's the one that did all the firing. She did all the hard-core firing. She was the one that implicated [sic] all the firing. If the supervisor didn't do it, she would come in and do it."

Williams said he ran into Barbero once after he had left Captain D's and Barbero told him the truth about what he had long suspected. "I saw her one day downtown and she was talking to me, and she told me that she was under the orders to get rid of the blacks, but she couldn't let me know that at the time. . . . She told me that she wasn't privileged to tell me what was going on at that time because that was her livelihood," Williams recalled.

Williams would later become one of the first nine named plaintiffs in the class-action lawsuit against Robertson Investment, Shoney's, Inc., and Ray Danner, claiming he had been illegally terminated because of his race and that he had been denied further promotions at Captain D's due to the company's discriminatory policies.

At a deposition in July 1989, the attorney for Robertson Investment, Rebecca Conlan, brought up Williams's 1976 discharge from the Navy. Was it true, she asked, that he had been accused of selling drugs at that time? He said it was. And was he aware, she asked, that there were rumors he was using and selling drugs at Captain D's? Williams said yes, Jan Suggs had told him about those rumors when she fired him, but he said the rumors were false.

Conlan pressed further: "Mr. Williams, is it possible that they were trying to protect you, that they had a reasonable belief that you were, in fact, either using drugs on the premises or selling drugs on the premises, they had a good faith belief that you were, in fact, doing that, and they really didn't want to prove it because of the impact it would have had on you? Is that a possibility?"

"No, it's not," Williams replied.

"Why do you think it's not a possibility?" Conlan asked.

"Because I'm here telling you that I wasn't doing that," he said.

"I understand that you say that you didn't and I'll even go so far as to say that you weren't," Conlan continued. "But my question is: If two—one or two reliable employees went to Mr. Robertson and went to the Suggses and told them that you were, in fact, using drugs and selling drugs, wouldn't that be a basis for firing someone?"

"No," Williams said. "Again, I wasn't convicted. They can say what they want to say, you know. No, it's not how the law works. People say things about people all the time. . . . In my situation, the job that I had, the money that I was making, I think I should have been proven guilty, or at least if they thought that I was doing something wrong, I should have been counseled on it and come to some type of agreement, not just come to me and fire me for something somebody said. No, I don't think that's fair."

Later in the deposition, Conlan asked Williams how he had suffered from being fired by Captain D's. "Tell me a little bit about the mental humiliation, anguish, and distress that you have suffered," she said.

"It's just—" He started and stopped. Since losing his assistant manager's job Williams had been working as a day laborer for the city, holding down a part-time cook's position at night, and doing yard work on the weekends. "It's been embarrassing to my family," he said. "I went directly from a necktie to a shovel."

The attack on Williams's character was an example of a typical defense strategy in employment discrimination cases, according to Barry Goldstein, a leading civil rights attorney who later joined Warren to bring the case against Shoney's. It was a strategy Shoney's attorneys would use on witness after witness whenever they found any dirt from the witnesses' personal lives or somewhere in their employment history. The idea, Goldstein maintained, was to divert attention from the real issue, which was the charge of discriminatory treatment.

"It's very common to have them attack plaintiffs," Goldstein later said. "It's one of the things you have to counsel plaintiffs about, especially if you bring a big suit. But nobody's record is perfect. Nobody's a perfect employee. You don't have to be a perfect employee to be a successful Title VII plaintiff. Everybody's entitled to be free from race discrimination whether you're average, good, or barely passable as an employee."

FOUR

66 He Was the Boss.

He Was the Tyrant.

He Was the Dictator 99

"One of the things that really made this case unique, and the Elliotts are the best example at the start, was how white people who were exposed to the policy or made to implement it came forward and told the behind-the-scenes, the behind-the-closed-door secret," Warren told a reporter in 1993, during a breakfast interview at a Shoney's restaurant. "Many of these folks just really were purging themselves of the guilt they felt when they finally had a chance to tell their story. . . . A lot were born and raised in the South, like a lot of us were, in bigotry around them and racism, yet they knew it was wrong and they didn't want to do it and they were made to do it, and it made them feel bad, and when they had their chance to finally tell the story they told it, and it made them feel good."

By the middle of May 1988, Warren had collected more than a dozen sworn statements from those white witnesses, as well as from black workers such as Leonard Charles Williams, Lester Thomas, and the women fired or forced to quit the Marianna Captain D's in the weeks after the Elliotts left. What Warren didn't have were adequate resources to pursue the case. "I couldn't even ask these folks for a retainer to help on costs because I knew it would be ridiculous," he said. "The costs were well above what they could have paid at that point."

Warren's relationship with Spriggs, his former partner, had been strained by the time they ended the partnership several months before, and Warren didn't want to go back there for support. The first person he contacted instead was a man he barely knew, an employment discrimination attorney with the NAACP Legal Defense and Educational Fund, Inc.: Barry Goldstein. The LDF, known to insiders as the "Inc. Fund," was founded in the 1940s by the late Thurgood Marshall, former general counsel for the NAACP and U.S. Supreme Court justice. As the legal arm of the national civil rights organization and later as an independent entity, although it kept the NAACP initials as part of its name, the LDF over the years brought hundreds of public access, voting rights, educational opportunity, and employment discrimination cases on behalf of minorities. Goldstein, a tall, affable man, whom his colleagues would later describe in appearance and temperament as Harrison Ford to Warren's more angular Sam Shepherd (though they shared the same ex-jock's competitive bent) was litigation director of the LDF's Washington office and had developed a national reputation in employment law, starting with his first successful cases eighteen years earlier fighting U.S. Steel in Birmingham, Alabama.

The LDF had provided Spriggs with some limited financial support in the West Florida Monsanto case that Warren joined as a law clerk in the early 1980s, and he had met Goldstein at that time, if only in passing. He knew Goldstein's reputation, though, and was hoping through Goldstein to get some of the LDF's resources, although those resources had grown increasingly scarce during the Reagan years. Nonetheless, Warren had a case based on "the most easily understood form of discrimination," as he and Goldstein would later characterize it, a compelling case involving the sort of prejudice that appeared to be every bit as egregious and systemic

Goldstein, too, was struck by the egregious nature of the early
facts in Warren's case, as well as by what he called Warren's ambi-
tious "vision" for where the case was headed: not just against
Robertson Investment, but against the entire Shoney's corporation. For that, though, Goldstein told Warren the LDF would need
more evidence before it got involved, further discovery not only
establishing a direct connection from Robertson Investment up
the company ladder to Ray Danner, but also demonstrating the
corporate-wide nature of the case. Sure, there were a dozen sworn
statements and more coming in, plenty of anecdotes alleging racial discrimination in the Florida Panhandle, but the LDF, or anybody else, would need more than anecdotes to bring and win a
major class action if it was purported to involve hundreds if not
thousands of managers and company executives in dozens of
states across the South and Midwest. He would review Warren's
draft complaint to Shoney's, Goldstein said, and he would advise
the case in any way that he could, but the LDF couldn't commit
any resources right away.

Warren would joke about it later—"Barry was kibitzing around
with me"—but at the time he was keenly aware of the burden of
what he had undertaken. In the fall of 1988, as he still waited for
the LDF to make up its mind, Warren began contacting larger
firms for help with the case, working his years of connections in
the Florida legal community dating back to his football and law-
school days and his brief foray into state government as an aide to
former Democratic governor Reuben Askew in the early 1970s.
All of them turned him down.

Despite Warren's compelling early evidence, all said the risk of
taking on a major discrimination class action of the magnitude he
envisioned was too great, requiring a firm to put up an enormous
amount of money and time on a case that might not pay off. Moreover, after eight years of Ronald Reagan appointees, the federal judiciary and the Supreme Court had taken a hard right turn during
the 1980s, so the risk of such class actions was even further
heightened by the acutely conservative tenor of the times. And
darker times lay ahead, even casual observers noted, with several

major litigation appeals that could make it even more difficult to bring and win discrimination cases winding their way to the U.S. Supreme Court.

Warren knew he was swimming against the tide, but he still wasn't willing to accept the prevailing political notion that race discrimination was a thing of the past. "It's disappointing that these suits have to keep being brought," he told an interviewer early in the case. "One possibility is that discrimination is still out there. If so, then it's disappointing and disturbing that the number of class actions is dwindling. Another possibility is that discrimination is being eliminated, in which case it makes sense that there are fewer and fewer cases. Unfortunately that's not the case." The evidence against Shoney's proved just the opposite, he said: "Here you have a major corporation well into the late eighties running rampant with intentional discrimination. You'd like to think that it's an aberration, but I don't think that's the case."

At least one person agreed with him. Kathy Villacorta, Warren's wife, convinced her small firm to stake him office space and a secretary in their no-frills suite behind a corner pawn shop near downtown Tallahassee, but he knew as the case grew he would need a lot more support than that, and he would need it soon. It would be four and a half years, though, before Warren was paid for his own work on the Shoney's case—except for a bizarre period in the winter and spring of 1990 when Shoney's itself picked up his and Goldstein's legal bills. Even that money Warren put into an account to help defray expenses in the case.

In the meantime, he had those dozen sworn statements from black workers who said they'd been illegally fired, from two black assistant managers who said they had been illegally denied promotions, from several former white managers who said they had suffered retaliation when they refused to carry out discriminatory policies, and from several other white managers who said they did follow orders to discriminate—all of them, as Goldstein had pointed out, associated with the same Shoney's, Inc. franchise group. But Warren also had the Ray Danner connection raising the possibility of a corporate-wide policy of discrimination, which Warren knew he would have to prove unless he limited his case to Robertson Investment. And he did not want to limit the case.

The next step for Warren was obvious: the Florida Secretary of
State's office to research corporate records for Robertson Investment and Shoney's, Inc. If he was going to bring an employment
discrimination suit against them, he would have to first understand the business.

In his 1989 book *A Turn in the South*, novelist and travel writer
V. S. Naipaul included a section on a self-styled "good old boy"
named Campbell, a real-estate agent from Mississippi who offers
a lengthy and colorful definition of the Southern redneck. Campbell holds forth in the book about trailer homes, hunting dogs, Red
Man chewing tobacco, and messy divorces, then he shifts categories. "There's an upscale redneck and he's going to want it cleaned
up," he says. "Yard mowed, a little garden in the back. Old Mama,
she's gonna wear designer jeans and they're gonna go to Shoney's
to eat once every three weeks."

Naipaul, whose family is Indian but who was raised in Trinidad,
writes that he "had seen any number of those restaurants beside
the highways, but had never gone into one. Were they like Mc-
Donald's?" Campbell's blunt reply: "At Shoney's you'll get gravy
all over it. That's going to be a big deal. They'll love it. I know
those sons of bitches."

When Barry Goldstein stumbled onto that passage after agreeing
in the late fall of 1988 to join Warren as cocounsel in the case
against Shoney's, he thought the description fit perfectly. The
niche in the restaurant industry that Ray Danner had successfully
filled since the late 1950s was the one next to the highways and
interstates where travelers could count on an alternative to the
fast-food joints proliferating at every exit, a solid, economical,
home-style, American meal. It was also the type of place lower-
middle-class working families, Campbell's upscale rednecks,
would frequent for a Sunday dinner after church or for an evening's
dining out.

Danner echoed that description of Shoney's coffee-shop restaurants and their dual identity in a 1985 interview with the *Wall
Street Transcript:* "We go from the blue-collar worker, where we
are sort of a special restaurant to them, all the way up to a convenience restaurant for the more affluent."

In a 1976 article featuring up-and-coming entrepreneurs, *Time* magazine described Danner's restaurants, known at that time as Shoney's Big Boys, as "a sort of Howard Johnson's featuring double hamburgers." The Big Boy trademark, widely recognized by two generations of highway travelers, was a giant-size plastic sculpture of a wide-eyed, bubble-headed white boy in checkered overalls holding up one of the cheese-dripping doubles on a platter.

The Shoney's concept had originated during the 1950s with a Jewish businessman from Charleston, West Virginia, named Alex Schoenbaum, who saw highway traffic picking up dramatically with an end to gas rationing after the war, an expanding economy, which meant a quantum leap in the standard of living for middle-class Americans, and on the horizon, construction of the Eisenhower interstate highway system. Those travelers needed someplace to eat, Schoenbaum understood, someplace like home, familiar, dependable, and predictable, so he bought the rights to the Big Boy trademark from the Marriott Corporation for an eleven-state area below the Mason-Dixon Line, and in 1958 he started planting those Big Boys in front of a string of identical highway coffee shops across the South. Not interested in running the restaurants himself, Schoenbaum sold franchise agreements instead. For a fee up front, and a small percentage of gross revenue afterward, just about any prospective restaurateur who wanted could sign on.

One of the first in line was thirty-five-year-old Raymond Louis Danner, who had been working days as regional sales manager for Canteen Company of America in Louisville, Kentucky, and nights as a clarinet player in his own swing band. In 1958 he and a partner, Jim Craft, laid out cash for the rights to develop the Tennessee market. They had wanted Danner's home state of Kentucky, but since another franchisee had already snatched it up they settled on the state next door. Danner and Craft opened their first Shoney's Big Boy in the Nashville suburb of Madison in 1959, one of only ten franchised by Schoenbaum at that time. By 1965, six years later, they had expanded in the middle Tennessee territory to seven restaurants, with more planned.

They did it, Danner would later say, with little direction from Schoenbaum beyond the concept itself and, of course, the familiar

Big Boy trademark. "He really didn't know exactly what to do,"

Danner said of the man he called "Mr. Alex." "The demand for
growth was strong and he had not put together what you would
call an organized company. It was just sort of come in and you can
have a franchise, we'll open you a store.

"We had worked very hard from the day we opened the first store
and tried to organize and, you know, we were pioneers. We had to
develop products and ways of cooking food, delivering it, training
manuals, store designs."

Danner soon bought out his partner and in 1968 incorporated
his growing string of franchises as Danner Foods, adding a number
of Kentucky Fried Chicken restaurants along the way. Sales that
year were $8.8 million, but by 1971, when Danner forced Schoen-
baum into a merger with Danner Foods, they were up to $17 mil-
lion. Every single store turned a profit, with earnings tripling from
$526,000 to $1.5 million over the three-year period. Altogether in
1971, according to an article in *Business Week* noting Danner's
rapid ascendance in the market, he had 52 company-owned restaurants and 112 franchises, which were bringing in an additional
$63 million.

"All I want each day is one more customer and one more dollar,"
Danner told the magazine. Jack Massey, cofounder of Kentucky
Fried Chicken, said he was so impressed with Danner that he had
tried to hire him away as KFC president, but Danner turned him
down to run all of Shoney's Big Boy Restaurants as chief operating
officer, while Schoenbaum settled in upstairs—and out of the
way—as chairman of the board.

In the early years, and afterward, the company took on a person-
ality and a set of values that directly mirrored Danner's own forceful, hands-on, in-your-face management style. That style was key,
company executives and industry observers would say, in devel-
oping a restaurant chain from the ground up and ensuring consis-
tency and quality. If stories about the top executive shoving a
cook's hand into a vat of soup or dragging an errant manager into
the cooler by his necktie could keep employees on their toes, who
was going to complain?

Karyn Hudson-Brown, who started at Shoney's as a dining-room
supervisor trainee in 1972, when she was twenty-four, and had

risen to director of marketing for Shoney's Specialty Division by the time she left in 1987, described Danner as an intense, charismatic man who inspired a kind of fearful loyalty among his employees, but who always led by example. "Mr. Danner trained you in the company philosophy," she said. "He trained you in what he believed in. He trained in the customer comes first." She described Danner as a boss who would roll up his sleeves and clean toilets alongside his employees to show them how to do the job right. "You knew whenever he told you something or he was explaining something to you, that that's the way he wanted it done. And it set your values, it set your philosophy for how things were to be done in the company. And actually, in a lot of ways, it would set values and philosophy in your life."

Danner attempted to articulate his "Shoney's, Inc. Values" once in a memo for a wallet card one of his executives planned to distribute to company employees. In large block print—all capital letters riddled with spelling errors and no punctuation—Danner stressed a lean and mean, consumer-driven philosophy that included "Descipline of detail," the need to be "inovative," and a commitment to develop "great achivers from average people."

Gary Spoleta, chief operating officer and company president during the late 1980s (and the executive who solicited the memo), said Danner's success depended on "getting out of the office and into the units." Spoleta, another small, intense man, adopted his boss's blue-collar approach to the business wholesale, though unlike Danner, whose formal education ended with high school, he came to the company with a chemistry degree from Cornell. Spoleta ingratiated himself with Danner by calling him "Chief" and publicly hailing him in speeches as "the best field general" in the restaurant industry. Hudson-Brown agreed: "[Danner] did not hold a training class where we all sat down and listened to him speak or anything, but he was actively involved in training. And it was always hands-on, one-on-one, you know, in the stores."

And Danner, she said, always got his way. "If Mr. Danner came in your store and he felt that you needed to be reinforced on a point, such as fast service or clean dining room or proper supplies, yes, it made an impression, because (A) you wanted to please him, and (B) he would tell you right to your face. And it would just—it makes an impression," she said. "Sometimes, you know, he would scold you. And he was unique in this in the fact that he could scold you, but he could put you back together, too. He made you want to do it."

John Oglesby, the first manager at the Marianna, Florida, Captain D's, said he had heard about Ray Danner's reputation for hard-nosed management, but learned about the direct Danner style firsthand when he worked at one of the Panama City stores as an assistant manager. "The first time I ever met [Ray Danner] I near about peed in my pants," he said. "The girls didn't greet him when he came through the door. He came walking back and I was dropping fish. He asked me where a mop was. And I mean I almost literally did. And I couldn't say anything. And Tommy [Garrett, the store manager], this is right after we'd gotten promoted, Tommy told him, 'Back there,' told him where the mop was. He went and got the mop. Had a spill in the dining room, and he went out and mopped it. He said, 'You know, we pay sixty-five dollars a month for this Muzak system and the customers can't hear.' He said, 'You've got some good rock and roll going on back here.' We had the radio playing.

"After that radios were banned in the kitchen area."

To Barbara Cragg, at one time director of management services for the corporation, Danner was "a complete terror," she said in a deposition, a man who could be brutally intimidating to store-level employees and to area supervisors and other executives at the Monday morning managers' meetings at Shoney's headquarters in Nashville. "One time he came to the meeting and he had been out in the stores the day before and he had a little cooler in his hand," she said. "It was fish that was not cut properly. And he put a scale up on the table, and he slapped the fish up there and made Wayne Browning [a Captain D's vice president] read the weight of the fish. And every time he slapped the fish up there, it slapped—the fish juice hit Wayne in the face. And Wayne had on glasses, so it was very obvious. Then he took the fish and threw it at the area supervisors. So we all ducked and dodged fish. Then the other time that he came in he had Linus [Leppink, the director of purchasing], and he was holding Linus by the tie and pulling him into the room. And he had cabbage and go-ketchup with him.

And he took the go-ketchup and said, 'Mr. Browning, taste this ketchup,' and he did. He said, 'What does it taste like?' Mr. Browning said 'Shit.' And then he had the other people taste the ketchup, and then he reamed everybody out about the ketchup and about the cabbage.'"

Danner was keenly aware of the deliberate effect he had on others, Cragg said. "He stood up in [another] meeting and he said he got a letter from a lady, and the lady said there was some mean little man over there chewing out the waitress, and he said, 'I know that mean little man was me.'"

Keith Roberts, Danner's personnel director in 1971, said that one of the primary reasons for the company's success, after Danner's hands-on, field-general management style, was his penchant for hiring college dropouts. "It's difficult to find a college graduate who's willing to get his hands dirty," said Roberts, who had dropped out of Vanderbilt himself. "The guy we want didn't finish college and knows he has to work a little harder to keep up with his classmates who got their sheepskins."

Danner, who was both proud of his working-class background and defensive about his lack of formal education, made it a policy to start those people in bottom-level jobs and then promote them through the ranks and into executive positions. It was both a calculated personnel decision and a desire to build a company populated by employees created in his own image. "When you say Ray Danner doesn't have a college degree, no, no, I don't," he told an interviewer in 1991. "But I would say that other than maybe for some English and some history, and a few of the liberal arts types of things, I've got one twice as good as most people who go to college on today's market." In the business world, he said, what you need more than a degree are "personal integrity, the personal drive, the personal control over your emotions, your life, how long you will work, how much energy you put into it."

His own education primarily came in a six-month crash course in the U.S. Air Corps Aviation Cadet School at the end of World War II, Danner said. "When I say we went to school for six months, it wasn't like our kids go now for two or three hours a day and have the weekends off. We went from 8:00 in the morning to 5:00 in the evening, then had a couple hours off for a dinner break. We

studied the books from 6:00 until 10:00. I would say that six
months certainly was equivalent to two years of a normal life at
most of our colleges."

He went on to flight school, gunnery school, and radio, navigation, and radar training, but never served overseas. The war ended
and he was discharged at twenty-one. Right away, he went into
business back in Louisville. "In business, there is no limit on how
far you can go," he said in that 1991 interview, "because if you
perfect something that works, you can have [something simple
like] cookie cutters, so to speak—more and more and more."

In a 1992 deposition, Danner listed some of the company executives who, like him, had started at the bottom and worked their
way up in the company and in the world: Steve Sanders, from busboy to president of the Shoney's division ("I think at the time [he
was hired] he said he was sixteen. He was a pretty big old boy. Later
on he told me he was only fourteen and he needed a job bad"); Jim
Arnett, from cook to chief operating officer; Chuck Porter, from
manager trainee to president of the Captain D's division; Don
Christian, from Captain D's cook to company vice president.

Danner's biggest success story, for a time, was Dave Wachtel, an
on-again, off-again student at the University of Tennessee who
started as a busboy in Danner's first Shoney's in 1959, began the
Captain D's division in 1969, and worked his way up to CEO in
1982 as Danner's hand-picked replacement. It didn't work out,
though; Danner was never one to give up control easily, and he had
the board of directors fire Wachtel after a year at the helm. Wachtel, a musician like his boss, always ready to grab the stage and
blow his trumpet at company parties, was cynical about that termination several years later when he testified in a deposition
about working for Danner. "Well, I guess the first thing he taught
me how to do was bus the tables in 1959. And the last thing he
taught me to do was how to leave. So he taught me everything,"
Wachtel said.

"What was his motto? Tell me and I might remember; show me
and I'll try to remember; do it with me and I will remember it forever," Wachtel said in a deposition. "And that's the way he did it.
He would stand right beside you and watch you do it and show you
how to do it. . . . He was very hands-on, used intimidation. There

wasn't a job too big that couldn't be done and if you didn't do it, he would do it. And he motivated you that way to make you want to do the job. He was kind of a Vince Lombardi type, I guess.

"His reputation, he was the boss. He was the tyrant. He was the dictator. He made things happen. If you associated yourself with him, you had a pretty good probability of being successful with the company."

That probability for success was evident not only from the executives whom Danner promoted through the ranks, but also from his franchising practices, especially early on when there was no franchise office and Danner often handed out the lucrative rights to Shoney's, Captain D's, and Lee's Famous Recipe Chicken restaurants to relatives, business pals, golf buddies, and politicians. Former Nashville mayor Richard Fulton and former U.S. congressman Bill Boner were among those given sweetheart franchise deals by Shoney's or its larger franchisees at minimal cost, according to published accounts in the *Nashville Tennessean*. Franchises were also the golden parachutes for some executives when they retired or resigned, and when Danner divorced his first wife a major part of the settlement was a Shoney's franchise property.

Danner took full control of Schoenbaum's business in 1976, assuming the mantles of both CEO and chairman of the board (though Schoenbaum stayed on with the title of senior chairman), and began an even more aggressive program for marketing new "concepts" that would diversify the company and allow it to expand into areas where the Shoney's Big Boys were restricted by Schoenbaum's old trademark agreement with Marriott. He had started Captain D's in 1969 (reputedly from a brainstorming session with Kentucky Fried Chicken figurehead "Colonel" Harland Sanders), backing in slowly, the way he approached everything new, but then, once he'd had Wachtel test the idea, moving quickly to dominate the market. By 1976, *Time* magazine was reporting that Danner had a personal fortune of $25 million, owned 231 Shoney's Big Boys, and was grossing $100 million from all his restaurants combined.

Even before he dropped the Big Boy trademark in 1984, Danner was testing Shoney's restaurants—without the identifying Big

Boy—in states outside the marketing area granted by Marriott. He
liked what he saw, and even though another Big Boy franchisee
failed in the courts to restrict Danner's expansion, he paid Marriott $13 million to terminate the Big Boy agreement. Customers
knew the Shoney's reputation, he had discovered, with or without
the checkered-pants boy out front. Rapid growth in company-
owned restaurants and in franchising followed through the 1980s,
as Danner also branched out into a chain of chicken restaurants,
Lee's Famous Recipe, and further into more upscale specialty
houses such as Pargo's and Fifth Quarter, and Shoney's Inns, a
motel chain.

The *New York Times* took notice in a front-page business story
the year Danner ended the Big Boy agreement, reporting that at the
end of May Shoney's, Inc. had turned in a remarkable and unprecedented record of what it claimed were one hundred consecutive
quarters of increased profits and revenues as Shoney's spread that
year to fifteen states. "We haven't had a market we went in where
we haven't done well," Danner said. "We'll be growing in a ring-
type fashion where you go out a little further each time and by the
time your restaurants get there, your reputation is already there."

The *Times* article focused on Shoney's top-heavy store management as essential to the chain's success: "The commitment
to close restaurant supervision runs deep. Each Shoney's coffee
shop has seven managers, two or three more than many of its competitors. Middle-level and senior-level executives tend to come
up through the ranks, ensuring they will be familiar with company practices. Division directors, normally responsible for up to
twenty-five restaurants, are given decision-making authority."
Gary Spoleta told the *Times* that control of the restaurants went
directly from the no-frills executive offices in Nashville to those
division directors in the field: "They can paint the restaurants
green if they want to. We have no strategic planners. No MBA's.
We have no layers."

"Shoney's is probably the single best-managed company in the
industry," Prudential-Bache Securities analyst Mike Culp told the
Wall Street Transcript a year later when the publication honored
Danner as the top CEO in the restaurant industry. "Twenty-five
years without a down quarter is a record that nobody has matched

in the industry, including McDonald's. It is unusually profitable on the coffee shop side." In a 1986 article in *Business Week*, Culp predicted earnings would grow by at least 22 percent a year through 1991 as the company continued its rapid expansion. *Business Week* writer Pete Engardio noted that profits had already leapt 30 percent from the year before in what were by then twelve hundred coffee shops, seafood restaurants, and fried chicken outlets that Danner ran either directly through the company or through franchisees. Overall sales in 1985 approached half a billion dollars, and profits were $30.2 million. Incredibly, four years later Shoney's various divisions had spread to thirty states and those sales and profit figures had doubled.

"More than anything else, outsiders believe Shoney's will succeed because of Danner's tight control of everything from food quality to corporate staff," the *Business Week* article concluded. "Headquarters regularly dispatches 'mystery shoppers' with orders to squeal on waitresses who don't greet a seated customer with a smile and a water glass within two minutes. Corporate executives make numerous spot visits to restaurants, occasionally pitching in by washing dishes or busing tables when the outlets are busy."

For thirty years, as the self-styled "godfather of this company," the hard-driving Danner never let up. During one period of uncharacteristically flat sales during the mid-1980s, he personally graded every single one of the thousands of shopper's reports from those paid diners that executives dubbed "mystery squealers." He even had them shipped to his vacation home in Naples, Florida (a sort of Nashville South for the Danner family and Shoney's executives), so he wouldn't miss a single opportunity during that period, which lasted several months, to identify the trouble spots and order them fixed.

In May 1985 he turned his full attention to the Captain D's division when he decided it wasn't performing up to company expectations. In a speech to 250 Captain D's franchisees and company operators, he outlined what he wanted done to improve service and sales, and then he ended with a typically direct warning: "Participate. I mean right now, here at this convention. I will

make a list of those who don't, and then I'll come and visit your
stores."

No one doubted he meant what he said. "I visit twenty restaurants a day to see that things are shipshape," he told a Louisville
business reporter in 1987. "For restaurants located a ways from
here, I hop in my plane at 7:00 A.M., visit two or three, and return
about eight or nine that night." Danner's own term for his approach was "floating management," but to former company officials such as Dave Wachtel and Barbara Cragg it was also management by intimidation. Not that Danner seemed to mind. Publicly,
at least, he never questioned that hard-nosed myth about himself,
the Danner legend adopted in industry publications and the popular press, where what primarily informed business reporting was a
company's bottom line.

Tommy Warren's early research quickly dispelled any illusions
about whom he was up against in bringing a major discrimination
case. Shoney's was one of the giants of the restaurant industry, and
Ray Danner ranked among the wealthiest and most successful
businessmen in the country. Warren and his wife talked long and
hard about what he would be getting into once he committed to
the case, and when they learned at the end of the summer that
Kathy was pregnant with their third child, the stakes rose even
higher.

"It became real obvious that it was going to be an enormous undertaking," Warren said, "and that I was going to spend not only
many years of my life from that point forward working on this, but
expending enormous resources of me and my family."

FIVE

" I Was Pretty Sure at That Point That There Was Going to Be War "

The Elliotts couldn't find work.

For weeks after they were fired both Billie and Henry knocked on doors, filled out applications, and waited for calls that never came. They filed for unemployment compensation. They grew frustrated with what they believed was a wall of prejudice that had suddenly gone up in white Marianna. Billie applied for her old job as a waitress at Union 76 but never heard anything, then she tried at a host of other restaurants, stores, and offices: Winn Dixie, Super C, Piggly Wiggly, TG&Y, The Movie Gallery, Payless Shoes, Russell Athletics, Sunland (a state facility for the severely mentally handicapped). Word had spread quickly around the small town about Captain D's, though, and suddenly no one seemed to be hiring.

Billie was furious. "How do you think it affects you when you go and you put in a job application, and you have to write on there why you were fired?" she said at a deposition hearing in 1989.

"And people turn around and look at you when they read it. And there is a lot of racist people still in Marianna. You think I can get a job when I tell them the real reason why I was fired? They are not going to hire me.

"If you could have seen the look in some of those people's eyes when I went in to apply, and they read my application and they looked at me. And they say, 'We don't have any positions open.' . . . There has been little snide comments made by some people that I don't even know or how they know how we got fired; things like, 'There is too many black people in that store.' One lady who did my hair said something to the effect that she didn't want to eat in a store where there are all blacks, and she didn't know how I could hire all black people."

When Billie applied in person at one local grocery store, the manager gave her what had become the typical response: nothing available. Before she left the office, though, a woman came in who worked for the school system locating jobs for students in vocational education. Billie had met the woman before, and they spoke briefly. "As a matter of fact, I worked with her at Captain D's in placing some people," Billie remembered. "And just before I walked away, she said to [the manager], 'If you need anybody, this lady is very good. I recommend her highly.' He just looked at me, after he already told me he did not have any positions. He just sort of looked at me. And I turned around to walk away. As I walked away I heard him tell her, 'Yes, send me seven more girls.'"

In late May, after six weeks out of work, Billie finally landed a job as a part-time cashier twenty-five hours a week at a local Revco drug store. She stayed there through most of June until she took a full-time job waitressing at Simbo's Truck Stop off Interstate 10 in nearby Bonifay. That lasted only another month, though, until business slacked off at the end of watermelon season and they cut back her hours.

Tommy Warren, meanwhile, was pressing forward with the case, and in early June called the general counsel for Shoney's, Inc. in Nashville—as a courtesy more than anything else—to advise them about the potential litigation. He would be sending a draft complaint, he said, along with copies of the sworn statements and a request for company employment records. Shoney's counsel gave him an address to send the complaint and little more was said.

Shortly after, though, on June 13, Billie Elliott received a letter from Robertson Investment offering her old job back at the Marianna Captain D's. It was a no-brainer as far as she was concerned. She contacted Warren, talked it over with Henry, then turned them down cold. At her 1989 deposition, Shoney's attorneys wanted to know why, and Billie was happy to tell them. "If you were to go back under a loaded gun, that's the atmosphere I would be going back under," she said. "My record was clean. I was a good worker. I worked hard for that company, and my record is clean. And if I went back to that company, there could be people coming out of Nashville right and left and write me up on nitpicky stuff, left and right. And they would have a reason to fire me for the little simple reasons, and I would be gone. They had no reason to terminate me before."

What made the Elliotts' termination even more difficult to accept, she said, was that in better times, before the orders to get rid of their black workers, before the 70:30 directive, Charlie Robertson had offered to make them his area supervisors when he expanded his Captain D's operations into Tallahassee. They would have been making good money, could have bought a house to replace their trailer, could have advanced further in the company instead of hustling for any minimum-wage service job they could find. At Robertson's urging they had even traveled to Tennessee on a vacation where they visited Dollywood, caught a show at the Grand Old Opry, and toured the Shoney's, Inc. headquarters in Nashville with Roger Danner as their guide. But they should have known then that something was wrong with the company they worked for, Billie testified in her deposition: "Roger did not introduce us to any black people. We went through all the company offices. We went through Shoney's warehouse. We went through the salad dressing place. . . . I saw no black people."

It took Henry Elliott well into the summer of 1988 before he could find work. He had been with Robertson Investment Company for ten years, his entire adult life, and took it hard when he and Billie were fired. He got depressed. He stopped eating and had trouble sleeping. "He just went into like a Twilight Zone," Billie remembered. Having to look for another job and explain what had happened to his career at Captain D's was painful, Henry said.

"It's not a whole lot of fun going out and applying for jobs, and they say, 'Why was you fired?' You say, 'Well, I was fired because I wouldn't fire the blacks.' And they kind of give you a funny look, like it would have been easier to fire the blacks than to hire them, or it would have been easier to do that rather than get fired." Henry said he struggled with "the humiliation of getting fired and having to write that down and tell everybody, 'Yes, I got fired.'"

At his own deposition a year later, Henry was asked how he knew what prospective employers thought about his job applications: "Has anybody said anything to you directly regarding whether you fired blacks or didn't fire blacks at Captain D's, or are you just assuming that's what everybody is thinking?"

No, Henry said, he didn't have to assume anything. "A lot of people said, 'I can't believe that. I can't believe that,'" he recalled. "It makes me look to be a liar. They are saying, 'I don't believe it. I don't believe it. I don't believe it.'"

Henry applied for more than a dozen jobs in the weeks after he was fired, including work as a Coca-Cola route salesman, as a cook in the federal prison, and as a driver for Flowers Bakery, which had advertised a route opening up in the Blountstown area. The bakery manager refused to give him an application. "He just hemmed and hawed around and beat around the bush, and I left it at that," Henry said. "He told me that he couldn't give out no more than two applications at a time, or they are cutting back on paper costs: 'I can't give out applications just to anybody who wants one.'"

Tru-Value Hardware said they didn't have any openings, but Hardee's was advertising for a couple of assistant managers. They interviewed Henry for one of the positions and said they'd call, but never did. Like Billie, Henry applied at Sunland, Payless Shoes, Super C, Russell Athletics, as well as Capital TV, Lehigh Furniture, Unimac Washing Machines. He finally landed a job as manager of a new Subway sandwich shop just opening in Marianna. It helped that the owners were from out of town, but Henry almost lost the job when they called Captain D's for a reference.

Paul Suggs had apologized the day he fired Henry. He regretted having to do it, he reportedly said, but he had no choice since he was under orders. Henry testified that Suggs assured him, nonetheless, that if Henry ever needed a recommendation he would be happy to provide one. So Henry had listed the area supervisor as a reference on his Subway application along with the Marianna Captain D's phone number. It was a mistake, Henry said in his deposition: When one of the Subway owners called for a recommendation, the person answering the phone at Captain D's said everyone at the store had been ordered not to talk about the Elliotts.

Henry got the job anyway. The owners started him as a manager trainee for a probationary period, and in August 1988 he was able to hire Billie as a sandwich maker for $3.75 an hour. Already they had other problems to deal with, though. A rift had developed between Billie and her sister's family when the new Captain D's manager, Debora Newton, offered Billie's nephew Mike Groover his job back as assistant manager and Mike took it. Relations between Billie and her sister, already strained, were now an open wound with neither side talking to the other. The Elliotts had fired Mike themselves, but they still couldn't believe he would align himself with Newton and the Suggses.

All the African American workers fired by Newton and the Suggses said they struggled after they lost their jobs at Captain D's. Gwendolyn Smith was unemployed for nine months before getting a job with Zebra Day Care for $3.30 an hour (she later found a better job at Chipola Aeronautics, where the pay was $4.70). Stephanie Cooper had been making $3.35 an hour working the counter at Captain D's. The mother of twins, she had gotten off welfare when Billie hired her but was forced to go back on AFDC after she was fired. She eventually landed another job at Russell Athletics making $5.50 an hour.

At fifty-seven, Madeline Herring had been working steadily for more than forty years and was still at Captain D's the day Paul and Jan Suggs came into the store to fire Henry. "Mrs. Suggs said something that I still think it was a rude remark," Herring said in her deposition. "She said it was too many niggers in the kitchen. She had to get rid of some of them. I don't think that was nice." Nor did she think it was nice the way the Suggses had Debora Newton

scale back her hours until she could no longer afford to work. They
should have at least told her to her face that they wanted to get rid
of her, Herring said, and if they didn't want blacks working in their
restaurant, then why did they let them in the front door to spend
their money?

"It still makes me feel bad because I never been fired off a job in
my life," she said. Herring was out of work for weeks and struggled
to cover her bills and to provide for her daughter, a high school
senior then a month away from graduation. It wasn't until June
1988 that she finally got another waitressing job at a restaurant
called Majapolos, where she made $170 a week for the next two
years, until it went out of business.

Deborah Bell, who claimed that the Suggses had forced her out
of Captain D's earlier, also by cutting her hours, was able to find
work as a cashier, a sales clerk, then as a cosmetologist, but Lester
Thomas, who lost his assistant manager position shortly after
Mike Groover came back to work, was unemployed until September, when he got a job working at a peanut mill in nearby
Greenwood.

Others said they struggled, too, including some of the white
managers who had signed sworn statements about carrying out
the company's discriminatory policies. For John Corley, who had
gone to court a few years before in an unemployment compensation dispute with Robertson Investment, that struggle took a bizarre turn in the fall of 1989 when he contacted Charlie Robertson
for a job recommendation, and Robertson, Corley alleged, offered
him a deal.

"[Robertson] wanted to know why I gave a statement in this
lawsuit," Corley testified under oath in his deposition. "And I told
him that, you know, that they asked me what I knew, and I told
them what I knew, and gave them a statement. And he told me,
'Was it true?' And I said, 'Yes, it was true.' And he said for a job
recommendation that if I would change my affidavit that I'd get a
job recommendation. . . . That's all he said. Change my statement,
saying I was coerced into making the statement."

Corley told Warren about Robertson's alleged offer, and Warren
had Corley contact the FBI in Panama City, where an agent named
Paul Maxwell was assigned to the case. Maxwell spoke with both

Warren and Corley several times, and at one point suggested the possibility of wiring Corley and then having him hand-deliver a bogus letter to Robertson recanting his testimony to see if the franchise owner would incriminate himself. Corley agreed, but Maxwell said he first had to get approval from his supervisors. (Maxwell confirmed those contacts in an interview with the author.) For reasons that were never made clear to Warren or Corley, that approval never came.

Corley's testimony about the alleged coercion, which emerged during his deposition in 1990, appeared to come as a surprise to attorneys for Shoney's and Robertson Investment Company. "Can we take a quick break so I can find out what's going on?" one asked. After the recess, the corporate attorneys resumed the deposition: "I'm going to ask you a little bit about your contact with the FBI that you talked about a little earlier. When was that that you would have talked to Mr. Maxwell?" Corley told the attorney the date of the conversation.

Q: And you said you talked to him generally about your conversation with Mr. Robertson?

A: Yes.

Q: All right. Did you ever give Mr. Maxwell, or anyone else with the FBI, any writings, or notes about your conversation?

A: No. I didn't.

Q: And you said you talked to Mr. Robertson by phone?

A: Yes.

Q: When he tried to make you change your testimony?

A: Uh-huh.

Q: Was anyone else listening to that conversation?

A: No.

Q: Was that conversation tape recorded?

A: No.

Q: Are you getting anything out of this lawsuit?

A: No. I'm not.

Q: Have you been told you're in any way a member of a class, or intend to become a plaintiff in this lawsuit?

A: No.

Q: That's about all I have.

Years later in a telephone interview with the author, Robertson's first response when asked about Corley's allegation was,
"That wasn't proven." After interrupting the interview to consult
with his attorney, he amended his statement: "That's already been
taken care of in the court case," he said. "That's just absolutely
not true. I don't think that was ever used in the case." Robertson
refused to comment on any of the racial allegations against him
except to say, "Most of that was in the company," meaning, apparently, that most of the discriminatory policies were alleged to have
taken place in stores owned by Shoney's, Inc., and not in the franchises. And, he added, "Several guys, supervisors and everything,
said I didn't even carry out orders. Are you going to write that?
There were three or four depositions. If you're going to write the
bad you better damn sure write the good." Indeed, in Robertson
Investment's response to the charges against the franchise company, the attorneys included affidavits from five then-current
managers, including Paul and Jan Suggs, denying the allegations of
racial discrimination.

The Equal Employment Opportunity Commission's Atlanta office reached a different conclusion. In one of the few actions to
come from the commission in the four-and-a-half-year case
against Shoney's, Danner, and Robertson Investment, EEOC regional officials issued a dozen "cause findings" against Robertson
Investment in 1990 after investigating the charges of Robertson's
Panama City and Marianna employees: determinations that there
was "reasonable cause" to believe that Robertson Investment had
illegally discriminated against Billie and Henry Elliott, Lester
Thomas, Leonard Charles Williams, Donna Mongoven, and seven
other African American former workers: Patricia Spires, Stephanie
Cooper, Deborah Bell, Hampshire Peterson, Julia Hunter, Gwendolyn Smith, and Madeline Herring.

In their determination on behalf of Billie Elliott, the EEOC concluded: "The pattern of evidence developed during the investigation overwhelmingly demonstrates that [Robertson Investment]
implemented discriminatory policies or practices, which adversely affected blacks as a class, as well as persons of other races
opposed to those policies or practices. [Robertson Investment's]
discriminatory policies or practices impacted hiring, assignment,

promotion, termination, constructive discharge, terms and conditions of employment (harassment and hours of work), and retaliation."

The EEOC also found that Robertson Investment's discriminatory "policies and practices" constituted "continuing violations of
Title VII," meaning that the EEOC investigators believed the discrimination had continued "unabated over time and [were] not
discrete events occurring at only one moment."

By June 23, 1988, Tommy Warren was ready to move against Shoney's. He had consulted with an economist at the University of
Kentucky, a labor analyst named James Freeman, about the kinds
of data necessary for an impact analysis of the system-wide racial
discrimination policies that he believed he had uncovered. He had
finished his preliminary research on the corporate structure of
Robertson Investment and Shoney's, Inc. He had spent hours on
the phone with Barry Goldstein refining a draft complaint, organizing his sworn statements, preparing a tentative round of interrogatories for company officials, and drafting a request for Shoney's employment statistics.

He put all these materials in a package, sent the package to Gary
Brown, Shoney's general counsel, and then he waited. A week later
he got the first conference call. It was Brown and an associate with
a few routine questions, a few points of clarification, not much
more. A week after that, another call came in. This time it was
Shoney's chief labor counsel, an attorney out of Birmingham, Alabama, named Charles A. Powell III, whom everyone called Butch
and whom Warren would come to know all too well over the next
four years.

Powell wanted to know what Warren was seeking to get out of
the company. Warren said he needed the employment statistics he
had cited in his request for documents, and only after he had an
opportunity to study them would he be able to discuss his ideas
for an appropriate settlement and injunctive relief—the sort of
agreement necessary to stop the alleged discriminatory practices—on a class-wide basis.

Powell said that executives at Shoney's would need to study the
material Warren had sent before deciding what employment sta-

tistics could be released. He agreed to toll, or extend, the statute of limitations on any civil rights charges while the company con-sidered the request. Warren let it drop that Barry Goldstein and the NAACP Legal Defense Fund would possibly be joining him in bringing the case.

Again, it was a polite conversation, and Warren came away op-timistic, not that there would be an immediate settlement, but that Shoney's was at least willing to engage in a reasonable discussion and examination of the evidence. Warren would be kept waiting for another two months, however, before getting a response to his request for documents at a terse face-to-face meeting in Tallahassee.

Periodically during the summer, while he waited for a response from Shoney's attorneys, Warren made sure to punctuate his calls to Goldstein with formal letters to the LDF asking for help in the case. But no class as large or as widespread geographically as the one Warren proposed had ever been certified in a discrimination case, Goldstein knew, and the LDF still insisted that it needed stronger discovery supporting Warren's vision of a corporate-wide class of plaintiffs. The LDF was interested, and Goldstein continued to provide help and advice, but for the time being Warren continued on his own.

On August 10, he agreed to meet with a battery of attorneys representing Robertson Investment Company, but nothing came of it. The lawyers made what to Warren were feeble overtures toward a settlement, then he didn't hear from them again. The only word coming out of Butch Powell's office, meanwhile, was delay, and Warren's initial optimism dimmed into something more realistic. "At that point none of them were taking it as seriously as they ultimately took it," he said. "They probably thought I couldn't pull it off, or that they could defend the case."

It wasn't an unreasonable assumption. Shoney's, Inc. was the tenth largest restaurant chain in the country (and the second largest family restaurant business), with virtually unlimited legal and financial resources, while Tommy Warren was just some southern attorney, working on his own, making broad class claims with limited evidence. When Butch Powell ran into Barry Goldstein at

63

The
Black
O

a meeting in Washington that summer, he tried to joke with Gold-stein about a small-time Florida attorney named Warren who was "bandying your name around as possible cocounsel in a suit against Shoney's." To Powell's apparent surprise, Goldstein said that yes, in fact he and the LDF were considering entering the case.

Warren's own formal introduction to Powell finally took place on September 1. The meeting was scheduled for the conference room at the offices of a downtown Tallahassee law firm, one of at least four firms, Warren soon realized, that Shoney's had already brought in on the case, an indication that they were taking it more seriously than they let on. Warren came with a single ally, attorney Jerry Traynham, who wasn't involved with the case but had agreed to accompany Warren as a favor. The corporation was represented by Jann Johnson Hart, a Tallahassee lawyer whom Warren knew socially; by Benny Ball, the director of personnel for Shoney's, Inc.; by Charles Burr, an employment attorney from Tampa who had been assigned to the case by his senior partner, an old friend of Butch Powell; and by Powell himself, a dark, bearded man.

The meeting didn't last long. According to Billie and Henry Elliott, who were later told what took place, Powell offered Warren $30,000 to divide among his clients in the Florida Panhandle, "and something on the fees to be handled separately." Warren countered that it was premature to even be discussing a settlement figure without a detailed analysis of the corporation's employment figures, which Powell had said he would bring to the meeting but didn't. On top of that, Warren said, there was the issue of injunctive relief, legally binding assurance that Shoney's would immediately stop its discriminatory practices and that it would agree to an affirmative-action plan to counter the years of previous discrimination. But Powell refused to negotiate. He cited a few broad figures, what he claimed were overall totals for minorities in the corporation, then he said, "That's all the statistics you're going to get."

Warren stood. "I can't believe you made me wait two months for this," he said, and he and Traynham walked out of the meeting. As soon as he got back to his office he started calling larger firms in what initially proved to be a fruitless search for support in

bringing the case against Shoney's. It didn't matter. He was angry
and he was tired of waiting.

He was determined to track down witnesses in every state Shoney's operated in, and he was going to put together a case so strong
that Barry Goldstein and the Legal Defense Fund wouldn't have
any choice but to join him.

"I was pretty sure at that point," he said, "that there was going
to be war."

SIX

66 This Is What You
Hire Niggers For 99

Barry Goldstein wasn't surprised when Warren was "stuffed," as both later called it, in his first attempt at a settlement in the Tallahassee meeting with Butch Powell. "It has been my experience that you usually can't get a company's attention in an employment discrimination suit," he said, "until you hit them over the head with class certification," official recognition by a federal judge that the common issues in a case affect a broad group of individuals and that the interests of that group can be best represented by a select number of named plaintiffs. To continue the case, therefore, Warren would need to identify plaintiffs who fit federal court requirements, and he would also need witnesses both outside the Florida Panhandle and in other Shoney's divisions besides Captain D's. On top of that, he would have to establish—and fight off increasingly hostile challenges to—his ability to adequately represent the class.

Clear about where he needed to go next, Warren didn't waste any time tracking down new witnesses, throwing himself back into discovery mode the day after the Tallahassee meeting and tapping into an informal network of civil rights attorneys around the South for possible leads. On September 7, a series of phone calls led him to a Nashville attorney named Pat O'Rourke. O'Rourke had information about an African American former Lee's Famous Recipe manager who had sued Shoney's and settled for a few thousand dollars after claiming he'd been illegally terminated from what company officials purportedly called the "nigger store" in a predominantly black area of Nashville. O'Rourke gave Warren the manager's name, Eugene Grayer, and Warren started what turned out to be a months-long process of tracking the uncooperative Grayer down.

On September 8, Warren found out about another lawsuit, this one in Montgomery, an hour from Butch Powell's Birmingham office, which Powell, as Shoney's labor lawyer, had managed to settle in 1985. One of the plaintiff's attorneys, Vanzetta Penn McPherson, who had since been appointed federal magistrate in central Alabama, agreed to send Warren the complaint and depositions in that case.

A third "hit" that soon followed was contact with an attorney named Greg Stein at a Mobile, Alabama, firm that had handled a number of early voting rights cases in the South. Stein told Warren about a gender discrimination action a lawyer in northern Alabama had brought against Shoney's. That lawyer had received a list of Shoney's employees in the northern Alabama stores, and Stein agreed to have a paralegal telephone the workers to inquire about possible racial discrimination on top of the gender claims. The instructions to the paralegal, Warren said, were to first ask if the individuals on the list still worked for Shoney's, and if they did to hang up immediately; under the rules of the federal court that had jurisdiction in north Florida, where Warren would ultimately file his case, plaintiffs' attorneys were restricted from directly soliciting testimony from current employees.

Most of Warren's effort during the fall of 1988 followed that pattern of working the phones and tracking down leads. He spent hours at night and on weekends watching his children and calling potential witnesses, because that was when he could catch people at home. The Elliotts had practically hand-delivered witnesses during May and June who could testify against Robertson Investment, but it was grunt work now, and the payoff wasn't always immediately evident. Warren eventually found Eugene Grayer managing a Wendy's in Nashville, but Grayer either wouldn't take his calls or, if he did, would quickly hang up after agreeing to send material from his lawsuit—which would never arrive. Toward the end of September, though, while Warren was still waiting for hard evidence—copies of the documents he'd been promised by Vanzetta McPherson and Grayer, more names to follow up on from Greg Stein—he caught a break: hit number four.

"It was a serendipitous call from a former client, a guy named Jim Miller who had been the NAACP chairman from Fort Walton Beach," Warren said. "I had handled a lawsuit for him at Eglin Air Force Base where he ran the officer's club back in 1982. He was managing the NCO club at England Air Force Base in Louisiana now and had called just to shoot the shit."

Miller asked Warren what he was working on, and when Warren told him about the Captain D's case and Shoney's, Inc., a surprised Miller said he'd just hired a white man named Elias Brown as a cook at his club who had a similar story: he'd either been fired or forced to quit his job as a kitchen manager at a Shoney's in Alexandria, Louisiana, he claimed, after he wouldn't cave in to pressure to get rid of some of his black workers.

Warren immediately contacted Brown, although like a lot of potential witnesses Brown refused to give a sworn statement about what had happened. He didn't want to get involved. Brown did agree to put Warren in touch with his former store manager, though, another white man named Mickey Vidrine who told Warren the same story and who in turn said they had received their orders to discriminate from a Shoney's division director responsible for dozens of company stores in that area. Most important, Vidrine was willing to go on the record.

The investigation was picking up speed. In short order Stein, working out of Mobile, found two more witnesses who could testify to racial discrimination at Shoney's, Inc. Then came the material Warren had been waiting for in the Montgomery case:

several depositions, an amended complaint, and a settlement
agreement that quickly convinced him the lid could have been
blown off Shoney's and its discriminatory policies years before. In
fact, it was difficult to tell from the documents now in front of him
why that hadn't happened, why what had been a $10 million lim-
ited class action ended up settling for less than $30,000. (A key
witness for Shoney's would later testify in a deposition that company executives were surprised themselves that they were able to
get off so cheaply in the Montgomery case. "You're not going to
believe this," then-Shoney's president Gary Spoleta was quoted as
saying about one of the plaintiffs' attorneys, "but the stupid fucking bitch has decided to settle the suit for about $25,000.")

The case started on New Year's Eve 1984 when a twenty-six-
year-old black woman, Sharon Johnson, was called in to work at
the West South Boulevard Shoney's despite the fact that she was
scheduled to have the night off. Her family needed the money,
though, so she left her two young daughters at home with her husband and went in. She was surprised when she got there. Three
other black waitresses were already on duty—Debra Smith, Flossy
Parks, and Gail Baldwin—and everyone at the restaurant knew
the company's unwritten rule: no more than two blacks at any one
time working the floor.

The night dining-room supervisor, a twenty-year-old white
woman named Pat Short, would later testify that she couldn't find
enough whites to work the New Year's Eve shift but didn't think
Gene Yager, the city manager in charge of half a dozen Montgomery Shoney's, would find out. The store manager didn't mind, but
the two-black-waitress rule wasn't his. Short and others later testified that it came from Yager and his area supervisor, Harvey Hester, and from their boss, division director Bill Long. All the company officials were white.

Short, who had been trained as a waitress by Sharon Johnson
two years earlier and then promoted past Johnson to supervisor,
had made the mistake once before of scheduling more than two
black waitresses. Harvey Hester showed up at the restaurant that
time and immediately sent one of them home, Short said in a
deposition, adding that both Yager and Hester had told her too
many blacks ran off white customers. According to Short and

other witnesses, the area dining-room supervisor, Janie White-head, also laid out race rules for the Montgomery restaurants. "She said that I was not to have more than two blacks on the floor at one time, and I was not to have a black cashier or a black person to seat the floor, period," Short later testified. Despite those orders, Short had once asked Johnson to run the register, and she got caught by Hester that time, too. Short testified that Hester told her he "wasn't going to have a nigger run his cash register."

Sharon Johnson and the three other black waitresses had been on duty for several hours that New Year's Eve, 1984, when things fell apart. Half an hour after midnight, barely into January 1, 1985, Pat Short and Richard Finsterbush, the store manager, got a call from another Montgomery Shoney's telling them that Yager and Hester were on their way over to check out the West South Boulevard store. Short knew she was in trouble with four black waitresses working the same shift, so she grabbed the first one she could find and in a panic asked her to hide in the restroom. That waitress was Sharon Johnson. At a deposition eleven months later Johnson described what happened:

"I was on the floor and as I was leaving off the floor going on the waitress line, Pat came right behind me. You know, she was—I almost kind of stumbled because she was so close up on me. And I turned around, and I said, 'What is wrong, Pat?' And she looked at me, she said, 'Sharon,' she said, 'Please go and hide.' She said, 'Harvey and Yager is here.' And we was facing each other, and I just looked at her. I just stared at her, because I couldn't say anything. Because I couldn't believe she was asking me. I just stared at her. And she said, 'Please go hide. I will lose my job. Please take Debra Smith with you.' And that is what I did."

Short and other witnesses confirmed Johnson's story. "The only reason she went was where I would not get into trouble," Short said.

Debra Smith sat on a stool in the women's restroom. Johnson dragged in a chair and they locked the door. "I was crying," Johnson said. "I was sitting there, I was mumbling and mumbling and crying, you know, and saying all kinds of things. [Debra Smith] was just sitting there. She was saying, 'Sharon don't cry, don't cry. . . .'"

finally left. For Johnson, the humiliation of having to hide in the
restroom because she was black was one humiliation too many.
She had seen white waitresses she had trained and who she considered her friends, people like Pat Short, continually promoted past
her onto the register, or into hostess positions, or up to dining-
room supervisor. No blacks ever got those jobs, and that night
wasn't the first time Johnson had been slapped in the face with
their two-black-waitress rule. A few years before, a different
dining-room supervisor scheduled Johnson and two other black
waitresses to work, she said in a deposition, and when Gene Yager
found out he exploded at Johnson's boss. "What are you doing with
three tokens on the floor at the same time?" he shouted, loud
enough for Johnson to hear. The dining-room supervisor suddenly
realized Johnson was standing nearby and put her hand over her
mouth. Yager turned and saw Johnson, too, and walked away,
Johnson claimed.

After Johnson and Smith finally unlocked the door and left the
restroom New Year's Eve, Johnson told Finsterbush and Short she
was sick of the discrimination at Shoney's and refused to finish her
shift. They took her into the manager's office and apologized, but
it wasn't enough. She did not quit her job, but the next day Johnson, who had never spoken with an attorney in her life, went looking for a lawyer.

The first two she contacted were white attorneys she found in
the Yellow Pages. Both told her she couldn't sue because she had
"hurt feelings" and declined to take her case. After that she decided to try black attorneys in Montgomery who might be more
sympathetic; several more firms turned her down, though, before
she found one who agreed to look into her allegations. That attorney was a slight, balding, bespectacled black man named Larry
Raby who reminded Johnson of the TV detective Columbo because of his rumpled suits. She liked him right away, she said,
though his inexperience in civil rights litigation was immediately
apparent; he acknowledged it himself. But at least he was willing
to take the case.

On February 11, 1985, Raby had Johnson file a charge of discrimination with the federal Equal Employment Opportunity
Commission, the necessary first step to bringing a civil rights

lawsuit. On July 18, they added another charge, claiming Johnson was being systematically harassed at work, criticized and written up for minor infractions or for none at all. As it turned out, Johnson wasn't just being paranoid. A white kitchen manager, Ellen Nix, would later testify that she and other employees were ordered by Gene Yager to "make it tough" on Johnson, to "keep on her black ass so she will quit." Nix also swore that she was told by Yager's assistant, Harvey Hester, that Shoney's executives had assured them that as long as Hester and Yager "stuck to their story that Johnson was a poor worker and an unreliable employee, they would be taken care of—that their jobs were secure and their lawyer fees would be paid." Those executives, Nix said she was told, were Ray Danner, Gary Spoleta, and the division director, Bill Long.

Despite the alleged harassment, Johnson refused to quit her job, and on August 19 she received her Notice of Right to Sue from the EEOC. On October 1 Raby filed a class action on behalf of all black waitresses at the West South Boulevard store, with Sharon Johnson as the sole named plaintiff, against Yager, Hester, Long, and Shoney's, Inc. The other black waitress who had hidden in the restroom, Debra Smith, stayed out of the case. According to Johnson, Smith said her family didn't want her to get involved. In the suit, Raby and Johnson requested a court order forcing Shoney's to end its discriminatory practices in hiring, promotion, and treatment of black employees, and they sought $1 million in compensatory and punitive damages.

Knowing the case was more than he could handle alone, Raby brought in a more experienced civil-rights attorney to help with the litigation, Vanzetta Penn McPherson. Even Johnson saw that it was a good decision. "[Larry Raby] was new to the field," she said. "But when we got into the depositions McPherson was strong, she was powerful."

Those depositions took place in November and December 1985, and pitted McPherson and occasionally Raby against an aggressive team of Shoney's labor lawyers led by Butch Powell. When McPherson was questioning Pat Short about orders from Yager and Hester to limit the number of black waitresses, for example, Powell typically jumped in. "We're going to object to the form," he

said. "Are you asking her about Hester or asking her about Yager
or are you asking her about a hopscotch?"

McPherson responded evenly: "I said Yager."

"Well, you were on Yager," Powell said, further interrupting the
deposition, "then you went to Hester and now you are back on—"

McPherson cut him off. "I said Yager," she repeated.

One of Powell's associates interjected at that point: "Well, then
we object to you assuming facts not in evidence."

"What facts?" said McPherson.

"Many facts," said Powell.

The transcripts show that, while McPherson may have been
occasionally flustered, she largely held her ground. And as the
testimony piled up against Shoney's and its Montgomery-area executives, she and Raby grew more and more confident. Short's
deposition proved to be particularly damning. She testified that
Johnson had been an excellent waitress and would have made a
good dining-room supervisor, but that company officials refused
to promote any blacks to positions of responsibility. She also said
that Hester had pressured her to help protect Shoney's officials
from Johnson's failure-to-promote charge after she filed her complaint. "He said they were going to have to try and cover their
asses," she testified. "He made me sign a piece of paper that stated
Sharon had never asked me for a supervisor's position," though
those positions were never publicized, she said, precisely so black
workers wouldn't be able to apply for them.

Another dining-room supervisor, Brenda Johnston, confirmed
that company officials repeatedly told her and other supervisors
not to have more than two black waitresses, or "tokens," on the
floor at any one time. Johnston said she was told by Yager that
"there should be no niggers working at the cash register, and no
niggers seating customers" because "niggers are not intelligent
enough to do either of these jobs." Johnston said racist attitudes
were rampant in the corporation, and she testified that she heard
Shoney's president Gary Spoleta refer to blacks as "niggers" on the
several occasions he visited the Montgomery store. She said Spoleta chided her once about performing menial tasks in the store,
saying, "Why do you do things like that? This is what you hire
niggers for."

Cathy and Harrell Shaw, a former Shoney's dining-room supervisor and a store manager, respectively, also testified to the company's discriminatory practices in the Montgomery stores, and they named Yager, Hester, and Long as the officials giving the orders to limit the number of black workers and keep blacks out of supervisory positions. The highest-ranking black employee ever in Montgomery, Cathy Shaw said, was a breakfast-bar manager who finally quit after six years because he was continually passed over for further promotion.

Harrell Shaw testified that the problems in the Montgomery stores weren't limited to racial discrimination. He said Hester and Yager were also lending money to workers and then in effect garnishing the employees' wages by making the workers cash their paychecks at the restaurant so Yager and Hester could take the money owed them off the top. He once clashed with Hester, Shaw said, over Hester's alleged treatment of a black employee. "Harvey had taken most of the guy's check and just given him the balance," Shaw testified, "and the guy was real upset because he had to pay somebody down at the courthouse. And I got into it with Harvey about it to just let the guy pay so much. And he just said he wasn't nothing but an old nigger anyway."

Yager, Hester, and Long denied all the charges, even when Raby and McPherson had Johnson go public with her charges on a local TV news broadcast, but the pressure on the company was mounting. Raby and McPherson, meanwhile, amended their complaint, upping the demand for damages to $10 million.

And then, suddenly, the case disappeared.

Late in December 1985, a year after she had been forced to hide in a restroom to cover the fact that there were "too many" black waitresses on duty at a Montgomery Shoney's, Johnson agreed to her lawyers' recommendation that she accept a settlement offer of $20,000, with $2,000 each for a handful of other black claimants at her store. To get the money she had to quit her job and sign a nondisclosure clause, which meant she was barred from talking about the case publicly. Shoney's, for its part, agreed to fire Gene Yager and post future job openings in management at the Montgomery restaurants, but there would be no admission of guilt. (Though she had signed the nondisclosure clause in 1985, Johnson agreed to talk about her case for this account since all the documents from her lawsuit—the charge of discrimination, the complaints, the depositions, the settlement agreement, and the consent decree—were entered into evidence in the subsequent case Tommy Warren brought against Shoney's and discussed in open court proceedings.)

Johnson said she felt let down by her attorneys, and that she had wanted her case to go to trial. She said it took her a year to find another job, and that was part-time clerical work in a state government temp pool.

What never made it onto the court record, though, or into the settlement agreement, was that Johnson had apparently derailed the lawsuit with comments she made in a phone conversation with one of the witnesses in her case. She was speaking on a pay phone at the West South Boulevard Shoney's in December 1985, after the depositions, and those comments were overheard by another waitress, who then passed them on to Shoney's attorneys.

The charge: that Johnson had promised to give away some of the money if she won the lawsuit. Faced with what they believed was credible evidence that the conversation had taken place, Raby and McPherson advised Johnson to accept Shoney's small settlement offer, even though they were still convinced of the truth of Johnson's charges of discrimination as well as the truth of the depositions of the other Montgomery witnesses against Shoney's and its white managers.

In a 1994 interview Johnson acknowledged having the conversation, but still maintained that what she said was taken out of context and distorted by the lawyers. She says one of the witnesses had told her his family was having "bad times," so Johnson said she would help out. "Shoney's tried to twist it around that I was paying people to lie for me. . . . I think that's what made it go down some, but for that reason it shouldn't have gone down that much because it was all still true facts," Johnson said.

Johnson's attorney Larry Raby (who only agreed to speak about the buried circumstances of the settlement after Johnson signed a waiver of the attorney-client privilege) confirmed that the overheard phone conversation did in fact hurt the case. "Sharon did admit that she was talking to some people," Raby said, "that she

had told them that once the case—this was before we had final-
ized the settlement—and she told them that once it was over that
she was going to give them some money. . . . That was one of the
main factors, the main factor that prompted the settlement."

Still, he noted, there was some consolation in the agreement
that Shoney's would post notices of all future job openings in management, a practice that had never before been in place and that
had contributed to the exclusion of black workers from promotion
opportunities. They were also able to take some satisfaction in
Shoney's agreement to terminate Gene Yager for his racist treatment of black employees and his discriminatory policies.

The only problem was, Yager wasn't fired, not right away. As
Tommy Warren discovered after subsequent investigation, Shoney's executives actually placed the Montgomery city manager
on leave without pay for several months so he could collect on
$40,000 worth of stock options that hadn't yet matured. In return,
Yager had to sign a nondisclosure clause similar to Johnson's, guaranteeing the company that he wouldn't discuss any facts about the
Montgomery case or his actions as a Shoney's official.

There was even more to the story than that. When Yager's termination did finally take effect, Shoney's indicated in his personnel file that his employment had ended due to "Mental/Physical
Condition." Nothing in his record said that his firing had anything
to do with discriminatory racial practices in the workplace. Harvey Hester, meanwhile, was promoted into Yager's old job as city
manager, and Bill Long received a promotion to vice president of
the Shoney's division.

Warren would eventually track Yager down in Tallassee, Alabama, where he had opened his own restaurant after a stint of
managing stores for Golden Corral. The man Warren found was
edgy, nervous, defensive—and angry. Yager admitted to Warren
that Shoney's had let him keep his $40,000 stock option, but said
he was still upset about what he later alleged was the company's
betrayal in making him a scapegoat in the Sharon Johnson case,
especially, he claimed, after he had told "half-truths" in his 1985
deposition to protect other corporate officials. When Warren told
Yager that his personnel records indicated he had been terminated
for "Mental/Physical Condition," Yager agreed to talk, on the record. He subsequently drove to Florida to meet with Warren, and

after an all-day meeting signed an eighteen-page affidavit in which he named eight current and former Shoney's executives, including Bill Long, Gary Spoleta, Dave Wachtel, and Ray Danner, who he claimed had instructed him in what he alleged was the company's "unwritten policy and practice of discriminating against black persons in Shoney's, Inc."

All of those policies, Yager said he was repeatedly told, and witnessed for himself, originated with Ray Danner. On one occasion, he testified, Danner explained to him why black workers made poor managers. "Have you ever seen a black housing project?" Danner purportedly asked. "If you have, you have seen how blacks don't take care of anything and you would know why they don't make good employees." When Danner saw "too many" blacks working in a Shoney's kitchen, Yager said, he would make a point of letting managers know it by telling them, "It sure is cloudy in here."

Bill Long also used figurative language to complain about the number of blacks working at his stores, Yager testified. A typical Long comment, according to Yager, was "What are you doing, filming 'Roots' today?" Other times Long was more direct, according to Yager. "You've got too many God damn niggers working here today," Yager said he was told on one occasion. And on another: "I'm not having any motherfucking nigger in management in my area." Another executive, Joe Sanders, referred to blacks as "roids," Yager testified, and when he asked Sanders why, Sanders purportedly responded, "You get in trouble for saying 'nigger,' so you call them 'roids,' short for 'niggeroids.'"

One of the first things he was instructed to do when he started his career as a cook at Shoney's, Yager claimed, was to blacken in the "O" in the Shoney's name at the top of an employment application if the applicant was black. That way, he said he was told, a manager who might not be around when an application came in could easily identify the race of prospective employees when going through the files later—and make sure to avoid calling in black applicants.

In his affidavit, and later in his deposition, Yager admitted passing along what he alleged were orders from Bill Long to store managers to keep blacks out of supervisory positions and to limit the number of black waitresses to two per shift. Moreover, he said he was aware of the circumstances of the Sharon Johnson New Year's Eve incident. Yager then cited at least twenty examples from his 1985 deposition where he said he gave "half-truths" or "beat around the bush" in his responses under oath to the charges by Sharon Johnson, Pat Short, and the other Montgomery witnesses.

At a subsequent deposition, taken in January 1992, Yager again listed the numerous examples of "half-truths" and evasions from his deposition seven years earlier in the Sharon Johnson case. Yager also charged that he had been "hung out to dry" by Shoney's officials. "These people had only one concern," he testified. "To protect Shoney's. They didn't give a shit about Gene Yager."

Yager also swore in his affidavit to Warren that after Sharon Johnson's suit was settled, in late December 1985, he received the news in a phone call from Gary Spoleta. "When Mr. Spoleta called me, he told me that, 'Gene, make sure that all of the other phones in your house are hung up so no one can be listening to this conversation,'" Yager claimed. "After I told him that no one else was on the line, he said, 'You're not going to believe this, but the stupid fucking bitch [meaning Sharon Johnson's attorney] has decided to settle the suit for about $25,000.' He then told me that I should avoid any contact with the press or anybody else about the lawsuit because the settlement was going to be announced the next day or shortly thereafter. He told me to lay low until everything is signed. I took this to mean that I should not discuss the case with anyone. A few days later, still in December, I heard that the case had been settled for $25,000 and my job."

Spoleta denied all charges that he had used racial slurs or given discriminatory orders, and Shoney's lawyers eventually tried to use the Sharon Johnson case as proof of the company's forthright policy of responding swiftly and surely to charges of racial discrimination. Yager—or "Krager," as Butch Powell misidentified him at a hearing in 1991—was a single "bad apple" in an isolated pocket of discrimination, they argued, and they had gotten rid of him as soon as they found out. Moreover, they said, Shoney's president, Spoleta, had summoned dozens of supervisors to a meeting in 1986 where he told them that he didn't want any more incidents like the Sharon Johnson case and that they would be fired if they used racial slurs. Several Shoney's officials also said that that meeting had been called by Spoleta and had taken place.

At that 1991 hearing, though, Powell failed to mention the $40,000 stock buyout, the "official" reason for Yager's termination cited in his personnel file, the twelve months that passed between the time Sharon Johnson was forced to hide in a restroom and the time Yager lost his job, the promotions for Harvey Hester and Bill Long, and Yager's charge that several top Shoney's officials contacted him after learning he had given sworn statements against them to Tommy Warren.

In meetings, phone calls, and letters, copies of which went into the court record, the executives apparently tried to convince Yager that Warren was the true enemy. Yager's own conclusion: "I believe that all this contact from Shoney's and its lawyers was an attempt to keep me from coming forward and telling the truth about Shoney's race discrimination that occurred in Montgomery, Alabama, and elsewhere."

What the Montgomery case meant to Warren, in the fall of 1988, was more witnesses who could help build the larger case about Shoney's alleged corporate-wide policy of racial discrimination. All of Sharon Johnson's witnesses, and others Warren was able to locate—thirteen in all—could not only provide testimony about their own experiences but could also give Warren the names of other Shoney's managers and employees who might further corroborate their charges and help establish the "continuing violation" theory of the case—Warren's contention that the company had been systematically discriminating against blacks for years in hiring, promotion, and treatment and was still, in 1988, a full generation after passage of the Civil Rights Act of 1964, carrying out discriminatory orders in the workplace and maintaining an ongoing climate of discrimination against those who had been run off or hurt years before.

Many of the white witnesses repeated what Warren had heard in the Florida Panhandle, that they were relieved to be able to finally come clean about what they said they had been part of at Shoney's. Some echoed Debra Tompkins, a former area dining-room supervisor, on why they carried out the policies instead of coming forward sooner or challenging the company themselves: "I had to in order to keep my job. At that time I was the sole breadwinner of my family. My husband had opened up a bicycle shop, so therefore he didn't have a paycheck coming in. I had a mortgage to pay, a car note to pay, and I was raising two kids." She agreed to testify, Tompkins said, "because I feel like I want the employees of Shoney's that are working there now not to have to worry about compromising their standards like I felt we had to compromise ours."

Tompkins, one of the witnesses attorney Greg Stein located in Mobile from the list of employees in the earlier Alabama gender bias suit, repeated an increasingly familiar litany of orders to discriminate that she said came directly from her bosses, orders involving race-coded applications, limits on the "acceptable" number of black waitresses, and the exclusion of blacks from positions in management. Those practices, she testified, continued even after the Sharon Johnson case exploded in Shoney's face. "We were just informed to be more discreet about it," she said, because her supervisors "didn't want the same thing that happened in Montgomery to occur in Mobile."

Throughout the autumn of 1988, Warren made sure to send Barry Goldstein and the LDF summaries on each new witness, copies of all new evidence, and the names of every new Shoney's executive on the growing list of those charged with implementing Danner's policies. And the LDF, Goldstein told Warren, was starting to come around. By late fall, the two men were talking on the phone several times a week, plotting strategy together, and working out an idea of Warren's for tying all the disparate anecdotes of the case together. That idea, to send an investigator to survey 250 Shoney's, Captain D's, and Lee's Famous Recipe Chickens in the corporation's ten most populous states, had come to Warren while he and his family were eating dinner at a Shoney's. While there, he realized that thanks to the open layout of the restaurants and the different style of uniforms worn by different employees, an observer could stand just inside a Shoney's entrance for several minutes and in that time account for all the front-of-the-store staff on a given shift, and their race.

The survey Warren and Goldstein ultimately designed, with the help of a team of university economists and statisticians, would

be the thing that put the case over the top for the LDF and ce-
mented Warren and Goldstein's decision to file the case together
as co-lead counsels. Disparities showed up in all the stores, where
the site survey indicated that blacks tended to work in the low-
paying, non-customer-contact positions, but the numbers were
starkest in the Shoney's division. There, blacks at the stores sur-
veyed made up more than half of the busboys, salad-bar attendants, and kitchen workers but held fewer than 10 percent of the
jobs that could be identified as store managers, kitchen managers,
servers, and cashiers.

Shoney's, meanwhile, had ideas of its own about a Warren-
Goldstein partnership and about the participation of the LDF.
Dealing with Tommy Warren was one thing. To Shoney's counsel
in the early months of the case he was a two-bit southern lawyer,
small-time, a minor corporate irritant. But Barry Goldstein, with
his eighteen years at LDF, his experience arguing employment
cases before the Supreme Court, his first-rate skills as a litigator,
and his pristine national reputation—that was another matter
entirely.

So, concerned about a possible Warren-Goldstein alliance, Shoney's own lead counsel, Butch Powell, and Steve Tallent, a Washington, D.C., attorney who led the labor section for Gibson, Dunn
and Crutcher, one of the largest corporate law firms in the nation,
decided to fill Goldstein in on Tommy Warren's past.

SEVEN

" A Trick of All Trades "

In 1966, Tommy Warren was everybody's all-everything: All-City, All-State, All-South, Honorable Mention All-American. It was his senior year at Coral Gables High School and he had quarterbacked the football team to another state title the previous autumn. The year before that, with Warren playing halfback, they had been so good they were also awarded the mythical high-school national championship. Fifty-three universities from around the country waved scholarship offers, but Touchdown Tommy was too busy that spring playing baseball to worry about it too much. He had been a Miami boy all but the first two years of his life; his father, a former player in the Canadian Football League, had moved the family to south Florida to take a job as a stockbroker with Merrill-Lynch in 1950. Since he had grown up in the tropics, Warren had already decided he wouldn't attend college anywhere it was cold. In the end he agreed to visit only five southern schools: Georgia

the University of Miami, and Florida State. It snowed the day he
visited Atlanta, so Georgia Tech was out as quickly as that, and
since Chapel Hill was even further north he crossed the Tar Heels
off the list as well.

The University of Miami offered a baseball scholarship, the University of Florida wanted to give him one in football, but only Florida State was willing to let Warren play both, so it turned out to be a simple process of elimination. Moreover, under its celebrated coach Bill Peterson, Florida State had recently blasted onto the national scene with a string of bowl appearances featuring its high-powered, pro-set offense. Most of the Southeastern Conference schools were still grinding it out on the ground, meanwhile, and since Tommy Warren's strengths were reading defenses and throwing the ball, Florida State was the logical choice.

He made certain, though, to have FSU's athletic director put the agreement in writing that he could skip spring football to play on the baseball team. Between seasons, he planned to take full advantage of the deer and duck hunting on those north Florida game plantations, many of them owned by wealthy boosters of the Seminoles football team. And with the Gulf of Mexico only thirty miles from the Tallahassee school, he'd be able to work in plenty of fishing as well. Academics didn't figure greatly in his college plans.

As Warren approached his freshman year at FSU his future seemed to be set, and it was a bright one. Coach Peterson himself had sat in a north Florida duck blind all day long with him during one of Warren's three recruiting trips to convince the young star that he was FSU's heir apparent at quarterback, and when Warren traveled from Miami to Jacksonville in August 1966 to play in the Florida-Georgia High School All-Star game, he made a dramatic entrance. He'd recently gotten his pilot's license, and he flew in on a friend's private plane.

He was small by anyone's jock standards—5'10" and 155 pounds the day he arrived on the FSU campus—but Warren shined right away on the field as quarterback for the freshman squad. The state tourism office featured him in its promotional literature around that time: a handsome, butch-cut young man in a football uniform staring sideways at the camera, left arm raised for balance, or to ward something off, right arm cocked, ready to throw a painted ball with a smiling Sunshine State wearing sunglasses above the words "Friendly Floridian" stencilled in lowercase on the leather.

From the beginning, Warren enjoyed the perks that came with being a blue chip recruit, which included contacts—and frequent hunting trips—with businessmen, politicians, and other boosters of the football program. "I remember being horrified one time when he told me he'd gone with a couple of boosters to Mexico," said David Ammerman, an FSU history professor. "They'd killed three hundred ducks in one day by seeding a goddamn pond, which apparently was not illegal down there, and they justified it by saying they gave the ducks to the poor hungry peasants."

It didn't take long, though, before football changed for Warren. Like a lot of players just out of high school, he found he had to adjust to no longer being the biggest and most obvious star on the team. Here everybody had been the hometown hero. But it seemed to be more than that. Almost overnight the game he had loved while growing up quit being fun. Instead there was the drudgery of daily practices, which started every afternoon at two o'clock and lasted into the evening, followed by mandatory study hall and, finally, a rigid bed-check routine. Anyone caught violating curfew or any of a myriad of other team rules was subject to what the coaches called Dawn Patrol, running stadium steps at 5:30 in the morning under strict supervision by those same coaches who were doubly annoyed at having to be up that early and took it out on the players. Warren was never caught himself, but ran his share of stadium steps when the coaches thought the whole team deserved the early morning punishment. What Warren struggled with as much as the disciplinary tactics and the seemingly arbitrary team rules, though, was the dispiriting monotony of the routine, seeing the same faces day in and day out. The players all lived in the football dorm, they all ate at the training table, they all took the same classes. From what Warren could see, in the fall of 1966, they might as well have been in the military.

But the worst aspect of college ball at FSU was yet to come. Warren and the other freshmen players had heard plenty of stories about a conditioning class they were required to take winter quarter; once Christmas break was over they found out for themselves. The name was innocuous enough: referred to by older players simply as "pre-spring," it was officially listed in the school catalog as Physical Conditioning, PE 117, offered by the physical education department and ostensibly open to anyone. In reality, participation in pre-spring was mandatory and no one but members of the football team was allowed in, both flagrant violations of NCAA regulations. As Warren and the other freshmen discovered, pre-spring at FSU was also deliberately brutal and intense, what the coaches liked to think of as a gut-check experience to winnow out the weaker players. Some of those players, Warren soon realized, were staying in their beds all day instead of attending class because they were so worried about the afternoon sessions.

Two days a week during pre-spring were devoted to intense weight training. The other two days the players ran until they dropped, did exhausting agility drills, and then went into "the Room," a converted locker area that had been stripped bare except for old wrestling mats and a chicken-wire "ceiling" hanging down from cables four feet off the floor. Surrounded by their teammates and by a battery of assistant coaches, all screaming, two players at a time were required to fight under the chicken wire until one was clearly beaten and lying on the floor. The winner moved on; the loser fought the next player in line, and the next one after that, and the next, until he finally won and could crawl out of the cage. Warren attended one day and was ordered to fight 6'4", 210-pound Bill Cappleman, a sophomore quarterback.

"The only rule was that no one could hit below the belt," a player from North Carolina named Hod Verble later told the *Charlotte Observer*. "Two players would line up back-to-back and a coach would blow a whistle. They then turned around and just started hitting. They didn't make any attempt to separate the smaller players from the bigger players, so sometimes you would end up with a big defensive lineman.

"You would literally fight it out until somebody won. The player who lost had to stay in and fight again. You had to stay in until you won. I've seen people with blood completely covering their shirts—me too. You could be standing there puking blood and the coaches would just holler louder, 'Get tough. Get tough.'"

Another player, Mike Cadwell, told the same story to the *St. Petersburg Times.* "People were so mentally and physically exhausted they were staggering around like drunks, lunging at each other and missing," he said. "We'd be too tired to stay down and several times players stood up and were cut on the wire. People threw up constantly. The first day they told us if anyone threw up on the mat he would have to clean it up with his body. So for the first few days players just went off to the sides, because the mat didn't extend all the way to the walls, and vomited on the floor. Then the other players would step in it as they ran to get back in line. . . .

"The final loser of the day had to report at 6:30 Friday morning to run up and down the steps of the stadium. Everyone was so desperate to win we kicked, slugged, hit each other in the groin, did everything and anything. It was the cruelest thing I've ever seen, it was survival of the fittest. It was dehumanizing to the extent that you could be out there with your best friend, and you'd be trying to kill him."

After his one day in the Room, Warren knew he didn't want any part of pre-spring, so when Peterson tried to order him back in, the freshman quarterback pulled out his agreement with the athletic director. He would be playing spring baseball instead, Warren told his coach. Peterson was furious. He had never had a player defy him like that, certainly not one who stayed on the team. He tried to pressure Warren, threatened to drop him to the bottom of the depth chart, but Warren insisted Peterson honor the agreement. It was the first skirmish in what would be an ongoing battle of wills between the quarterback and the coach, the beginning of what Warren called his love-hate relationship with "Coach Pete," who admired Warren's skills and his quick football mind but never quite knew what to do with the rest of the player. Tommy Warren was a paradox: a natural team leader who for most of his college career counted none of his teammates as close friends, a gifted and skillful athlete who hated the limited and regimented jock lifestyle. And once he started questioning the role of the individual in big-time college football, he never stopped. Soon he would find himself questioning a lot of other things as well.

During that winter quarter his first year in Tallahassee, Warren did play FSU baseball—he started in the outfield and led the freshman team in hitting—and though he eventually came back around to football for regular spring training he was always clever enough to avoid Peterson's brutal pre-spring regimen. For a couple of years it was baseball. Another year, after he researched NCAA regulations and discovered Peterson couldn't actually require any of the players to sign up for pre-spring, he went out for golf instead. And the winter before Warren's final season, when Peterson finally thought he had his nemesis nailed, Warren was diagnosed with a mysterious case of high blood pressure and had to sit out pre-spring under orders from the team doctor, though he was well enough by the end of the school year to establish himself as the starting quarterback for the upcoming 1970 season.

Like many college coaches, Bill Peterson recruited a lot of quarter-backs, more than he would ever need in the position. One reason, in those days before NCAA scholarship caps, was to keep talent out of the hands of opponents. The other reason was that quarter-backs were usually the most gifted athletes on their high-school teams and could easily adapt to other positions, usually wide re-ceiver or defensive back. Peterson decided that Warren was no ex-ception, and since he was number four on the quarterback depth chart going into his sophomore year, Peterson switched Warren over to cornerback where he saw limited action on defense as a reserve. Warren hated it. "I was definitely more in the offensive mode, where you have an opportunity to run out of bounds or fall down," he said years later.

He managed to bulk up to 170, but he never stopped lobbying to return to quarterback. He was still the reserve cornerback at the end of the year, though, when the Seminoles played Penn State in the Gator Bowl, and as it happened, the starter at cornerback was injured early so Warren ended up playing most of the game. He had an interception, ran back a punt, and managed a spectacular, high-light-film tackle on a Penn State tight end who outweighed him by a hundred pounds. The play stuck in Warren's memory, he said, because what on film appeared to be him stuffing the runner at the line and planting him into the ground was actually a perfectly timed slip by the Penn State tight end, his cleats losing their hold on the loose Gator Bowl turf at the exact moment he would have otherwise run over Warren, the would-be tackler. The game ended in a tie.

The following year, Warren returned to quarterback. He was second string behind Bill Cappleman but also saw duty running back kickoffs and punts. Occasionally he went in for some downs as a running back. Peterson, known to sports writers for his humorous malaprops and general mangling of the language, even had Warren sprinting wide receiver patterns and catching the ball in practice one day. Impressed with what he saw, the coach remarked on his quarterback's versatility to a visiting reporter. "That Tommy Warren is a trick of all trades," Peterson said. The quote was widely reported.

Through five seasons at FSU, Warren chafed at the authoritarian system of big-time college football. He was smart enough and good enough to subvert the system in private ways even as he prospered, but he was also keenly aware of those who weren't able to survive, the players who quit going to class, the ones who dropped out, the ones who were pressured to give up their scholarships when injuries cut short their careers. "We had virtually no say in how our lives were controlled," he came to realize. "Even though if it wasn't for us there would be no games, no athletic programs, no revenue, no coaching jobs."

But the world of football was an insulated one, and though social and political change was rocking the nation in the late 1960s, life on the field and in the football dorm went on as myopically as always. There were classes, there was practice, there was study hall, there was bed check, there were games. In 1968, though, the FSU coaching staff, recognizing the success schools in other regions were having with black players, decided it was time to face up to changing social realities and start recruiting black players of their own. Former Washington Redskins head coach Joe Gibbs, at that time an assistant with the Seminoles, was sent to south Florida to find a good one, and he came back with Calvin Patterson, an All-Dade-County running back from nearly all-white Palmetto High.

The move was immediately controversial. With the exception of the private University of Miami, no other traditionally white

school in the South at that time had any black players at all, and
though Patterson and his parents received plenty of support when
he signed with FSU, they were also besieged by hate mail and even
death threats, many of the letters signed by the Ku Klux Klan. A
second black high-school player, Ernest Cook, had originally
signed to play at FSU that year, the idea being that no one black
athlete should have to break the race barrier alone, but the Klan
threats frightened him off. He switched to the University of
Minnesota.

Though he did well enough on the freshman team, despite being
switched suddenly from running back to safety, Calvin Patterson
never did live up to his promise or the heavy expectations placed
on him by white fans and by the black community, both in Tallahassee and back home in south Florida. In a 1995 retrospective on
Patterson in the *Fort Lauderdale Sun-Sentinel,* reporter Dave
Hyde noted that at the time there were only forty black students
attending FSU, fraternities still celebrated "Old South Weekend"
in honor of the Confederacy, and the school band still played
"Dixie" at football games. Once when the team bus stopped at a
small store on the way to a game, a man standing with a small
group nearby saw Patterson getting off with the other players and
asked them, "That boy with you?" Patterson struggled academically and socially just as he struggled athletically. Injuries, poor
grades, isolation, family problems—all piled up his sophomore
and junior years and he never played a down of varsity ball.

Seeing the difficulties Patterson was having, Warren eventually
approached the coaches and asked to be the younger player's room-
mate. The friendship that subsequently developed would change
Warren's life, but it wouldn't be enough to save Calvin Patterson's.

The intellectual foundation for the changes going on in Warren
came from an American Studies course he took in 1969 with a history professor named David Ammerman. "By the time I reached
my junior year I realized that my college life was passing me by,"
he later said. "I realized that I was really quite naive intellectually.
It's very disheartening to become stagnant in whatever you do. I
felt very stagnant."

The American Studies course, he said, helped break him out of that sense of stagnation. Ammerman, annoyed that so many varsity athletes seemed to be academically unprepared, congregating in the back of the room and sleeping through his and other faculty members' classes, had agreed to teach a special section of American Studies just for football players. The requirements: that they stay awake and that they attend class. Word quickly spread about the course, and when Warren took it the impact was profound. For the first time in his life he started reading books, and the eclectic and progressive list in Ammerman's class seemed to challenge every assumption he'd grown up with about race and patriotism, politics and class—and sports. They read *Winesburg, Ohio, Black Power, Catch-22, One Flew over the Cuckoo's Nest, The Adventures of Huckleberry Finn,* and J. William Fulbright's *The Arrogance of Power.* They attended lectures by black activist Dick Gregory, radical attorney William Kunstler, and Dave Meggyesy, a former professional football player who had become an outspoken critic of big-time professional and college sports.

The more he read, and the more he discussed it with Ammerman and other progressive faculty members at FSU, the better Warren was able to articulate for himself the questions that had troubled him since he first came to campus. He later described his intellectual and political metamorphosis as a "conversion" experience. "I had the sense that what we were taught to believe the first twenty years of our lives wasn't all there was to believe," he said. "There was a whole lot out there to explore."

As he told an interviewer in 1975, "It was the whole football experience that really started to radicalize me. Looking back, I really feel that I missed a lot of what I should have and could have gotten out of college by playing football. If I had to do it all over again, I wouldn't play.

"College is supposed to prepare you for when you're put out on the street four years later, but football takes you out of that. As a football player, you're not allowed to develop any sort of responsibility as an individual or learn the kind of things you go to college to learn. They insulate you from the rest of the students, from the rest of the world."

Not that Warren was ready to give up football at the time. He agreed to take a medical redshirt in what would have been his se-

nior year since Bill Cappleman, then in his final season, was starting ahead of him anyway, and though Warren's intellectual and
political world was rapidly expanding, he still wanted to get his
chance to quarterback the team. A serious shoulder separation in
a preseason scrimmage sealed the redshirt decision, and he spent
the fall wearing a headset on the sidelines, signaling in plays sent
down from the offensive coordinator in the booth, an assistant
named Dan Henning who became close friends with Warren and
later coached in the NFL.

Warren began rooming with Calvin Patterson that winter, and
quickly learned about the special pressures on black athletes, and
on African Americans in general. "In the black community you're
nothing unless you're a jock or have really made some very high
intellectual attainments, which is hard to do," Warren told a *Miami Herald* reporter in December 1975. "We'd be walking along
and Calvin would see a black kid bouncing a ball, and he'd say, 'Do
it right, kid, it's your only chance.'" (The *Herald* reporter misidentified Patterson as "Clarence" in the story.)

David Ammerman said that he and others could see the influence Patterson was having on Warren. "I think that played a part
in Tommy's social awareness," he said. "I saw him becoming more
and more uncomfortable with people using racial slurs and stuff
like that. He commented to me that he was finding it harder and
harder to put up with that kind of thing."

After Patterson broke the race barrier in 1968, other black athletes followed, including five the next year, three of whom later
played in the NFL: Charlie Hunt, Eddie McMillon, and J. T. Thomas. Their careers took off as Patterson's floundered, and despite
Warren's academic coaching Patterson eventually flunked out of
school. He was living in a bedroom at Ammerman's house and taking classes at the local community college when what would have
been his last year of eligibility came up in 1972. Patterson was
hoping to get back into FSU that fall, back to one final chance to
prove himself on the football field, but in August he got the bad
news: his community college grades weren't good enough. He
wouldn't be returning for his senior year to play football. His career was finished.

What happened next, Warren and Ammerman both theorized,

was Patterson's tragic attempt to save face with his friends and family back home in south Florida. On August 16, 1972, with no one else around, Patterson took a .38 revolver from a cabinet in Ammerman's house, sat in a living room chair, and shot himself in the side. He had apparently meant only to inflict a superficial wound and then claim that he had been shot by a would-be robber. It was to be his explanation to the world for why he wouldn't be playing his final season of football at FSU. In fact, police later learned that he had called a Miami friend before shooting himself, and said he'd been wounded in a robbery and wouldn't be able to play.

His angle, though, was all wrong. Instead of passing in and out of the fleshy part of his side, the bullet cut through his abdomen and struck his aorta. He was able to drag himself to a telephone to call for help, but when a police officer arrived Patterson was in so much pain that he begged the officer to shoot him in the head, to put him out of his misery. He died in an ambulance holding an attendant's hand.

The local paper, the *Tallahassee Democrat,* buried the story on an inside page under the headline, "Young Man Dies of Gunshot Wounds." A few players attended his funeral. Ten years later, at an FSU football game, Warren noticed that the plastic commemorative soda cups at the stadium carried a picture of J. T. Thomas, who had since become an all-pro defensive back in the NFL, and saluted him as the first black athlete to play for the FSU football team.

Warren sent a letter to the editor of the *Democrat,* which was published in 1983.

At a recent Florida State University football game, an inscription on a 'collector' drink cup stated that James 'J.T.' Thomas was 'FSU's first black football player.' This is incorrect. Calvin Patterson was FSU's first black football player.

Patterson, an extremely talented running back, came to FSU on full football scholarship in 1968. Like many blacks who have been the 'first,' he experienced indignities, hostility, and even personal threats while breaking the color barrier. He persevered in the face of these conditions.

After Patterson led the way in 1968, five more blacks attended FSU the following year. J. T. Thomas was one of these five. Thomas had a brilliant career at FSU; Patterson, for various reasons, never played a down of varsity ball. Yet Patterson's role in beginning what has become a long tradition of gifted black football players at FSU should not be overlooked.

It is unfortunate that Patterson did not live long enough to see and appreciate the full extent of what he began in 1968. He died a tragic death in 1972. And although his name does not appear in any FSU record books, his role in FSU football history has been significant. FSU fans owe him recognition and thanks.

Calvin Patterson never got his season of football glory, but Tommy Warren managed to get his. In the fall of 1970, two years before Patterson died, Warren was a fifth-year senior. He started the first two games of the season at quarterback but played poorly, winning one and losing one. Peterson yanked him late in the second game, and benched him in favor of his back-up, Gary Huff. The team continued to struggle without Warren in the line-up, though, and after five games the Seminoles' record was 2–3. In the sixth game, against what was generally recognized as an inferior South Carolina team, they quickly fell behind 13-0, and with Huff obviously ineffective Peterson was forced to give Warren another shot.

This time Warren was ready for his chance. He threw three touchdown passes that day in a 21–13 come-from-behind victory and went on to lead the team to four more wins before being injured in the final game of the season. Several years later, the offensive coordinator, Dan Henning, told a reporter he was still struck by Warren's performance during the team's 1970 winning streak. "In my eight years in football those five games are the most efficient I've ever seen by any quarterback," he said in that interview, "and that includes Bill Cappleman at FSU, Don Strock at VPI, and Dan Pastorini when I was at Houston. I would be willing to stack that five-game span against any in the history of any FSU quarterback."

The Seminoles played Houston in their final game that season. Warren was tackled hard early in the contest and knew right away that he had reinjured his shoulder, but there was no way he was taking himself out. The team was 7–3 and the game was on national television. One more win would assure FSU of a bowl invitation. And perhaps more important to Warren, it was his last game ever and he wanted to play. It was the wrong decision, though. He stayed in the line-up but threw three interceptions in what turned out to be a lopsided defeat. The season, and his football career, was over.

There was a life after football, even if it took Warren some time to figure out what to do with it. He worked on a voter registration drive for eighteen-year-olds. He teamed up with a friend to organize a two-day bluegrass festival, sort of a mini-Woodstock that they repeated each spring for a couple of years, occasionally turning a profit. And, in a more conventional mode, some of his contacts in state government helped him get a job in the governor's office, where he served as then-Governor Reuben Askew's liaison to the Florida Highway Patrol. Warren soon set to work convincing Askew that the all-white force needed to be integrated, and to his surprise the lobbying effort was successful. Askew agreed to target 10 percent minority hires, despite protests from Highway Patrol officials that they couldn't hire blacks even if they wanted to because blacks didn't want to work in law enforcement. Warren was given the task of recruiting minority candidates and proving those officials wrong. That victory felt good, but the pace of change in state government was otherwise slow and incremental, if it happened at all, and it didn't take long before Warren was ready for something else, some other avenue for radical change.

Since Ammerman's class he had come to see what he called "the football syndrome" as a microcosm for other political struggles that were then swirling around him, chiefly the civil rights movement and the war in Vietnam. Established institutions thrived, just as college football thrived, by controlling the lives of the individuals who did most of the work but who had no voice. His allegiance and his responsibility, as Warren saw it, were to the poor and the working class, to minorities struggling against majority oppression, and, by extension, to the people of Vietnam fighting a war of liberation against the U.S. government.

Working with attorneys in state government had exposed him

to the idea of taking some of these political and ideological battles into the courts, since the law at least gave lip service to protecting the rights of minorities and individuals. The Civil Rights Act of 1964 had spawned dozens of legal challenges to entrenched discriminatory practices in many areas of American life, and those cases, Warren learned, which after several years were just then reaching the Supreme Court, were being brought by a small coterie of lawyers. He decided he wanted to join them, and after several months in the governor's office, where he said he stuck out like a sore thumb with his antiwar politics and his progressive ideology, he enrolled in the FSU Law School. He was ready to change the world, and he wanted to do it right away.

He wouldn't be able to walk away from sports all that easily, though. To help pay his bills in the fall of 1971, Touchdown Tommy Warren also signed on to do color commentary for the FSU football radio network.

It was a year after Warren started law school that Calvin Patterson died. Warren was devastated, friends say, but characteristically he kept his emotions to himself. Instead of outwardly grieving, he turned his attention to practical matters such as dealing with the police in the ensuing investigation and trying to find out, for himself and for Patterson's other friends, what had happened, and why. "I remember of course when Calvin killed himself," David Ammerman said recently. "Tommy came over and he was all broken up about it as of course all of us were. Tommy and Calvin, they just cared a lot about each other. They shared a lot, they lived together, when we had big dinners at my house they spent a lot of time together. And Tommy was familiar with the problems Calvin went through—the problems at home, the pressures he got from the white community, the pressures he got from the black community, and also, if you knew Calvin you couldn't help but really care about him. And to see the things that destroyed him, I think, had a big impact on Tommy."

A few months later, when several current members of the football team approached Warren for advice on how to deal with what they saw as the increasing brutality in the program, he was still grieving privately over Patterson's death, and he was ready once again to get personally involved.

Once before he had tried to do something about pre-spring, but the effort hadn't gone anywhere. During his senior year the team had started holding what they called "Dissension Meetings" to discuss their grievances with the program, and at the top of everybody's list was pre-spring practice. Warren, one of a cadre of "Dissension" leaders, was appointed the team's representative to talk to Peterson about pre-spring and the NCAA rules that it appeared to violate. To his surprise, Peterson said fine, anyone who didn't want to participate no longer had to. He even called a team meeting to announce that pre-spring would be voluntary from then on. However, everyone who failed to register for the physical conditioning class that winter quarter was immediately dropped to the bottom of the depth chart, which meant he had little chance of playing in the fall.

Peterson had left FSU after Warren's last season. Now, according to the players who had come to Warren for help, his replacement, Larry Jones, was trying to run off players he didn't like, and he was using pre-spring as a way to harass the unwanted players into giving up their scholarships. The Room had always been bad under Peterson, they said, but under Jones it was even worse.

Their first strategy, Warren and the players decided, was to publicly expose pre-spring for what it was: not some benign physical conditioning class but a brutal and illegal part of the FSU football program. To do that, Warren contacted the sports editor and a photographer from the college newspaper, the *Flambeau*, and together they paid a surprise visit to the Room one afternoon when he knew players would be fighting under the chicken wire. The assistant coach running the drills when they came in was Bill Parcells (who like a number of FSU assistants later went on to coach in the NFL). He stopped the drill as soon as Warren and the student journalists entered. "Tommy, you can't be here," he said. "You're out of here, *now.*" They left, but not before the photographer snapped pictures of the Room, which subsequently appeared in the *Flambeau* along with a story about pre-spring and the players who said they were being unfairly forced to give up their scholarships.

Later that spring, *St. Petersburg Times* reporter Fred Girard contacted Warren. He wanted to follow up on the *Flambeau* story with a more extensive investigation of his own, he said, and he needed help doing it. Warren agreed to cooperate, and he eventually was able to line up two dozen players, most of whom were willing to talk on the record, for what turned out to be a controversial three-part series of articles exposing abuses in the FSU program: the degrading combat drills in the Room; the mandatory and illegal pre-spring practice; the twenty-eight scholarship players who had been forced off the team to make room for Jones's preferred junior college transfers; and the allegations of untreated injuries and medical conditions. Warren, who served as a kind of graduate spokesman for the players, was quoted extensively throughout the series.

The coaching staff and the university president denied the illegal policies and improprieties alleged in the *St. Petersburg Times*, but after a subsequent investigation the football program ended up being placed under severe sanctions by the NCAA. Perhaps not surprisingly, much of the public reaction to the players who had come forward was negative, and Tommy Warren, once celebrated as a football hero in sports-crazed Tallahassee, was lambasted instead for trying to destroy the system. With the publication of the *St. Petersburg Times* series, his alienation from the world that had first brought him to Tallahassee appeared to be complete.

Outwardly, Warren seemed to shrug it off. He finished law school, passed the Bar, represented the Young Socialist Alliance in a local First Amendment case (which he won), lobbied the legislature on behalf of the ACLU, and started defending small-time drug cases. Privately, though, he had problems.

All of which set the stage for what happened next.

On August 19, 1974, Tommy Warren, then twenty-six, and his twenty-nine-year-old brother John, a pilot for Eastern Airlines, were on board a seventy-five-foot shrimp boat named *Stormy Seas* in waters seven hundred miles south of the United States. Piloting the boat was a young fisherman named John Cruse from Appalachicola, a fishing town on the Gulf Coast in north Florida, an hour from Tallahassee. The boat belonged to Cruse's father.

At 6:30 that evening, as the *Stormy Seas* sailed south through the Windward Passage between Cuba and Haiti, a 210-foot Coast

Guard cutter, the *Steadfast,* sighted the shrimp boat and hailed it over. The *Steadfast,* which carried a cannon and a .50-caliber mounted gun, had left Guantanamo Bay to patrol known smuggling routes as part of Operation Buccaneer, an interdiction program recently initiated by the Nixon Administration to fight drug trafficking in the region. An official on board the *Steadfast* would later call the encounter with the *Stormy Seas* "a gratuitous bumping into."

Three Coast Guard officers, a Drug Enforcement Agency official, and a Customs Service agent all boarded the shrimp boat. Cruse identified himself as the captain and handed over the ship's enrollment papers. The officials were suspicious, not only because the *Stormy Seas* was a "lookout boat," a style of craft included on a list of suspect vessels the Coast Guard was watching out for, but because the enrollment papers failed to show that the *Stormy Seas* was bound for any foreign port. Tommy Warren told the officials they were on an expedition to buy land. John Warren said they were planning to fish and scuba dive. When the officers got Cruse off alone, though, he broke down and said the Warrens had promised him $10,000 to take them to Santa Marta, Colombia, to pick up a load of marijuana.

A search of the boat turned up three guns, a .22-caliber pistol and two .38s, plus $41,500 in undeclared U.S. currency and 46,800 Colombian pesos. The money was hidden in brown envelopes spread flat under Tommy Warren's mattress. In the hold, tucked behind a panel, was a Sears Kenmore trash compactor and a couple of hundred plastic garbage bags. The officials also discovered a lawyer's yellow legal pad belonging to Tommy Warren with the names of Colombian contacts and lists of equipment to be used to load and package marijuana. His passport showed that he had visited Colombia two weeks before the *Stormy Seas* set sail.

Cruse and the Warrens were read their Miranda rights, arrested, and then ordered to board the *Steadfast,* which brought them to Miami for arraignment before a federal magistrate. The charges were possession of undeclared currency and conspiracy to import marijuana. Law enforcement officials later determined that the Warrens had planned to smuggle in ten tons.

When the federal magistrate asked if they had an attorney, Tommy Warren said that he had recently passed the Bar and that

he would be representing his brother and himself. The magistrate
shook his head. "Son," he said, "it looks like your law career is
getting off to a mighty shaky start."

At the time, Warren was defiant, and in a 1975 interview with
the *Miami Herald,* shortly before his case went to trial, he seemed
unrepentant. "I'm not going to let the system suck me in," he said.
"They're sucking me in right now, but they're going to have to spit
me out some day."

He would spend the next six years of his life, though, in a daunt-
ing series of battles over the constitutionality of the Nixon Administration's interdiction program, the admissibility of much of
the evidence seized, and other legal aspects of his case. Originally
convicted in a Miami federal court on conspiracy charges in November 1975, the Warrens and two others who had not been on
the boat were sentenced to eighteen months in federal prison.
John Cruse, identified in court records as an "unindicted co-
conspirator," testified against them. But the case ground on long
after that. Every appeal meant waiting months, sometimes as
much as a year, for a hearing. Every new hearing meant waiting
still longer for a ruling, and then for subsequent appeals to play
themselves out.

In the meantime, Warren landed a job with civil rights attorney
Kent Spriggs back in Tallahassee, where he kept a low profile
while working as a paralegal on Title VII discrimination cases. His
own case was a roller coaster—the conviction overturned by a
panel of appellate judges at one point, only to be reinstated several
months later—but on August 19, 1980, exactly six years to the day
after the arrest, the ride ended.

The Warren brothers entered a minimum-security federal prison
at Eglin Air Force Base in Pensacola, Florida, to begin serving their
conspiracy sentences which had been ultimately upheld, although
mitigated to a year and a day in one of their final appeals. "It didn't
seem like more than eight or nine years, though," Warren would
later say. They were paroled after four and a half months and released from prison on January 5, 1981.

That was the story Shoney's attorneys wanted to make sure Barry
Goldstein knew when they contacted the LDF attorney in his
Washington, D.C., office months before the Shoney's case was

filed. Goldstein, though, had already done his homework, and he already knew the Tommy Warren story, including the part that came later. In August 1981, Warren won reinstatement to the Florida Bar. He had spent the seven years since his arrest working for Kent Spriggs and quietly making a positive name for himself in the Florida legal community. Thirty-five people wrote letters in support of his reapplication to the Bar. They included a former president of the American Bar Association, an agent for the Florida Department of Law Enforcement who had directed part of the drug investigation against Warren, and dozens of other friends, attorneys, members of the business community, his high-school football coach.

"I asked around about Tommy," Goldstein said. "And I liked what I heard."

Shoney's attorneys would continue to focus on Warren's past at other times as the case went forward, as part of the ongoing challenge to the adequacy of plaintiffs' counsel. On one of those occasions Butch Powell brought up Warren's record during a hearing in Pensacola, Florida, before the federal judge eventually assigned to the case. It was a highly charged moment, but in Goldstein's eyes it backfired in the same way as that first private attempt to bring up Warren's past had backfired with him.

"I think it hurt Powell," Goldstein said. "Tommy paid the price—everybody understood that. He paid a big price for what he did. And he had some of the leading lawyers in Florida to say just that, and to say that he'd had a stellar ten years after this happened. He'd been sort of a model person after that, working as a paralegal, doing very good work, and the state supreme court and the Bar of Florida agreed with them. And that was ten years before, and now to bring it up again? . . . It was hardball. It was tough-assed. But I don't think it was effective. It damn sure didn't intimidate Tommy Warren or me."

Plaintiffs' counsel Tommy Warren, standing in a warehouse in Tallahassee, Florida, with all the legal documents from *Haynes v. Shoney's, Inc.* (Photograph by Mike Ewen, *Tallahassee Democrat*)

Barry Goldstein, co-lead counsel for the plaintiffs, spent two decades as an attorney with the NAACP Legal Defense and Educational Fund before joining a private firm in Oakland that specializes in discrimination cases.

Days after the $132.5 million settlement in *Haynes v. Shoney's, Inc.*, many members of the Black Business Community in Nashville turned out for a tribute to Ray Danner. (Photograph by Ricky Rogers, *Nashville Tennessean*)

Len Roberts was hired by Shoney's, Inc. after the lawsuit was filed but didn't learn about the case until he had been installed as CEO and chairman of the board. (Photograph by Mike Dubose, *Nashville Tennessean*)

Josephine Haynes, whose name appears first among the named plaintiffs in *Haynes v. Shoney's, Inc.*, was twice turned down when she applied for jobs at Shoney's restaurants in Pensacola, Florida, where the case was filed. (Photograph by Mike Fuhrman)

Sharon Johnson brought a lawsuit against Shoney's in 1985 after she was forced to hide in a restroom during a surprise visit by area supervisors because "too many blacks" were on duty that night at the Montgomery, Alabama, Shoney's restaurant where she worked as a waitress.

Billie and Henry Elliot were managing a Captain D's seafood restaurant in Marianna, Florida, when they were ordered to reduce the number of black workers in their store. They refused and were subsequently fired. They took their case to civil rights attorney Tommy Warren.

Carolyn Cobb, one of the named plaintiffs in *Haynes v. Shoney's, Inc.*, worked for twenty years in the kitchen of this Shoney's restaurant in South Carolina. (Photograph by Wade Spees)

Ray Danner, longtime CEO and chairman of the board of Shoney's, Inc., in front of the restaurant chain's old Big Boy trademark. (Photograph © Jack Corn)

EIGHT

"Into the Belly of the Beast"

March 2, 1989. Tommy Warren is on a plane to Nashville. All the signs for months have been pointing him there. "Into the belly of the beast," he calls it, though residents prefer "Music City" or "The Buckle of the Bible Belt" because of the saturation of local churches. So far, though, everything seems to be going wrong. Heavy thunderstorms cancel his connecting flight in Atlanta, so he's hours late by the time he finally lands at the Nashville airport. On top of that, he can't find the woman who is supposed to meet him, a paralegal named Carol Condon who works for civil rights attorney Pat O'Rourke and who's been trying, unsuccessfully, to locate key Shoney's witnesses in Ray Danner's backyard for Warren to interview. He walks around the airport for half an hour before he and Condon stumble onto each another. Condon thinks Warren will want her to simply drive him to O'Rourke's house where he'll be staying, then the next day they'll get to work, but Warren has other ideas.

They drive to O'Rourke's, all right, but immediately Warren talks O'Rourke into taking him to see another attorney, Richard Dinkins, who knows the first man Warren needs to see: Eugene Grayer, the former Lee's Famous Recipe manager who has been promising, and failing to deliver, documents from the individual discrimination suit he brought against Shoney's, Inc. a few years before. Warren, calling from Tallahassee, has been able to get Grayer on the telephone, usually at the Wendy's restaurant he now manages, but for reasons Warren can't figure out, either Grayer will promise to send documents and then not send them, or he will put Warren on hold, claiming he's busy with something else, and then never return to the phone. Carol Condon has actually met with Grayer at his store but hasn't had any better luck convincing the black manager to cooperate. They speculate that Grayer is simply distrustful of yet another white attorney who wants to ask questions about his years with Shoney's, Inc. He had been manager of the Jefferson Street Lee's in a predominantly black area of Nashville for a couple of years in the mid-1980s, and even though company officials had decided it was acceptable to have black managers in that and other "nigger stores," Grayer claimed he was denied promotions because he was black and ultimately fired by the company for undisclosed reasons, which he also believed to be racist. Shoney's had settled his claims for $2,000. The labor lawyer who handled the case for the corporation was Butch Powell.

It's already late when Warren and O'Rourke find Richard Dinkins, but Warren is able to talk Dinkins into accompanying him to Grayer's restaurant that night to make the introductions and to help convince Grayer to work with Warren in tracking down four other former Lee's managers, white men, in the Nashville area. All four had given statements supporting Grayer's charges of discrimination against Shoney's, but none of the statements were sworn, and now Warren wants to get them on the record.

Grayer, a light-skinned black man, short, stocky, in his mid-thirties, is wearing a typical manager's white shirt and tie when Warren and Dinkins pull up to the Wendy's minutes before closing time. He's obviously surprised to see Dinkins, and just as obviously suspicious of Warren, but once Dinkins makes the introductions he relaxes and agrees to talk. The men sit in the Wendy's dining area for an hour discussing plans for finding the three white managers whose statements Warren has already seen from Grayer's case—Terry Toney, Jim Usrey, and a man named Jandrokovic—plus a fourth, whose name Grayer says is Danny White but whose statement no one has been able to find. Using city directories, driver's license records, the Tennessee Highway Patrol, even the utility company, Warren has located addresses for two of the men and sent them letters, but he hasn't received any responses, so those addresses might be no longer valid. The only way to find out at this point is to go to the addresses himself to try to pick up the trail.

The men are key witnesses because at least two of them said they received direct orders from Ray Danner himself to limit the number of black workers in their stores or to fire some black workers Danner didn't like. Warren has already amassed a considerable amount of evidence against Shoney's—dozens of Florida and Alabama witnesses, plus the results of the survey he and Barry Goldstein designed in the fall, enough to convince the NAACP Legal Defense Fund to commit itself formally to the case—but most of what he believes connects Danner to the case at this point is still secondhand.

This need to find witnesses who can directly connect Ray Danner to the company's discriminatory policies is particularly acute now, because in seven days Warren and Barry Goldstein are scheduled to meet with a California attorney named Guy Saperstein, a legend in Title VII law who has created one of the nation's few top-line firms dealing almost exclusively with discrimination cases on behalf of women and minorities. Large settlements in a handful of major class actions have given Saperstein the ability to take on large corporate firms, with their virtually limitless resources and their tendency to bury outmanned plaintiffs' attorneys in protracted litigation, and to beat them at their own game. Now Saperstein wants to hire Goldstein away from the LDF, and Goldstein, after eighteen years, is ready to go, on one condition: that he be able to take Shoney's with him, and that Saperstein agree to support the case.

Shoney's, Danner, and Robertson Investment already have half a dozen law firms working on their side of the coming litigation before a single motion has even been filed, and the cash-strapped LDF is stretched too thin to keep up for very long, a concern that is heightened for Warren and Goldstein by the potential costs of litigation. When Butch Powell's firm defended General Motors in an employment discrimination suit in the mid-1980s, that litigation "often degenerated" into "acrimonious bickering," according to the decision handed down by the federal judge who heard the case—which General Motors lost. The judge charged that GM "injected needless work and expense into this case by adopting an 'afterthought' defense," and he said the company had been "stubbornly litigious and [had] adopted an obstructionist policy in responding to discovery," a policy that prompted him to allow more than double what he said would ordinarily have been the fees for the plaintiffs' attorneys in such a case.

Warren knows they'll need Saperstein's resources, on top of what the LDF can provide, to be able to effectively bring their own case, and the Nashville witnesses, he hopes, will be the thing that ices the agreement with the California attorney, just as the survey back in the fall put them over the top with the LDF.

So on that first night in Nashville, Warren tells Grayer he'd like for him to come along to help convince the former white managers to give him sworn statements about what they know—once he and Grayer are able to find them. Grayer, who impresses Warren as "a fast-talking, well-educated man, a college graduate," eventually says okay. He also says he thinks he remembers an address for Usrey, so maybe he can take Warren there while he's in town.

It's well past midnight before Warren finally lets Grayer and Dinkins go home. Warren himself ends up working 16.5 "billable" hours that day, a double shift. In the course of the four-day trip he'll toll more than sixty hours on the job, sleeping no more than a few hours each night at O'Rourke's place. On some of those nights, Carol Condon remembers, Warren will show up for dinners with her and O'Rourke, who are dating at the time, but he'll inevitably take off in search of witnesses as soon as they've eaten.

"Tommy is a bloodhound," she says. "He has an obsessive singularity of purpose. I've never seen anybody who's as good as he is. . . . Tommy, once he gets his teeth into something, he's not

going to let go. He's just like my Chow dog. He's just going to sink
them in and hold onto it for all he's got."

Her comments are an echo from earlier times. After Warren's
conviction on conspiracy drug charges back in the 1970s, one of
his law school professors wrote a letter urging the judge to be le-
nient in his sentencing. He characterized Warren as "immensely
sympathetic to social issues and to the deeper and more universal
claims of justice," but said Warren's "one weakness" was "the
need to be psychologically dedicated to the pursuit of one holy
grail or another."

March 3, 1989. Warren is back on the trail early the next morning
early, going solo in O'Rourke's car, a blue Chevy Blazer with a car
phone and four-wheel drive. He refers to it as O'Rourke's "urban
assault vehicle." Carol Condon has managed to get Warren an address, "somehow," for one of the former managers, Terry Toney,
"an almost unfindable place out in the boonies of Nashville," as
Warren remembers it. Unfortunately, the house turns out to be de-
serted, as he might have expected. Even after he finds Toney and
convinces him to be a witness in the case, Warren will have difficulty keeping track of the man as Toney moves three times over
the next three years. After one of those moves, Warren will again
have an "unfindable" address in Nashville and no luck at all locating it on a city map. In desperation, he will call a Pizza Hut, explain that he's given them a lot of business over the years, and ask
for their expert help in finding Toney's latest address. The Pizza
Hut dispatcher, properly cajoled, gives him the right directions.

This first time, though, Warren is stuck going door-to-door until
he finds a neighbor who knows something. That neighbor con-
firms that Toney and his family have moved, and then mentions a
cabinet business he thinks Toney once ran at a nearby strip mall.
Warren drives there and finds the storefront that had apparently
been Toney's shop, but it's vacant too, so again he goes door-to-
door to the neighbors. Another merchant eventually puts him in
touch with the building landlord, and the landlord tells him Toney
lost the store when he was forced to declare bankruptcy several
months before.

Warren keeps pressing. He goes to Richard Dinkins's office to call the bankruptcy court in Nashville, and when the clerk asks for a case number, which he doesn't have, he talks her into checking the records by name instead. She does, but comes back with bad news: no Terry Toney, and only recent bankruptcy records are available in her office. The Toney bankruptcy must have been too far back to show up in the records she can access. Sorry.

Warren isn't ready to give up yet. Surely she can look a little further back? he says. It's vital to his case, he's there from out of town, he doesn't have much time. . . .

Maybe, she says, there *is* somewhere else she might look. She puts Warren on hold, for a long time. When she finally gets back on the phone, though, she says she's found it: Toney's lawyer's name, his lawyer's phone number, and Toney's address.

That night Warren picks up Grayer after he finishes work at Wendy's, and together they drive to the apartment complex in Nashville where Toney is supposed to be now living. At first there's no answer when they knock, though lights are on inside, but after a minute a man's face peers through the curtains. It's Terry Toney, hesitating, but then recognizing Grayer, whom he hasn't seen in three years. It's enough to get Grayer and Warren in the door, though, where Toney introduces them to his wife and children then, reluctantly, sits down to talk. Bright and mild-mannered, Toney has a master's degree in industrial technology and says he taught high-school shop classes for a number of years before moving over into restaurant work. He strikes Warren as honest—and scared.

Slowly and methodically, though, Warren wears down Toney's resolve not to talk. He speaks evenly but insistently about the need to put an end to what Shoney's has been doing and about the people, white and black, who have been hurt by it. Eventually, Toney agrees to tell his story. Warren credits him for having the spine to stand up to the corporation—with a little prodding—but Carol Condon, who will spend much of the next several months taking notes and writing up declarations during meetings Warren has with a dozen other critical Nashville witnesses, says much more of the credit goes to Warren himself.

"He's the one that got all those people to talk," she says. "You can't say no to Tommy, but you don't realize that he's manipulat-

ing you. He's exceptional. It's amazing to me. I watched him work
those people, and they absolutely would not talk, and then the
next thing you know you're sitting there in a little meeting and
you got your little notepad and there they are just gabbing away.
All those people, they were absolutely, 'No, I will not talk to you.
No way in hell.' And then they would talk to you, and then they
would say to you, 'Absolutely no, I am not going to sign a declaration.' And the next thing you know there it is with their signature on it."

His own introduction to Shoney's racial policies, Toney tells Warren (in an account he will later repeat in a deposition), happened
his first day on the job as a Lee's Famous Recipe manager. The
previous manager was leaving the store just as Toney and his area
supervisor walked in. "Just for curiosity, if you can say, why is he
leaving?" Toney said he asked.

"Well," the supervisor purportedly said, "he wasn't very good as
far as hiring, because he hired too many blacks and he wouldn't
make the ratio with whites to blacks as far as the neighborhood
correct, so he had to be let go." He then added, "I hope you don't
make the same mistake."

Several weeks later, according to Toney, Ray Danner and the
same supervisor came into the restaurant, one of dozens in Nashville. They summoned Toney to join them in the dining room.

In his deposition, Toney gave the following account of what he
claimed happened next: "Mr. Danner started telling me his phi-
losophies and theories of how he had started in a single store and
came up from there, and what he believed as far as how to make
the store run properly. And he said, 'The main thing I see here and
the main problem I see here at this store,' he said, 'you've got too
many blacks working here.' He said, 'You need to have the number
of blacks to coincide with your neighborhood ethnic group.' And
he said, 'This is a predominantly all-white neighborhood and
you've got way more blacks than you need. On top of that, there's
two types of blacks.' He said, 'There's blacks and there's niggers.'
And he said, 'You've got niggers working for you.'

"I was just kind of dumbfounded from the statement," Toney
testified. "And he said, 'You need to take care of this.' I said, 'What

do you mean?' He said, 'You need to get white employees in here.' He said, 'Don't get me wrong,' he said, 'blacks are fine. Their money is as green as anybody else's, but the white customers you have don't want to see black employees up front. It might be all right to have a cook or two in the back where they can't be seen, but as far as up front where they're seen, you need white people.' And he said, 'You need to get that taken care of. You have about two weeks to get this taken care of.' I said, 'Two weeks or what?' He said, 'Well, you're smart enough, you know what will happen if you don't take care of this.'"

Toney testified that later he asked his division director if they could get into legal trouble for what they were doing to black employees and job applicants. "Shoney's can't be beat in a lawsuit," he said the division director told him. "We just beat the United States government in a labor suit, and we've never lost a discrimination case in court."

So Toney said he followed Danner's orders. When vacancies opened up, he hired only whites. If black employees were even a few minutes late he wrote them up for violating company policy until the infractions were enough to justify their firing. Although in Toney's mind these were bogus, trumped-up charges, he was successful at it nonetheless. After several weeks, he said he remembered having only two black employees left, a cook in the back and "the one front-end girl," whose name was Valerie Maze and who Toney says was the best worker he had.

Maze, whom Warren would later find to corroborate Toney's account, was working the counter the next time Danner came into the store. "She seen Mr. Danner come in the front door," Toney testified, "and she had seen him before go off, you know, get upset and yell and things, and she was real nervous when she seen him walk in the front door. And you could see she was shaking a little bit."

Maze was so nervous that she dropped the chicken order for the woman ahead of Danner. Toney, who was also behind the counter, prepared another order for the woman while Maze apologized. "And, of course, Mr. Danner was standing there seeing all of this," Toney said, "and he just said, 'Don't charge her for that chicken. Refund her money. The service is lousy.' So the woman just didn't really know what was going on. He told the lady who he was and

she thanked him and she left. And then Ray Danner placed his
order and started talking to [Maze], saying how she needed to be
more careful with the food and how she needed to treat customers
and she couldn't be clumsy and all this. By this time the little girl
was all shook up, because he was doing it in a rather forceful, high-
pitched voice, and he sat down and she took his food out to him.
When she took his food out to him she apologized to him for what
had happened and said it wouldn't happen again. And he looked
up at her and the only thing he said was, 'Well, you don't have to
worry about it not happening again, because it won't.'

"And he went ahead and finished his meal and then he came
back to me and said, 'Let's go have a little talk.' So he took me in
the cooler, which is one of his famous cooler talks that he done
with managers. He took me in the walk-in cooler and just went
irate, went bananas and started saying, 'I told you to get rid of the
damn niggers weeks ago and you didn't do it.' He said, 'You've still
got them up there where people can see them.' He said, 'You didn't
do it. You're in a heap of trouble. If you can't manage this store, I
can. You can quit and walk out the door right now and I will just
take care of it for you.' I said, 'No, I can take care of it.' He said,
'Well, it doesn't look like it so far. You haven't followed my instructions like I told you.' He said, 'Now, you get rid of the damn
niggers or it's going to be your job.' He stomped out of the cooler
and left."

Over the next few days, Toney testified, every official over him
in the Lee's hierarchy, his area supervisor, the division director,
the division vice president, and finally Vearl Stearns, the Lee's
division president, all visited the store with the same message:
Toney hadn't gotten rid of all the blacks; Danner was upset; it was
time to finish the job.

So Toney fired Valerie Maze.

It wasn't enough, apparently. Two weeks later Toney's area supervisor came by the store and suggested they go for a drive. "Now,
there's two ways you can do it," the supervisor said, according to
Toney. "You can quit and I will give you a good recommendation.
Of course, don't expect Shoney's to give you one, but I will, personally. Or you can do it the hard way and I can fire you."

March 4, 1989. Warren never will find Jandrokovic, not on this trip, though he'll wear out Pat O'Rourke's cellular phone chasing down every possible lead. And as he starts off his third day in Nashville, it doesn't look like he'll find the other former Lee's manager, Danny White, either, though he still has the address Grayer claims to remember for Jim Usrey, which they'll check out later. He always pushes himself to make that extra call, though, no matter how thin the lead. The rationale is simple: You never know when it might be the one to break you through. Earlier, in Tallahassee, he had been trying to contact a Lee's executive named Jim Bland, the only black division director anywhere in the corporation. Warren had gotten a tip that despite his position in the company Bland didn't like the way he was treated by the other white executives, who viewed him as their token minority in management, so Warren called long-distance information in Nashville and asked for a home number.

The Jim Bland who answered the phone responded affirmatively to Warren's questions: yes, he had worked for Shoney's, Inc., and yes, he had experienced the company's discriminatory policies. As a manager for three years at a restaurant in Baltimore, he had been ordered on a number of occasions to limit the number of black workers, and he had carried out those orders. As Bland continued to talk about the corporation—he'd recently quit, he said, and moved from Maryland to Nashville—Warren realized that several things were amiss: the man on the phone had been a manager only, never a division director; he had worked for Pargo's, an upscale restaurant in Shoney's specialty division, not for Lee's Famous Recipe; and he was white, not black.

It was the wrong Jim Bland.

Not that Warren minded. It was more serendipitous proof of the broad reach of Shoney's discriminatory policies. The "wrong" Jim Bland turned out to be another witness who could testify about those policies and help expand the growing body of testimony into another division and state, further bolstering Warren's argument for the broadest possible geographical definition of the plaintiff class.

So, during his four days in Nashville Warren stays on O'Rourke's

car phone almost constantly, talking to a number of other potential witnesses while trying to track down the white managers,
Toney, Usrey, Jandrokovic, and Danny White. (O'Rourke will later
say it's Warren's kid-in-a-candy-store introduction to cellular technology.) Among the witnesses Warren is able to locate are black
ministers and other activists who were involved in the early days
of the civil rights movement and who can testify to what they al-
lege was Shoney's poor record of integration during the 1960s. The
list also includes Olympic great Wilma Rudolph, who after her
stunning three-gold-medal performance running track in the 1960
Rome Olympics returned to her hometown of Clarksville, Tennessee, only to be tear-gassed by police in 1963 while peacefully pro-
testing the refusal of a local Shoney's to seat black customers, the
last restaurant in her hometown to accept desegregation.

The memory burned inside Rudolph for the rest of her life, and
in a 1991 deposition she talked about returning to that same Shoney's almost three decades later. "I would say maybe a year and a
half ago I was back in Clarksville, and I had meetings [at the Shoney's restaurant], and the people that I had meetings with were not
from the area, so they did not know the history that I had with
Shoney's. . . . And with mixed emotion I went. . . . I was there about
fifteen minutes when I asked the people that I was having the
meetings with if we could please go to another restaurant.

"The memory was still too vivid as to what had happened to me
at Shoney's all those years ago, the humiliation I had felt. I had
never been tear-gassed before. And I just—I just wasn't very comfortable. I didn't see any blacks still in the restaurant from the
standpoint of being hostesses and things like that that you normally notice when you go in a restaurant. Especially with the history that I had with Shoney's, I was very uncomfortable."

Later in that same deposition, Danner's attorney, Don Partington, who was white, wanted to know if Rudolph had "ill feelings"
against Shoney's.

"I wouldn't say ill feelings, no," Rudolph answered. "I have uncomfortable feelings as to what happened to me at my last visit at
Shoney's, and I will probably at that particular Shoney's always
feel that way. It is something—I guess it is something that I'm

sharing, that you, yourself, would have to experience. I cannot begin to impress upon you how I felt as a black American when that happened."

Rudolph, who died in 1994, was introduced to Ray Danner at a banquet in 1991 at her alma mater, Tennessee State University, where she had been invited to give the commencement address at graduation. In her deposition later that year Rudolph said Danner asked where she had grown up, and when she told him, he said that he had once operated the Moonlit Drive-In Theater in Clarksville back in the 1950s. He asked if Rudolph had ever gone there. No, Rudolph answered. Blacks were not allowed into the Moonlit at that time. Danner quickly changed the subject, she said. He did not apologize.

Rudolph also testified that after corporate officials learned she would be a witness for the plaintiffs in the case against them, Danner's representatives contacted her to see if she would be interested in working for Shoney's as a spokesperson in some of the company's new marketing efforts. She said she would be willing to meet with Danner personally to discuss the offer, but nothing ever came of it. She never heard from Danner, his representatives, or Shoney's again.

The address Eugene Grayer remembers for Jim Usrey is in a trailer park, which he and Warren eventually find after considerable confusion. The trailer that's supposed to be Usrey's is dark, though, and there's no car outside. Warren talks Grayer into knocking, figuring if Usrey is inside he'd rather see a familiar face at the door instead of a stranger at this late hour, but no one answers so Warren goes to the trailer next door and this time knocks himself. The neighbors tell him what he already suspects, that Usrey has moved out, though they have no idea where. Warren thanks them, then goes back to Usrey's trailer to look around for a lead, which he immediately finds: a For Sale sign in one of the windows with a phone number on it.

Grayer says he knows another guy who lives nearby, a black man named Clifford Bell who also managed a Lee's for a while and who had an experience similar to Grayer's, though he didn't sue after he was terminated. Great, Warren says, they can talk to Bell tonight and call the number on the For Sale sign from Bell's house.

Grayer is convinced to go along, largely because, since Warren is
driving, he doesn't seem to have much choice. He gets them into
Bell's house, though, and then calls the number from the trailer.
They're in luck: Jim Usrey answers, and after talking to Grayer he
agrees to speak with Warren. He says he's not sure he wants to give
a sworn statement, but yes, he was an area supervisor for Lee's in
the Nashville area, and yes, he saw a lot of the racial stuff that
went on.

Usrey is a slender man in his early thirties, a heavy smoker with
a thick Tennessee accent, and when Warren meets him face-to-
face on a subsequent trip to Nashville, he has to travel miles
through the country outside Cookeville, Tennessee, to find Usrey's house. It is hidden deep in the woods and surrounded by acres
of land and his own stocked pond. Usrey's story turns out to be
similar to Terry Toney's. When he managed a Lee's in Nashville,
he says (and testifies in a deposition), he heard Danner on a number of occasions explain his philosophy that white customers
didn't like blacks, so blacks should work in stores in black neighborhoods and whites in stores in white neighborhoods. Other
company officials, Usrey claims, instructed him to code applications, schedule only white workers for Danner's Sunday inspections, limit the number of black workers in his restaurants
and hire as many whites as he could instead, no matter how poorly
qualified they might be. In fact, Usrey says, there was a joke often
made in the company about the single requirement necessary for
hiring white workers to avoid having to hire blacks. "The joke that
went around in the personnel department," he says, was, "[they]
told me that they was to stick a mirror under their nose and if they
fogged it up, to hire them."

When he was an area supervisor, Usrey tells Warren, he was
once instructed to go to the "nigger store" on Jefferson Street to
fire the black manager there, Eugene Grayer, on orders from Danner. "I don't know what was wrong, but something was wrong and
Danner said he wanted him gone," Usrey says. "I was told we had
another token nigger to take his place."

Usrey tells Warren that he was also instructed to fire a white
manager named Danny Gibson, who had been lobbying company

officials to allow him to promote a black woman to dining-room supervisor or assistant manager. Gibson had been working as many as ninety hours a week and desperately needed help in his store, according to Usrey, but he wasn't able to find any qualified white applicants who could do either job. "Gibson kept pushing the issue and he was told to back off on it because he knowed how the policy worked," Usrey says. "He didn't back off and that's when I was ordered to terminate him."

As it turns out, the "Danny White" Warren has been trying to locate for months is the Danny Gibson whom Usrey says he fired. When Warren gets off the phone that third night in Nashville, Grayer and Clifford Bell decide they've had the name wrong all along. Immediately Warren gets back on the phone, and late that evening he's somehow able to find Gibson, who lives twenty miles west of Nashville in Ashland City, a small town tucked into a bend of the Cumberland River. He'll meet Warren in the morning, Gibson says; they can talk over breakfast at the Hardee's in Ashland. Warren is scheduled to return to Tallahassee the next day but thinks he can work in one more quick trip, so he agrees.

What he hasn't counted on, though, is the heavy storm that breaks that night. By morning the rivers are up and there are reports of flooding all along the Cumberland. Still, O'Rourke's urban assault vehicle has four-wheel drive in case he gets stuck, and there's always the cellular phone for serious emergencies. So Warren keeps the appointment with Gibson.

The story he hears is the one he's been hearing for the past three days: Lee's officials routinely telling yet another manager to hire whites and to keep blacks in the back if he has to have them at all. Gibson, then twenty-five, had worked his way up from Shoney's busboy to Lee's manager over six years since starting with the company in 1980. During that time, he says, and repeats later under oath, he also got the message straight from Ray Danner, who purportedly told him, "I don't like niggers and I don't want them in my stores."

March 9, 1989. Tommy Warren and Barry Goldstein leave their American Bar Association conference hotel on Amelia Island, a resort town on Florida's Atlantic Coast, to drive to nearby Fernandina Beach where the nearest Shoney's restaurant is located. With them is a slightly built Californian with a trim white beard. His name is Guy Saperstein.

Saperstein has never been to a Shoney's—they don't have them yet in California—so on the way over for lunch Warren explains what they'll see. A woman will greet them once they walk inside. She'll be the hostess, who will seat them, and she'll be white. Near the register they'll see either a man or a woman in a white shirt. That will be the manager. He or she will also be white, as will their waitress and most of the other waitresses in the restaurant. At some point during their meal, Warren says, a man or woman will come out of the kitchen to service the salad bar. That employee will be black. The young men who dart out of the back with deep plastic trays to bus the dirty tables will also be black, and if Saperstein looks closely when the kitchen door swings open, he might be able to see the cooks and prep workers, hidden from the customers' view. Most of them will be black as well.

When the three men sit down at the Fernandina Beach Shoney's, the tableau unfolds exactly as Warren predicted it would. Saperstein, who as a young attorney lived for a while in Colorado migrant labor camps so he could understand the lives of the workers he was then representing, agrees on behalf of his firm to support the class-action racial discrimination suit that Warren and Goldstein intend to file in early April against Ray Danner and Shoney's, Inc. Over the next three and a half years his firm will spend more than $700,000 to make good on that promise.

Later, back at the ABA conference on Amelia Island, Barry Goldstein, who is an officer in the Bar Association's Labor and Employment Section, manages to tweak one of the other conference participants, Shoney's attorney Butch Powell: Goldstein sticks him on a session panel with one of Guy Saperstein's partners, a Berkeley social activist named Brad Seligman. The issue is ethics.

NINE

" We're Going off Tackle, and You Can't Stop Us "

On April 4, 1989, nearly a year after Henry and Billie Elliott were fired from their jobs, Barry Goldstein left his NAACP Legal Defense and Educational Fund office to walk several blocks across Washington, D.C., to the well-appointed Connecticut Avenue offices of Gibson, Dunn and Crutcher, one of the largest and most powerful law firms in the country. He was hand-delivering a package to a man he'd known socially for some time, the corporate lawyer Stephen Tallent, immediately recognizable with his white beard and hair, corpulent figure, and omnipresent pipe. Tallent's predecessor in Gibson, Dunn and Crutcher's labor division, William French Smith, had left the firm several years earlier to take over as Ronald Reagan's attorney general, and Goldstein had spent a considerable amount of time during the 1980s countering Smith in the national debate over affirmative action. Today, though, his business was with Tallent, who had informed Goldstein months

before that he would be joining Butch Powell as labor counsel for
Shoney's in any employment discrimination case that might be
pending, and who had also "warned" Goldstein about working
with Tommy Warren. As a courtesy, Goldstein was now bringing
Tallent the first public copy of the class-action complaint he and
Warren had drawn up against Shoney's, Inc., Robertson Investment Company, and Ray Danner.

To Goldstein, the evidence in the case was already "overwhelming" and the legal issues "not that technical": clear violations of
Title VII of the Civil Rights Act of 1964 and of Section 1981 of the
U.S. Code, which for nearly a hundred years, since Reconstruc-
tion, had made racial discrimination in the formation of employment contracts illegal. Because Title VII restricted awards to back
pay and limited plaintiffs' options to bench trials, that is, trials
held before a federal judge only, Goldstein and Warren had decided
to file their case as a class action under Section 1981, which per-
mitted jury trials and allowed for punitive and compensatory
damages.

The "quintessential class issue" was straightforward: "Did Shoney's maintain and implement a direct and overt policy of discrimination against blacks by limiting their job opportunities and
by retaliating against white managers and others who opposed or
refused to implement this policy?" To the plaintiffs' attorneys, the
answers were clear.

At the same time Goldstein was delivering the personal copy of
the complaint to Tallent, Tommy Warren was filing the document
formally at a red-tiled federal courthouse in Pensacola, Florida,
which was home to the U.S. District Court for the Northern District of Florida. The nine named plaintiffs in the suit, Warren and
Goldstein were prepared to argue, represented two classes of employees at Shoney's, Inc.: an indeterminate number of all past,
present, and future black workers affected by the corporation's "illegal discriminatory employment policy and practices," and all
white employees who had been subjected to illegal retaliation for
refusing to carry out those policies and practices.

The nine had all worked, or applied to work, at Captain D's or
Shoney's restaurants across north Florida. All had strong, representative claims and, just as important, all had agreed to let

Warren and Goldstein put their names on the complaint, knowing they would have to face attacks on their past, their work history, and their character that were certain to follow. Five had been employed at Robertson Investment and had been among the first Warren had interviewed the previous spring: Billie and Henry Elliott, Leonard Charles Williams, Lester Thomas, and Donna Mongoven. The other four had specific claims against company-owned Shoney's restaurants in Pensacola and Tallahassee.

Josephine Haynes, an aspiring cosmetologist who was black, said she had applied at two Shoney's in Pensacola and been turned down for waitress jobs at both, even though the stores appeared to be hiring. Shoney's attorneys would later claim she was a "set-up plaintiff," a tester sent into those restaurants by Warren or someone acting on his behalf. Because she was listed first, the suit against Shoney's would bear her name: *Haynes et al. v. Shoney's, Inc.*

Denise Riley, another young black woman, had worked in a Pensacola Shoney's for two years but said she had been repeatedly passed over for promotion by less qualified whites and illegally forced to quit when her hours were severely reduced. Shoney's would eventually succeed in having most of her charges rejected, not because they weren't valid, but because Riley hadn't exhausted all administrative procedures by first filing her charges with the EEOC under the established deadline as required by federal law.

Dewitt Nelson had been a cook for four years in two Tallahassee Shoney's, both within a mile of Warren's office, and said he had also been passed over repeatedly for better jobs in those stores on account of his race. He also claimed that he had been illegally fired by Shoney's a week after he filed a charge of discrimination against the restaurant with the EEOC. Shoney's contended in court documents that he had been dismissed because of allegations that he had harassed female employees. He would prove to be the most problematic of all the named plaintiffs.

Buddy Bonsall, who had been one of Nelson's store managers, said he had been pressured by his supervisors to reduce the number of black employees who worked for him—and to fire Dewitt Nelson without cause. When he refused, he said, he suffered retaliation from those supervisors, who included Bill Long, the Shoney's vice president who had been charged with giving similar discriminatory orders in the 1985 Sharon Johnson case in Montgomery, Alabama. Long, Bonsall testified, called him a "nigger lover" after he refused to fire Nelson and said he would quit himself instead. The retaliation against Bonsall culminated in August 1988, he claimed, when his division director came to the store and took him into the walk-in cooler to berate Bonsall for being too soft on his black employees. "This is how you talk to them," the official purportedly said, after which he allegedly grabbed Bonsall's tie, pulled Bonsall close to his face, and then said, "'Listen you goddamn nigger, if you can't get to work on time stay the fuck out.'" The restaurant's kitchen manager, John Pender, said he witnessed the scene. Bonsall, who had worked at several Shoney's over the years and said he had experienced discriminatory policies at all of them, quit the next day.

In addition, though they weren't cited in the original complaint, dozens of other witnesses, including the three white former managers Warren had located in Nashville, had already given sworn statements, or filed their own charges of discrimination with the EEOC, to back up the class action brought by the nine named plaintiffs. Alerted by an aggressive Legal Defense Fund publicity campaign, more than sixty newspapers around the country reported on the filing of the lawsuit, though in many of those reports the case was mischaracterized as simply involving nine unhappy former Shoney's employees. In fact, the putative classes, that is, the two classes as Warren and Goldstein sought to have them defined, geographically and temporally, numbered in the hundreds of thousands. LDF director Julius Chambers characterized it in the *American Bar Association Journal* as "the largest employment-discrimination class action ever brought by private attorneys against a private company."

The most significant aspect of the filing was an LDF press release announcing a tollfree hotline for other witnesses or discrimination victims to call. Warren had recruited a battery of Florida State University law students to work the phones, and he converted his office into a virtual telephone bank to handle what, given the scope of the case and the extensive nature of the alleged discrimination throughout the Shoney's empire, he anticipated would be an avalanche of responses.

And the calls poured in, from black applicants who said they had been turned away despite posted job openings, from low-level black workers who said they had been passed over for promotions and had never known why, from black employees who said they had been terminated without cause or forced to quit when their hours were inexplicably cut back, and from white managers like the Elliotts who said they had been fired themselves for not following the racial directives. Calls also came in from other white managers, even from some former company executives, who said they had been among those responsible for carrying out what they alleged were Shoney's discriminatory policies. Warren would spend the next several months convincing these people to give sworn statements that would hold up in court. The law students in Tallahassee, sitting in the attic room over Warren's office where it was always too warm or too cold because of a faulty air conditioner, took down all the names and all the stories for Warren to investigate further, and the "dec sheets," spiral-bound compilations of those initial declarations, grew as thick as phone books.

The Warren family was growing at the same time. On April 12, 1989, Warren's wife gave birth to the couple's third child, a daughter whom they named Bridget.

As the investigation moved into this new phase, Warren's vocabulary and his knowledge of the underside of the restaurant industry expanded rapidly. Even before he and Goldstein forced Shoney's to hand over its employment statistics, he discovered what he contended was the "inexorable zero" in minority representation at the upper levels of Shoney's management; there were virtually no minorities at any level in the central office in Nashville. He learned that well-built black men at some stores might be referred to as "Arnold Schwarzenigger," that a "blue-gum nigger" was a black worker who seemed to be especially "African," "just off the slave boat," and that too many blacks meant a restaurant was "too cloudy" or that someone must be "shooting a jungle movie" or that it was "Little Africa." He learned a host of other names, too, which were purportedly used by a number of white Shoney's executives and managers to refer to black workers: "boy, coon, spear chucker, jungle bunny, monkey, iguana, welfare baby, black bastard, Buckwheat, Alfalfa, and black cat." The last term reportedly came from an area supervisor in Kansas City who, witnesses said, looked at a black employee on one occasion and then said to others present, "I don't like black cats. I like to hang them upside down and shoot them in the eye and watch them squirm."

Warren learned that hiring blacks back after you'd just "lightened" your store was known as "re-nigging," and he learned a new generation of racist jokes: "I smell a gar." "A ci-gar?" "No, a nig-gar." He learned that "nigger stores" in predominantly black neighborhoods like the Jefferson Street location where Eugene Grayer once worked in Nashville might have black managers, but that in many other stores the place for many minority applicants was "File 13," the trash can, according to witnesses. But there were other ways to note the race of black job applicants besides the standard blackened "O" on the Shoney's name, these witnesses said: a simple "A," for instance, which stood for "Ape." And witness after witness, black and white, testified that the last thing anyone wanted to hear was a version of the comment a supervisor told one manager about his restaurant: "You better put some cream in your coffee. Your kitchen is too dark."

The work pace for Warren and Goldstein was furious that spring and into the summer. When Goldstein left the LDF in June and flew from Washington, D.C., to Oakland, California, to start his new job at Guy Saperstein's firm, he joked that he billed twenty-seven hours to the case that day. He was not entirely joking. He had in fact been working on the Shoney's case that morning in Washington, and when he got off the plane in Oakland he went directly to Saperstein's office and continued with it until late that night. With the three-hour time delay, he and Warren working together were routinely able to keep up the action on the case for eighteen hours each day, starting at 7:00 A.M. EST and continuing until 10:00 P.M. Pacific. From February through May Warren reported 725 hours spent on the case; in June alone he worked more than 300.

In the beginning, there was a clear division of labor. Warren's role, for the most part, was handling discovery: chasing down new witnesses and leads, taking depositions, and doing background research on Danner and Shoney's, aided by a "Deep Throat" source he had developed in Nashville's city government. Goldstein, with the resources and personnel available to him in Saperstein's Oakland office, did most of the legal research and wrote the majority of the briefs, faxing copies to Warren in Tallahassee for his review.

For more than a year, Shoney's had been the only item on Warren's agenda, but during the spring and summer of 1989 Goldstein was juggling a great deal more than that: arguing a critical civil rights case before the Supreme Court in March; traveling with Warren on subsequent trips to Nashville and then filing the Shoney's complaint in April; preparing to leave the LDF and move his family to the West Coast; spending ten hours a day alone in a room at his house during most of May cramming six weeks' worth of study-course tapes into three weeks' time so he could pass the California Bar. He knew the pressure on the family was getting out of hand when his then-three-year-old son Nicholas wandered into the study one day while the tapes were playing, looked up earnestly at Goldstein, and said, "Work, Daddy, work."

As soon as Warren and Goldstein filed the original complaint in early April, they knew Shoney's would come back with a barrage of motions attacking their case, and the corporation didn't disappoint. There were immediate battles over preservation of records, requests for information, access to company documents, and the number of acceptable interrogatories (the formal lists of plaintiffs' questions to which corporate officials were required to respond). Shoney's, Robertson Investment, and Danner made various early motions to have the lawsuit dismissed, motions that never went anywhere, but which took up hours and sometimes days of the attorneys' time nevertheless.

Danner's lawyers argued that their client shouldn't be held personally responsible for whatever had gone on in Shoney's, because, as they wrote, "Mr. Danner acted only in his corporate capacity, not in his individual capacity." They filed objections to Barry Goldstein being admitted into the jurisdiction of the north Florida court as co-lead counsel in the case. The reason, they said in a two-page brief, was that Warren and Goldstein had supposedly violated a local court rule regarding "inappropriate" outside publicity when they approved the LDF press release and the tollfree number announcing the lawsuit. The press release, in naming Danner as a defendant in the case, had included his net worth, and that, his attorneys claimed, "was frightening to him because of concerns for his family."

Goldstein, who had never before in eighteen years with the LDF faced such an objection, nonetheless had to respond with a lengthy legal argument, affidavits from him and Warren, and copies of a dozen articles that had run in the Nashville newspapers and in the trade press about Danner's wealth, a subject Danner had apparently never been reluctant to discuss in the past. It was a pro forma exercise, and Goldstein was admitted to practice in the north Florida court with no legitimate problems, but concerns over the local publicity rule would have far-reaching effects on the litigation afterward. Because they were trying their case in the conservative north Florida district, Warren and Goldstein decided they would have to assiduously avoid most public comment in the future, though that meant turning down interview requests from the major networks and CNN, among others, and losing the chance of reaching even more potential witnesses. (When a major public-accommodations suit was brought against the rival Denny's restaurant chain by attorneys in Saperstein's office three years later, that complaint was filed in California's federal courts, which didn't follow the same local rules as north Florida. In that case, the attorneys were allowed to speak freely about the charges, and at least partially as a result, the Denny's suit and the charges of racist treatment of black customers stayed on the business pages and in the national press for months until it settled. The case against Shoney's, meanwhile, largely sank from public view after the initial splash of publicity.)

But Warren and Goldstein had enough to deal with without having to worry too much about that. There were the Nashville trips to meet with former top Shoney's executives, including the ex-CEO Dave Wachtel, to urge them to testify; there were ultimately fruitless meetings with the Equal Employment Opportunity Commission's Systemic Unit in Washington to discuss possible EEOC support for the class action; there were half a dozen Supreme

Court rulings in July, including the one that Goldstein had argued back in the spring, that they knew would have a critical impact on their case; and there was the first round of depositions with the Marianna and Panama City witnesses, many of which became a battle-within-a-battle between Butch Powell and Tommy Warren.

They weren't about to let up, though, not while they had the momentum going hard against Shoney's, forcing the play. On July 3, 1989, they submitted their formal request for class certification, under the three-month legal deadline after the filing of the original complaint. In most class actions, certification requests were honored by the courts "in the breach," or after the deadline, Goldstein and Warren knew, but they wanted to keep the pressure on Shoney's, and they wanted to show the court that they were ready to deliver everything they promised, and deliver it on time.

"We were largely approaching it like the Vince Lombardi Green Bay Packer offense," Goldstein said. "'We're going off tackle, and you can't stop us.' We were going to be very clear. We were going to promise a lot and we were going to deliver."

They would have to. Without class certification, which the judge held broad discretionary powers to grant or deny, the plaintiffs' only alternative would be to bring each of the thousands of possible cases individually, an impossible, decades-long task which would be prohibitively time-consuming and costly, for the plaintiffs' lawyers, as well as for the courts.

Nine days after Warren and Goldstein filed their class-certification request, though, Shoney's attorneys dropped their first incendiary bomb.

On July 12, 1989, they abruptly filed an "emergency motion for protective order and the imposition of sanctions" against Warren, charging that he had improperly contacted witnesses and threatened a Tallahassee Shoney's manager over the phone to get her to testify for the plaintiffs. They argued that the court should impose "substantial fines" on Warren for violating the rules of attorney conduct, that Warren and Goldstein not be allowed to talk to any current Shoney's managers in the future, and that they be forced to hand over all discovery material from discussions with any managers in the past. Even contact with former Shoney's managers, the motion stated, should be restricted.

From the plaintiffs' perspective, most of the allegations were
easily dismissed. Either the employees hadn't occupied managerial positions or they had been contacted by other witnesses, not
by Warren. In any event, Warren and Goldstein contacted the Florida Bar for an opinion, and consulted with three law professors
who specialized in legal ethics—all of whom supported Warren in
those cases.

The one allegation that remained, that Warren had twice called
Tallahassee Shoney's manager Tanya Catani and threatened her if
she didn't cooperate in his investigation, was the most disturbing
charge, and potentially the most damning, except for one thing:
Warren claimed he never made the calls.

Of course, Shoney's attorneys weren't simply attacking Warren.
In bringing the ethics charges, which would hang darkly over the
litigation for the next three years, they were also laying the
groundwork for a challenge to the overall adequacy of plaintiffs'
counsel, a challenge that, if successful, could conceivably kill the
class action.

At the time the suit was filed, a longtime Shoney's insider named
J. Mitchell Boyd was in the third year of a three-year plan to replace Ray Danner as CEO and chairman of the board. Boyd, the
original franchise director for Danner after he bought out Alex
Schoenbaum in the early 1970s, had gone into a sort of Shoney's
exile when a management rival, Dave Wachtel, briefly ascended to
the Danner throne in 1980. That exile was a lucrative one, the
northern Virginia franchise area, which Boyd accepted as part of a
management buyout package and subsequently developed into
one of the most profitable franchise groups on the spreading Shoney's map.

Danner had originally intended to tap the corporation's chief
operating officer, Gary Spoleta, as his next successor after the
Wachtel experiment failed, according to Boyd. Spoleta, however,
was arrested and charged with possession of cocaine in 1983 and
sentenced to six months probation. His record was ordered ex-
punged at the end of the probation, but the plaintiffs' attorneys in
Haynes entered copies of the arrest warrant, the receipt from his
bail, and the expungement order into the court record as part of a

motion late in their case to allow them to depose Spoleta. Spoleta kept his positions as Shoney's president and chief operating officer despite the arrest, but he never made CEO.

After Dave Wachtel left, Danner himself returned as chief executive officer through the early 1980s but in 1986, still on the lookout for a successor, he asked Boyd to give up his franchises and return to the company fold. Boyd agreed. For the first year, the plan was for Boyd to observe from the side and concentrate his efforts on the Shoney's division while Danner still ran the business. In the second year, they would work as a team, in effect, as co-CEOs. Finally, in the third year, Boyd would take over, with Danner still around as a senior adviser. Or, as Boyd himself characterized it, Danner "would run the company for a year while I watched, then we would both run the company for a year, and then I would run the company for a year while he watched."

The only problem was, Danner didn't like to watch, and Boyd quickly discovered that his boss wasn't going to relinquish control easily. Indeed, Danner continued to read most of the shopper's reports to chart customer satisfaction, and when Boyd made the unilateral decision to close all the Captain D's on Thanksgiving Day—a sound business move, he asserted, one supported by clear evidence, amply documented, that they lost money on meager holiday sales—Danner, he said, was furious.

The scheme Shoney's executives and Danner himself eventually agreed on for smoothing Danner's withdrawal from daily operations was a $728 million, leveraged recapitalization plan that paid shareholders a one-time twenty-dollar-per-share dividend. Since Danner was the single largest owner of Shoney's stock (he held 19 percent at the time) he picked up $111 million straight off, with another $3.3 million each year in interest on subordinated debentures also issued as part of the recap.

The recapitalization meant going hundreds of millions into debt, but Boyd and Chief Financial Officer Taylor Henry decided the company would have no trouble paying it off. A management buyout of Danner would cost at least a couple of hundred million dollars anyway, Boyd reasoned, so why not spread the wealth? The board of directors signed off on the plan, and by summer 1989 they were already $122 million ahead of the repayment schedule. It was a questionable move, however. Leveraging the company so Danner could have his cake and eat it too—that is, so he could receive $140 million but still keep his controlling ownership of company stock—meant losing all the financial flexibility the corporation had previously enjoyed. Keeping ahead of the competition required a ready supply of cash to routinely sink back into upgrading the restaurants.

From that point on, Boyd later said, he would struggle unsuccessfully with the tight-fisted board for money to maintain quality in the stores.

Still, the urbane Boyd, who once aspired to a Ph.D. in philosophy, was a marked contrast in style to the blue-collar Danner, though both were the only children of working-class parents. Fluent in French, Boyd had lived in Paris for a year in the early 1960s, working as a translator. The Nashville native had attended Vanderbilt University after three years in the Army as a psychiatric medical corpsman, then spent two years as a social worker in the rough Bedford Stuyvesant neighborhood of New York City before returning to Tennessee and starting his career at Shoney's, first as a manager trainee, then as a store manager.

In a 1995 interview, his first and only public comments on Shoney's since he was forced out as CEO in December 1989, Boyd was careful to distance himself from what he said were Danner's discriminatory policies, both as those policies existed when Boyd began working for Shoney's in the late 1960s and as he said they remained entrenched when he returned to run the company himself in 1986. He did say, however, that racial problems had long existed at Shoney's, and that Danner's "intense, consumer-driven philosophy" was the reason. "In my heart I do not believe that Ray Danner was a bigot," Boyd said. "Ray had a particularly strong business way of thinking about people. Not who they were or what color their skin was, but how they affected business."

If, for example, Danner had an employee with offensive body odor that drove away customers, Boyd said, he would order that employee to do something about the problem. If the employee didn't comply with the order, Danner would get rid of him. That was Boyd's analogy for Danner's attitude about blacks: Black workers were bad for business in predominantly white areas, so

Danner, Boyd said, felt he had to limit the number of black workers in those restaurants, especially blacks in customer-contact positions.

"In the sixties and seventies, and into the eighties, if there were too many blacks working in a restaurant, especially in the South, whites wouldn't eat there," Boyd said. The Civil Rights Act of 1964 and other antidiscrimination laws, he said, didn't take that into account. "The laws were written by social engineering standards—the way we'd like things to be. But Ray was not a social engineer, he was a restaurant engineer trying to get the most out of his business. This was reality. Ray didn't give a damn about social engineering. He cared about dollars and cents."

Boyd said that most blacks, especially in the South in the 1960s and 1970s, suffered from a lack of education, and "among themselves spoke a language whites couldn't understand." When black workers composed 50 to 60 percent of the employees in a restaurant, Boyd said, their language tended to dominate, and since whites had difficulty understanding that black language, they wouldn't want to work there—or eat there. To illustrate, he told the author about a stop he had made at a McDonald's drivethrough to order an Egg McMuffin. The voice of a black employee came back over the intercom, according to Boyd, who mimicked the employee's stereotypical "black dialect": "We ain't servin' breakfast no mo'." Customers, he said—presumably white customers—didn't want to hear "inappropriate" language like that and would take their business elsewhere.

Boyd said Danner "never understood" Title VII of the Civil Rights Act of 1964, which made discrimination in the workplace illegal under federal law. "He started the company, he ran it all his life with no bosses ever telling him what he could or couldn't do, and he was the law unto himself," Boyd said. "Ray fell victim to what we all fall victim to. He was a brilliant man who didn't understand how reality had changed. He couldn't treat people in the 1980s the way he had during his successful early years in the 1960s and 1970s."

And as Danner interpreted Title VII, according to Boyd, he believed that he couldn't be required to hire any more blacks at his stores on a percentage basis than there were blacks in the neighborhood population. Boyd was unable to explain why other corporate executives and attorneys were apparently unable to correct what he called Danner's "misunderstanding of the intent of affirmative action."

When he came back to Shoney's to replace Danner as CEO, Boyd said, he "worked underneath" to address the racial problems he saw in the corporation in the then-recent aftermath of the Sharon Johnson case in Montgomery. Though he avoided discussing any specific incidents in the company—he was never involved in operations, he insisted—Boyd did say that serious problems still existed at the time of the lawsuit, which he claims he tried to settle within months of the filing. "I felt we were culpable for some time," he said.

In the summer of 1989, already convinced that Shoney's had "no way to win" the lawsuit, Boyd said he went to some members of the board of directors to "test the idea" that they offer the plaintiffs $50 million to settle the case.

Shoney's founder Alex Schoenbaum confirmed that there were settlement discussions in the company during the summer of 1989, but he said he didn't remember the $50 million that Boyd said he suggested. "That was without the knowledge of the board," Schoenbaum said. "It was probably done with the officers of the company and not necessarily with the board. I don't think the board knew about it." Schoenbaum added that for years the Shoney's board had been divided into two camps. One was led by Danner and his friends Wallace Rasmussen and Dan Maddox, the retired chairmen, respectively, of Beatrice Foods and of Associates Corporation of North America, according to Schoenbaum. The other camp he referred to as the "outsiders," which consisted of men like Schoenbaum himself who lived elsewhere and who were given little say in the direction and operations of the company.

Tommy Warren says the plaintiffs never knew about any of the early settlement discussions that Boyd and Schoenbaum mentioned, nor did the plaintiffs know about the understanding that Boyd says he had that the company was "culpable." Both Warren and Goldstein added, though, that it would have been difficult to turn down a settlement offer of that magnitude—$50 million— especially so early in what everyone knew would be a brutal and protracted litigation. What the plaintiffs *were* aware of, the attorneys said, was that Shoney's hadn't taken any action against executives such as Bill Long, the former division director accused by several witnesses of being the architect of the discriminatory policies challenged in the Sharon Johnson case, and that under Boyd, Long had actually been promoted to Shoney's division vice president. The plaintiffs also claimed that the charges of discrimination they were hearing had continued during Boyd's three years at the helm.

When Shoney's did finally act to address the racial climate within the company, according to Boyd, and to combat the bad publicity from the lawsuit, an important focus was on public relations. The centerpiece of the PR campaign was a "covenant" with the Southern Christian Leadership Conference, a corporate promise announced with great fanfare in August 1989 that Shoney's would do $90 million worth of business with minority-owned firms over the next three years and that it would target management jobs and franchise ownership opportunities for blacks. Shoney's had never had any sort of affirmative action program, several corporate executives acknowledged in their depositions, and all the news reports remarked on the curious timing of the SCLC pact.

In an August 19, 1989, article in the *Atlanta Constitution*, Barry Goldstein charged that the covenant, which had been drafted in a single meeting between company officials and the SCLC, was not legally enforceable. "That's so much garbage," he said. In the same article, Mitch Boyd denied that the covenant had anything to do with the lawsuit. "There's no real connection between that and what we've done with the SCLC," he said. After the settlement, however, Boyd said that the covenant and other corporate donations to minority causes made after the lawsuit was filed constituted what in one interview he called "a payoff to the black community." He later amended his remarks to the author, saying he intended to describe those actions as "a pay *back* to the black community."

The SCLC covenant served Shoney's purpose well. It received extensive press coverage, and according to Goldstein many potential witnesses were convinced that it meant the class action had been settled. Shoney's executives later acknowledged, and subse-

quent audits showed, that the company had included no clear definition of "minority" and were counting millions of dollars worth
of contracts with two Italian-American-owned companies as fulfilling some of the terms of the corporation's "covenant."

Other questions about the covenant were raised when a request
for company documents by the plaintiffs' attorneys produced a
September 29, 1989, memorandum from Benny Ball, director of
personnel, to then-Shoney's president Gary Spoleta concerning
what was labeled a "Partnership Agreement" with SCLC executive director Joseph Lowery. The document discussed waiving the
standard franchise requirements in order to give Lowery half-
ownership of a Shoney's restaurant which the company would
then run. The memo, in its entirety, read as follows:

The concept would consist of the following:
1. The partnership would consist of Shoney's, Inc. and Joseph
   Lowery. Each partner would hold 50 percent of the partnership.
2. The initial capital would be provided by the partnership.
   Joe Lowery would sign a note to the partnership for his half
   of the initial capital.
3. Partnership pays the standard franchisee fee.
4. Shoney's, Inc. keeps all books.
5. Lowery's note payment would be taken out of the profits
   of the store.
6. Shoney's, Inc. would be responsible for the management of
   the store.

The author of the memo, Benny Ball, when asked in a subsequent
deposition if Shoney's had discussed a partnership agreement with
Lowery, responded, "Not to my knowledge." He said the memorandum was an "example" of a type of agreement Shoney's was
considering using to increase minority franchise ownership.

In a later deposition in the case, Ray Danner said he knew of
only one minority-owned franchise in either the Shoney's or Captain D's divisions prior to his retirement as chairman of the board
in March 1989, and he was unable to explain why, on a compre-
hensive list of franchises for those two divisions, the name of that
purported owner wasn't included.

Warren and Goldstein said they tried to contact Lowery to express their concerns about the unenforceable nature of the SCLC agreement and the harm the publicity could do to the lawsuit when they first learned of the organization's covenant with Shoney's, but were never able to get through to him. Lowery, in a 1995 interview, said the SCLC never heard from the plaintiffs' attorneys, and in any event the SCLC, on advice from its own lawyers, steered clear of any employment issues in the covenant, focussing instead on promoting franchises for minorities and Shoney's business with black-owned companies. He said the discussion about making him a franchise owner was never serious.

"I recall at one meeting [Mitch] Boyd said something about I ought to be interested in a franchise," Lowery said. "We were pushing him about helping blacks qualify financially for franchises. . . . In the process we were pushing them to make possible the financing to help blacks qualify for ownership of franchises. And in the conversation I remember Mitch Boyd saying, 'You ought to get a franchise.' That was the only time I ever heard of that.

"It was not a serious discussion. I never heard anything more about it from them, and they never heard anything more about it from me. And this is the first I've heard of these memos. They never copied me, and I never heard another peep about it. Nor did I inquire about it because I never did consider it a serious proposition.

"I'm a little surprised that they were serious enough to write a memorandum about it. But there again I don't know what their purpose was because they never discussed it with me. At no time did they ever discuss the things you mentioned in the letter. At no time. So I don't know what their purpose was, whether they were trying to fool somebody in the company or—I don't know what they were doing. I really don't.

"There was no way under God's sun that our sense of ethics nor our common sense judgment would we have made ourselves that vulnerable to enter into an agreement like that with them."

The covenant negotiations with Lowery and the SCLC had been initiated by a public relations firm from High Point, North Carolina, called B&C Associates, which was run by two black conservatives, Bob Brown and Jim Patterson, with ties to the old-line civil-rights leadership and to the national Republican Party. Bob Brown had served on the SCLC board of directors. Their specialty was corporate image makeovers, and when they contacted Shoney's after the lawsuit was filed, Mitch Boyd said he was immediately interested.

Brown advised an aggressive PR response right away. In a July 21, 1989, document titled "Shoney's, Inc.: A Corporate Image Campaign," B&C pushed for $3 million in radio, newspaper, and television ads, all touting Shoney's as "A Place To Start, A Place To Grow," with special emphasis on images of and opportunities for African Americans. They recommended Whitman Mayo, who played Grady Wilson in the TV show "Sanford and Son," as a company spokesman for one set of commercials, and "well-known passages from such famous personalities as author James Michener or baseball legend Hank Aaron" for others. One proposed radio spot, to be aired on black stations in the top ten markets, was to feature Michener reading a text, apparently designed to encourage minorities to apply for management positions at Shoney's, written in a sort of free-verse form replete with spelling and mechanical errors:

Let me say
that I have a real commitment to excellence;
but I think the motivations is,
clear and simple,
I think an individual ought
to make the most of his talents,
perfecting them,
enlarging them
if they are too parochial.
But he really is committed to making a contribution
and it can be in the widest variety of forms.
I am very, very conservative in my tastes,
and I like a good baker
who can bake a good loaf of bread,
or a man who runs a good fishing boat here,
or people who run a good restaurant.

I have never believed that I was engaged in a profession
that was in any way sacrosanct or privileged.
I think I could have done just
as good a job as a banker
or a newspaper editor,
or a college professor.
I think they work
in a very difficult "ambient"
and a lot of them handle it very well, indeed.
And I think that could
have been a challenge to me.
In other words,
I really believe that one ought to capitalize
upon the talents he has
and ought to try to make a contribution.
It's as simple as that.

The ad never ran, but B&C got its contract. In addition to running the minority ad campaign, Brown and Patterson were paid $5,000 a month to oversee the SCLC agreement and to recommend minority contractors. One of those they recommended, according to Boyd, was a black-owned travel agency in Atlanta. Boyd said he subsequently sent two Shoney's executives to Atlanta to talk to the woman who ran the agency about handling some of the corporation's business. When the executives returned to Nashville, Boyd said, they told him they were impressed with the woman and her business, that they thought they would be able to work with her, and that she was very active in a number of social causes in the Atlanta area, including what one called the "United Nigger College Fund."

The executive meant well, Boyd said, but the oral slip was yet another indication of how far the company would have to go to change its racial attitudes.

Meanwhile, even B&C was calling into question aspects of Shoney's compliance with the SCLC Covenant. In a May 2, 1991, memo discovered by the plaintiffs' attorneys and entered into the court record as a deposition exhibit, Jim Patterson raised that issue and also the issue of the company's "system" for counting minority employees and reporting that number to the government. That memo read, in part: "1. Your system for head counts for the official EEO-1 reports is subject to question, and should someone bring up the origin of head count data, it could prove difficult to explain. 2. The amount of business done with minority suppliers includes sub-vendors that were in place without any direct action on the part of Shoney's, and that mixing could prove difficult to explain." Lowery said B&C never told the SCLC that there were any concerns over the implementation of the covenant, and he said no one had ever informed him that Shoney's counted contracts with Italian-American-owned companies as fulfilling some of the terms of that agreement.

Over the next few years B&C would continue to advise Shoney's and Ray Danner on ways to improve their corporate and individual images. What that largely meant, besides the ad campaign and the SCLC covenant, was handing out money to black organizations. The Nashville newspapers and other media around the Southeast, African American–owned papers in particular, regularly received press releases and photos featuring a white Shoney's executive standing between two African Americans. One of the two, shaking the executive's hand, would be a representative of the organization accepting the check; the other would often be a tall, older black man with glasses, a deeply receding hairline, and a Rotary Club mien: Bob Brown, smiling over his handiwork.

Once, at Brown and Patterson's suggestion, Shoney's "donated" a fax machine to the Martin Luther King Jr. Center for Nonviolent Change in Atlanta. In return, they received a letter of thanks from Coretta Scott King, widow of the slain civil rights leader. Corporate documents uncovered by the plaintiffs' attorneys later showed that the fax machine hadn't come from Shoney's, but had instead been provided, at the insistence of a corporate executive, by an office supply company that did considerable business at the restaurant chain's Nashville headquarters.

TEN

" Due Diligence "

A few days after the original class complaint was filed, in April 1989, Tommy Warren received an unexpected call from Henry Elliott. Debora Newton, the woman who had been brought in to replace Henry as manager of the Marianna Captain D's, had just contacted him, Henry said, and she wanted to talk.

Warren agreed to meet with Newton, but only if she came to him on her own initiative, so Henry passed on the message and shortly after that Newton herself called. She had something to confess, she told Warren: she had misled EEOC investigators in her original response to their questions about the charges of discrimination against Robertson Investment. The truth, she said in a sworn statement, was that she had been ordered by her area supervisors, Paul and Jan Suggs, not to hire black workers after the Elliotts were fired, and then was encouraged by Jan Suggs to lie about it to the EEOC.

Newton was speaking out now, she said, because her circumstances had changed dramatically in the past year, and she was afraid for her own job. Her husband had been killed in a truck accident, leaving her to raise a three-year-old daughter by herself. At some point after her husband's death she had started a relationship with James Stephens, one of the black Captain D's employees, the same James Stephens who had allegedly overheard Paul Suggs ordering the Elliotts to reduce the number of their black employees in order to achieve a 70:30 white-to-black ratio. When the Suggses found out she was seeing Stephens, Newton claimed in an affidavit, they began harassing her, and now she was afraid she might be fired. She wanted Warren to represent her as part of the class action, she said.

Newton was clearly frightened, Warren said, and her story fit with the others Warren had heard from Robertson Investment employees, so he agreed to take her on. New statements were drafted; new affidavits were sworn; and Debora Newton became a witness for the plaintiffs. She even contacted the EEOC to retract her earlier comments and give them a new statement alleging discrimination at Robertson Investment.

Months later, though, in August, nine days after Shoney's lawyers filed their emergency motion against Warren alleging improper contact with managers, Robertson Investment's attorneys followed suit with an emergency motion of their own. Warren's talks with Newton, they charged, constituted a similar violation of the rules of attorney conduct. He had to be stopped, they said, and he ought to be punished.

Those and other challenges to the way Warren and Goldstein brought their case, many of them aimed specifically at Warren, would continue throughout the litigation, taking up hundreds of hours of the attorneys' time. Warren, in later interviews, was typically stoic about how he was affected by the attacks. "In the kind of cases that we do, the defense always tries to take shots at you," he said. "The point I tried to raise is, I went to the Florida Bar when I was accused and they exonerated me. But the defense isn't interested in the truth. It's a tactical thing." Carol Condon, the paralegal who had worked closely with Warren taking statements from Nashville witnesses during the early phase of discovery in the case, said she doubted he was surprised when the attacks came. "He was ready for it," she said. "He'd been steeled against that since day one because he knew they were amassing troops and ammunition. Plus you knew just from talking to these people that they were totally, totally ruthless."

Charlie Burr, a Tampa, Florida, attorney who did extensive work on the case representing Shoney's, said he was always impressed with Warren's ability to stay calm under the Shoney's fire: "I never saw Tommy Warren play football but I always had this impression of him as one tough guy, the quarterback hanging back in the pocket, taking whatever comes at him, totally focused, like a Joe Montana." Burr, the lawyer who had actually drafted Shoney's emergency motion for sanctions, a motion that had the potential not only to force Warren off the case, but also, if granted, could have led to his disbarment, said he later apologized to Warren.

In one of the ironies of a litigation replete with irony, Burr, who said as a college student he had joined civil rights marches led by Dr. Martin Luther King Jr., quit his lucrative corporate labor practice in early 1992 after more than three years defending Shoney's full-time under Butch Powell. When he left, he said, he walked out with boxes of Warren and Goldstein's motions and briefs filed in *Haynes et al. v. Shoney's, Inc.*, which he intended to study as a textbook example of how to bring discrimination class actions.

Then Burr contacted officials with the Florida NAACP, offered them his services, and began working on civil rights cases solely on behalf of minority plaintiffs.

There were, of course, specific consequences to the motions Shoney's defense attorneys filed while the case was going on, not only to Warren, but to witnesses such as Debora Newton, whom Warren was eventually forced to abandon as a client and as a member of the plaintiff class under the judge's strict interpretation of the rules of the court.

After being dropped from the suit, Newton changed her statement yet again, testifying during a hearing in the case that she had lied in her affidavit on behalf of the plaintiffs. In fact, she claimed, reversing herself for the second time, there had been no orders to discriminate against black workers, and she had only been harassed a little by Jan Suggs for dating James Stephens, the black employee whom she later married. She still said Jan Suggs had occasionally used racist language, but she insisted that she and the Suggses were good friends and that Jan Suggs was only concerned about Newton dating a black man because it might be bad for business. Newton said she never should have signed her statement with its charges of discrimination against Robertson Investment because, she claimed during that 1991 hearing, Warren had "worded it totally different" when he wrote it up for her, distorting what she had said to make things sound worse than they really were.

The cross-examination, by an attorney out of Goldstein's office named Laney Feingold, took less than two minutes. Feingold began by handing Newton a copy of her 1989 declaration in which she admitted lying to the EEOC. "I want to show you what has been marked as Exhibit 46 to Document 109 and ask you whether that is your signature on the last page, page 6," she said.

"Yes, it is," Newton responded.

"Paragraph 16 of this declaration," Feingold continued, "refers to the fact that you called the EEOC investigator in Atlanta to tell him that you hadn't told the truth when he first came to Marianna. Is that correct?"

"Yes, I did."

"Who was present when you called the EEOC investigator?"

"Nobody."

"You said you went to talk to Mr. Warren because you were afraid of losing your job?"

"Yes, I did."

"Is your job security with [Robertson Investment] still important to you?"

"Yes, it is," said Newton, who by this time was crying hard on the witness stand. Feingold said she had no further questions.

"That was one of the more dramatic things I've seen in the courtroom," Barry Goldstein said later. "When she started to cry. What they had done to her. It was really short. It was sort of a very elegant examination. That was a mistake the judge made, I think, in basically not allowing Tommy to keep talking to her. She was really exposed and unprotected."

Not long after that 1991 hearing, Newton, who had been employed by Robertson Investment Company for fourteen years, was fired from her job as manager of the Marianna Captain D's.

○   Starting with the motion to keep Goldstein off the case and continuing through the series of ethical charges against Warren, Shoney's kept up its challenges to the plaintiffs' attorneys with the federal judge assigned to the class action, a former Navy pilot and 1983 Reagan appointee named Roger Vinson, a staunch Republican with a reputation for starched, straitlaced conservatism. "I think that what they were trying to do with Judge Vinson," Goldstein said, was "to create any situation where he would somehow buy into some argument they had that there had been some impropriety in this case or how it was established, and that would divert the court's attention from the merits of the case. They were throwing out maybe twenty different arguments. All they needed was the judge to latch on to maybe one of them, so we had to treat every one of them seriously."

Things grew tense, and sometimes heated, between Warren and Shoney's lead counsel, Butch Powell, and it was often up to Goldstein to act as a pressure valve. Warren might lose his temper briefly, he might storm around his Tallahassee office next to the corner pawn shop, but he'd soon be on the phone to Goldstein in his friend's Oakland office suite with its panoramic plate-glass view of the San Francisco Bay, a place Warren started referring to as "Utopia."

"It was always a standing joke that Tommy would call me and say, 'Okay, Goldstein, what are you going to do now that they're coming after me like this?'" Goldstein said. "And I'd say, 'I'll do whatever I can from three thousand miles away.' He'd say, 'How come it's always my ass on the line?' and I'd say, 'Well, we all have our jobs to do.'"

When joking didn't work, Goldstein would remind Warren to keep his eyes on the prize. "Early in my career," he said, "when I was arguing cases in Birmingham, Alabama, with Demetrius Newton, who is currently the city attorney in Birmingham, we had an incident where I was quite pleased with myself because I had successfully argued a case on appeal on some procedural matter. . . . I was in the first few years of my practice. Demetrius, who was an old, experienced, very good trial lawyer who had tried about fifty capital cases, said to me, 'Barry, it doesn't count unless you and your client can fold it up and put it in your pocket. And the only way you can do that is if you can get to the merits of the case.' "

So, late in the summer, Tommy Warren started pushing for just that. Why sit around and wait for more sideshow attacks from Shoney's? he said. The plaintiffs' evidence was so strong and focused so emphatically on "the most easily understood form of discrimination," why save it for trial? Why not steal a page from the defense book and file a motion for summary judgment? Why not lay it all out now, all they had so far, anyway, which was considerable? It would show Judge Vinson how serious they were, and how confident of their case, and it would put extraordinary pressure on Shoney's to try to settle early. After lengthy discussions with Guy Saperstein, followed by even lengthier conference calls with both Saperstein and Warren, Goldstein agreed to go along with the idea. He called it "a daring move," but thought it might work. At the very least it would be a shot across the bow, a strong message to Shoney's about how seriously they should be taking the case.

Warren and Goldstein filed their summary judgment motion on July 24, 1989. In it they offered "voluminous and compelling direct evidence that Shoney's, Danner, and RIC [had] acted in a viciously racist manner," including testimony from more than two dozen white former managers and supervisors in thirteen different states, plus charges from nearly fifty current and former black employees representing every division in the Shoney's empire. "The plaintiffs' proof establishes a paradigm of discrimination," they wrote; "Blacks may enter some doors to work in restaurants located in black areas or in the kitchens of other restaurants, but as to other doors, such as those leading to positions dealing directly with the public or leading to managerial positions, the Defendants, in effect, have erected signs reading 'Whites only.' "

The most dramatic testimony in the summary judgment motion came from one of the new witnesses, Jerry Garner, a former Captain D's division director who had overseen operations at as many as twenty restaurants at a time during his ten years with the company. It was Garner who said that he had been present at what became known as "The Fish Incident," when Ray Danner brought an underweight fish into a Monday morning supervisors' meeting in Nashville and then, Garner alleged, threw it against a wall. According to Garner, Danner then denounced the store's black manager as responsible, saying, "That's a prime example of black management in our company." "The message was crystal clear," Garner concluded in his sworn statement. "We were not to have blacks in management positions in the company."

Several months later, in a meeting with one of Shoney's lawyers, Garner apparently equivocated and said he wasn't certain who made the racist statement after Danner brought the fish into the conference room. A stenographer recorded part of that session with the Shoney's lawyer, but Garner refused to sign the transcript or swear to its accuracy. In a subsequent deposition, however, with attorneys from both sides present, Garner disavowed the statements attributed to him in the unsigned document, and he reiterated the testimony he had originally given in his sworn statement for the plaintiffs: that it was Danner who threw the fish, and Danner who denounced "black management in our company."

In his own deposition late in the case, Danner himself acknowledged that he had conducted the inspection of Ron Murphy's Murfreesboro Captain D's referred to by Garner, that he had found underweight fish, and that he had put the fish in a cooler which he brought back to Shoney's headquarters for a Monday morning meeting. He denied ever throwing the fish.

A Shoney's vice president named Don Christian claimed in his deposition that it was another executive, Wayne Browning, who threw the fish, not Danner. Linus Leppink, a longtime Shoney's executive who had been the corporation's vice president for purchasing, said in an interview with the author that though he wasn't at the meeting he was aware of the incident at the time it occurred, and he said he was told that Danner had thrown the fish and denounced "black management" as in Garner's account. Browning, who didn't address the incident in an affidavit he gave the plaintiffs during the case, said in a recent interview with the author that both he and Danner threw underweight fish during that Monday morning meeting, but that he didn't recall any racial slurs being used. "I think what was said was, 'This is what happens when we don't properly supervise our restaurants,'" he said.

Shortly after the plaintiffs filed their motion for summary judgment, Tommy Warren received a call from Shoney's general counsel, Gary Brown. "If you were trying to get our attention, it worked," he said Brown told him. The company wanted to talk settlement.

Not long afterward, Barry Goldstein got another call that was even more surprising, this one from Jim Neal, the former Watergate prosecutor and one of the top corporate defense lawyers in the country, renowned for his skills in the courtroom and for his integrity as a negotiator. Neal, whose high-profile clients included Ford Motor Company in the controversial Pinto case and the Exxon Corporation in the Exxon Valdez disaster, was also dean of the Nashville legal community; he had been brought into the Shoney's case, he said, to get Warren and Goldstein to agree to a litigation moratorium while they negotiated a settlement. According to Goldstein and Warren, Neal said he had done his "due diligence" (that is, he had studied the case closely), and he realized there was "cause for concern" at Shoney's. Perhaps, he suggested, with his help they could soon get those matters equitably resolved.

Goldstein was impressed that Neal was suddenly involved in the case, "out of the blue," but he was reluctant to accept the moratorium proposal. "We were knocking ourselves out," he said. "We had the momentum. We were really ahead of these folks." A moratorium, he knew, could simply be a defense tactic to slow them down so Shoney's could catch up, and even after a subsequent call from Steve Tallent to assure him the company was serious about entering into negotiations, he was skeptical about the company's motives.

"A lot of cases don't settle until you have the class certified," he said later, because without class certification, a trial would be unlikely. "We told that to Tallent and Neal when they called us in August of '89. I was very frank. I said, 'I find it very hard to believe that this company is ready to make a significant settlement at this early stage in the litigation. It would be very intelligent for them to do it, and I think they would save themselves a lot of problems down the road, and they'll get a much better deal than if they settle after class certification, but it's not often the case that companies act that intelligently.' And they assured me that the company was prepared to do that.

"I believe there were some people in the company, and I can't say who, who wanted to do just what Tallent and Neal said. I don't know. We were also dealing with Ray Danner and his group. But I don't second-guess us relying on the integrity of Tallent and Neal."

Before the plaintiffs would agree to the moratorium, though, Goldstein and Warren insisted that Shoney's turn over computer tapes of all the company's employment records, which would be critical in determining any settlement figures. They knew they faced a major battle getting their hands on the statistics otherwise, and if they were going to take on the risk of a moratorium, Shoney's would have to make it worth their while. Once they had the tapes, the moratorium gave them the opportunity to get Guy Saperstein's statistical experts in California to take the years of employment numbers and "crunch them," so the plaintiffs could counter any statistical case Shoney's might later make and so they could check their own anecdotal information against their witnesses' documented employment histories. The tapes also gave them the names of others who had worked with their witnesses, which meant more people who could corroborate the stories they had already heard about the "paradigm of discrimination" at Shoney's, Inc.

On August 21, 1989, Judge Vinson issued an order to stay the proceedings. It meant all litigation was halted while the parties tried to negotiate a settlement. It also meant the charges against Tommy Warren would be held in abeyance—for a while.

The next three months were a blur of research for Warren and Goldstein, starting with an intense session in Oakland in early September. Armed with Shoney's employment data, they could begin figuring out more precisely the number and circumstances of the putative class members in light of a variety of issues such as back pay and compensatory damages. They studied precedents, approaches, and amounts from other cases, and considered a number of possible terms for their own settlement, including an aggressive, legally binding affirmative action plan with all aspects clearly defined.

Any settlement, they concluded, would have to involve current and former employees not only in all company-owned stores in each of the Shoney's, Inc. divisions, but in all franchise operations as well. Moreover, Warren and Goldstein were prepared to argue, the overwhelming direct evidence they had amassed proved the "willfulness" of the discriminatory policy, which would necessarily drive up the settlement cost, as would their "continuing violation" theory that no claims against the company were time-bound because the policy had been ongoing. In other words, a person suffering from the discriminatory policies ten years before could make the claim that he or she was still a victim of bias years later since those racist practices were still in place.

On the other side, unknown to the plaintiffs, Shoney's was in a state of chaos. The CEO, Mitch Boyd, had brought in Jim Neal not only to convince Warren and Goldstein to agree to the moratorium, but also, he said, to bring some semblance of order to the various factions of the defense "team," who actually represented a host of often competing interests. Danner's lawyers wanted to sever him from the lawsuit and argued that he shouldn't be held personally accountable for what might have happened in the company; Robertson Investment's attorneys didn't want their client, as a franchisee, lumped in with the corporation and Danner; and Shoney's lawyers knew the company didn't want to pick up the entire settlement tab itself, since the recapitalization that had put them into such a debt hole in the first place had been taken on at least in part to line Ray Danner's pockets.

What the plaintiffs also didn't know was that Mitch Boyd was having problems of his own. Some members of the board of directors said he had taken a position that they viewed as too aggressive and expensive in responding to the lawsuit, Boyd said. The SCLC covenant, the black PR firm and ad campaign, and the $50,000 Boyd spent on sensitivity training for executives to address racial issues in the company—these looked like public admissions of guilt, Boyd said he was told. In addition, and perhaps a more serious problem for Boyd at the time, there were the ongoing battles over money to put back into the stores; desperately needed funds, Boyd said (and Alex Schoenbaum agreed), that the board was reluctant to release because of the amount of debt the company was then carrying.

By December 1989, Warren and Goldstein had completed the bulk of their research and were ready to enter into direct negotiations with Shoney's. By that time, though, Mitch Boyd was on his way out, and the Shoney's board had lined up a new CEO. To the astonishment of everyone associated with Shoney's—for thirty years one of the most inbred companies around—they had decided to go outside to fill the position. Their choice: Leonard Roberts, a bright, hard-charging Chicagoan who in the previous five years had engineered one of the more remarkable turnarounds in the restaurant industry as head of the once-failing Arby's chain. Roberts, no stranger to controversy, was coming in bruised from his own highly publicized battles with Arby's owner, financier Victor Posner, who in a fit of pique earlier in the fall had fired Roberts for what Posner's spokesman said was "insubordination." That had been difficult enough for Roberts to deal with, but not entirely unexpected given Posner's reputation in the business community. Now, though, with a Shoney's corporation that was hundreds of millions of dollars in debt, struggling to separate itself from the iron-fisted Ray Danner, and facing the largest class-action race discrimination suit in history, Roberts was about to step off the edge of the known corporate world.

There were three face-to-face negotiation sessions during the month of December. The first, on December 4, 1989, in San Francisco, had Tommy Warren, Barry Goldstein, and Guy Saperstein on one side of the table, Butch Powell, Steve Tallent, and Jim Neal on the other. Central issues were the interpretation of the employment figures, the temporal and geographical definition of the classes, and the nature of the affirmative action plan the plaintiffs insisted the company adopt as part of any consent decree. The parties discussed formulas for determining an appropriate amount for settling the suit, and the plaintiffs made their opening case. Due to what they maintained was the systemic and egregious nature of the discriminatory policy and the willfulness with which it had been carried out, the plaintiffs' attorneys argued, there was in all instances a presumption of discrimination. Because of that, Warren and Goldstein said, they sought to use the maximum definition of both classes of plaintiffs, white and black, and the starting point for negotiations was $400 million.

The second session, on December 12 in Washington, D.C., was an extension of the first. The plaintiffs let it be known that there were more witnesses, former high-level Shoney's officials, lining up to testify against Danner and the corporation, and that they had even more damaging testimony to place before the court than had come out in the original complaint, the class certification request, and the motion for summary judgment. Tallent, Neal, and the Shoney's officials who joined them in Washington talked a lot about "business necessity" and what they claimed were the dire financial straits of the corporation. As far as the money was concerned, Shoney's attorneys said, they would make their first offer at the third negotiation session scheduled for a week later in Nashville.

Though Butch Powell had taken part in all the sessions and would be present when the talks shifted to Jim Neal's office for three days in Nashville, Steve Tallent and Jim Neal were the central figures for Shoney's in the negotiations, partly because that was their forte, and partly because of the apparent enmity between Powell and the plaintiffs' attorneys.

In June 1989, for example, while deposing Buddy Bonsall, a former Tallahassee Shoney's manager who was one of the original named plaintiffs, Powell began jabbing toward Bonsall's face with his pen to punctuate his questions. Bonsall objected—"Don't point the pen," he said—and Warren stepped in to caution Powell.

"Calm down," Warren said. "You are not going to harass the witness. You are not going to try to intimidate him. I know you are used to being a bully. You are not going to do it here, or we are going to stop the deposition."

Powell snapped back: "You can stop the depo if you want to. You can filibuster. I am trying to straighten out the confused—"

Warren cut him off. "Sit back and relax and ask him the question," he said.

"When I relax, I will relax," Powell countered. "It will have nothing to do with your instructing me as to whether or not to be relaxed."

The argument continued:

Mr. Warren: We may not get through today.

Mr. Powell: We won't get through here today. We already established that.

The Witness: Please keep the pen from pointing at me.

Mr. Powell: I am sorry. Does that intimidate you?

The Witness: No sir, it doesn't.

Mr. Powell: Are you uncomfortable?

The Witness: I will be honest, yes.

Mr. Powell: Any time you feel uncomfortable, you are free to walk out, get a drink of water, relax, do whatever will make you comfortable. We want you to be comfortable.

The Witness: Not really, you don't. I am not stupid, sir.

In another incident, when Warren brought a young lawyer named Sam Smith into the case as an associate several months later, Smith, only a year out of law school, soon found himself pitted against Butch Powell in his first deposition ever.

When his witness sat down, Smith asked the standard opening question: "Would you state your name for the record?"

Powell immediately interrupted. "We object to the form of the question," he said. "It calls for hearsay."

Smith tried to ignore Powell's objection and simply repeated his question to the witness: "State your name for the record." Powell, though, broke in again, calling it hearsay, presumably intending to rattle the inexperienced Smith, who nonetheless managed to get through the deposition.

In 1991, the plaintiffs' attorneys found a witness named James Larry Marks, a former truck driver who had worked in the Shoney's commissary in Nashville and had agreed to testify about what he alleged was racial discrimination in that operation. Marks, who at the time of his deposition was running a landscaping business and moonlighting as a rodeo bull rider, testified that whenever blacks applied for jobs driving trucks for Shoney's they would be given a driver's test on a specially rigged semi kept in a far corner of the lot. That truck had a reverse gear box, Marks said, so of course the black applicants, who didn't know, would fail miserably when they tried to drive it.

Butch Powell, who represented Shoney's at the deposition, at one point demanded that Marks hand over a list of all his landscaping clients. The witness refused. "I don't think that's none of your business," he said. Powell told Marks that in fact he was required by the court to turn over the business documents, including his telephone records going back several years. Marks would have to drive the thirty miles back to his house to get them, Powell said, or else be compelled to produce the records under subpoena.

Marks argued. He would mail the material to Powell, he said, but he had business to get back to, and he was losing money already by taking time off for the deposition. Powell wouldn't budge. He demanded that Marks return home immediately for the documents, and then called for a recess. Unaware that the court reporter was still recording the proceedings, Marks, a big man who had come into the deposition dusty from work, wearing chaps and a cowboy hat, leaned over the table.

"My own personal thinking, off the record," he growled, looming over Powell, "I think you're an asshole." He then angrily left the room.

Once he returned from the recess with his phone records, Marks had the final say: "For the record, I brought these back not to comply with your little subpoena, which I doubt if the District Court of Florida would punish me anyway, or Tennessee. I need a vacation anyway. I brought it back because it's about time somebody stood up against corporations stepping on the little guys."

To Barry Goldstein, Powell was a familiar type of defense lawyer, aggressive, confrontational, and for the most part successful. Powell had never lost a case for Shoney's, and on at least two occasions had so thoroughly destroyed complaints brought by the EEOC that the government was ordered to pay Shoney's attorneys fees. Goldstein said he got along passably well with Powell because he saw Powell for what he was and dealt with him professionally on those terms. Warren said he did the same, and publicly that seemed to be the case, but when all the lawyers gathered in Nashville for the third negotiation session, and Shoney's first settlement proposal, the enmity spilled out into the open.

The first couple of days in Nashville were spent talking around the edges of the settlement agreement, a sort of elaborate buildup to the company's offer. Before that happened, on the second or third night in Nashville, Warren and Goldstein returned to their hotel late after a couple of hours listening to a bluegrass band at a local club, trying to catch a break from the frenetic pace of the intense negotiation sessions.

As it happened, Powell and Tallent were staying in the same hotel and were sitting in the hotel bar when the plaintiffs' attorneys walked through the lobby. They called Warren and Goldstein over and invited them to sit down for drinks. The conversation was amicable enough at first. Then Powell confronted Warren.

"You know what I want out of this case?" he said. "I want to get your license."

The conversation stopped. Goldstein tried to defuse the situation. "What do you want his driver's license for, Butch?" he joked.

"No," Powell said. "I want his law license."

Goldstein and Tallent left the table as Powell apparently had more to say.

Warren, the ex-quarterback, dropped back in the pocket. He folded his arms across his chest, sat deep in his chair, and listened in silence.

Warren and Goldstein brought Pat O'Rourke along with them to Jim Neal's high-rise office in downtown Nashville. In all the negotiation sessions so far they'd been considerably outnumbered by Shoney's people, lawyers, company officials, and various assistants crowding the conference rooms. "Two little lawyers versus a cast of thousands," as O'Rourke put it, so they thought they would add some bulk to their own entourage. O'Rourke, the Nashville civil rights attorney who had been "Tommy's local eyes and ears," helping locate Nashville witnesses, had run what he described as a "boutique" law practice for years, many of his cases referrals of individual Shoney's discrimination complaints, which he had been largely successful at settling with some compensation for his clients. The class action, though, went way beyond his resources and his experience.

He was awed right away, O'Rourke said, by Neal's "power office," all wood and leather and glass, with a giant eagle on a credenza against the wall behind Neal's chair. "It would have scared the shit out of me to be up against these guys," he remembered thinking as he sat with Warren and Goldstein.

Shoney's attorneys made "a substantial settlement offer" that stunned O'Rourke, "like winning two Powerballs at the same time," he said, referring to the popular lottery game. But Warren and Goldstein merely "dead-panned." They thanked Neal, said they would certainly consider the offer, and then left the office to walk down the street to a nearby seafood restaurant to talk it over. O'Rourke said his knees buckled when he tried to stand.

Shoney's offer actually consisted of two options, according to Len Roberts, who was just coming in as Shoney's new CEO. The first was a fairly straightforward $32 million: take the money and make the lawsuit go away. The second was the Shoney's franchise rights to the state of California.

ELEVEN

"The Niggers Are Going to Get This Company. Thank God You're on Board."

Len Roberts says he didn't know the full extent of the lawsuit when he was hired as CEO and elected chairman of the board of Shoney's, Inc. He had heard rumblings, and remembered reading something about it back in the spring, but with the moratorium Roberts, like many who were outside the company and not involved in the litigation, thought it had gone away. "At the time it didn't sound like anything major," he says. "It sounded as if there were pockets of racial discrimination as there are in any large corporation. The only time it was an issue was when I was elected, and this may be my stupidity because I hadn't looked into it and all that, but I sort of trusted if it was big I would have heard about it."

Roberts, then forty, had researched the business side of the company after members of the board of directors began secretly recruiting him for the CEO position in September. Candid disclosure about the discrimination suit, though, didn't come until December 21, 1989—a few hours too late.

"It was at the board meeting, after they installed me as chairman of the board with all those little ceremonies, and everyone was shaking hands. And then Gary Brown [Shoney's general counsel] came up to me—and I knew Gary because he had negotiated my deal—and then Gary said, in his own inimical way, 'Are you up to date on this lawsuit?' I said, 'Not really.' He said, 'Has anyone told you anything about it?' I said, 'Not really.' And he said, 'Well I think you need to get up to date on this lawsuit.' He gave me some transcripts, he gave me some depositions, whatever was available at that time. He gave me the complaints, and I took that stuff home with me that first day. It was the way Gary said it. He did it in such a way that he was shocked that no one had told me about it. It was that night that I really read it, and as you know it's fascinating stuff. You don't find it much. That's when I knew it was a big issue. Either it was all false, or if there was any truth in the matter then this was a big issue I had just inherited. I really felt very discouraged."

The racial divisions in the company hit Roberts directly, he said, when he paid his first visit to the corporate headquarters, a long, low, nondescript building east of Nashville on Elm Hill Pike. He actually drove past it twice, Roberts says, thinking it was a company warehouse. Only when he stopped to ask directions did he discover his mistake. He also discovered that there were virtually no blacks working in any office jobs at the headquarters complex.

"The notion that was out there at the time was that I was actually hired by Shoney's, Inc. to resolve the lawsuit," Roberts says. "That notion was incorrect. First of all there's nothing in my track record to indicate that I would be someone to clean up a situation of major racial discrimination, although certainly I've always been very sensitive to those issues. I was brought in to grow the business, because under Mitch Boyd it had gotten stagnant."

In interviews during December 1994 and January 1995, Roberts, now working for the Tandy Corporation as president of Radio Shack, was unequivocal about how he would have responded had he known about the lawsuit earlier: "The question has been asked, if I knew how serious this litigation was would I have joined Shoney's? The answer is definitely not. Absolutely not."

His last few years, after all, had been spent publicly fighting his old boss, Victor Posner, in what Roberts described as a sort of battle for the soul of Arby's. He had become leery of controversy, Roberts said, and when one of the board members, while courting him for the Shoney's job, began denigrating then-CEO Mitch Boyd, Roberts balked.

"I'd been around enough to know that there was some real political something going on here between Mitch and the board, and I ain't going to get in the middle of this stuff," he said. "I mean I came from that kind of place. What I was looking at were clean opportunities for me. I wasn't going to get involved in another mess, and quite frankly it turned me off when he started talking about that stuff. And I thought professionally I couldn't afford another crazy situation." He took the job, he said, because he was drawn to the larger challenges of marketing multiple divisions and "growing a diversified company" that had stagnated in recent years. In late December 1989, though, he was stuck.

At the time Roberts was installed as CEO, Tommy Warren and Barry Goldstein were still considering Shoney's first settlement offer. The $32 million was clearly insufficient, given the size of the plaintiff classes, but they had to explore in good faith the other option, so they hired an investment banker to assess the viability of accepting the California franchises. They even went so far as to contact an associate of Victor Posner, ironically enough, to explore the possibility of Posner's DWG corporation running the West Coast Shoney's for the plaintiffs. That avenue led nowhere fast. It would take so long to establish and turn a profit on the stores that it could be years before the plaintiffs received any real compensation. And the question of who would run the restaurants couldn't be effectively answered.

"It was a stupid idea in the first place," said Warren. "And after we studied it, it was still a stupid idea." He and Goldstein did agree to come down considerably to settle the case—to $250 million—but they also threatened to call off the moratorium if Shoney's, who seemed to be stalling, didn't get serious about the negotiations. Goldstein even told Shoney's lawyers at one point—jokingly, he later claimed—that the corporation would have to pay his and Warren's legal fees to cover their time spent in subsequent negotiations as a further condition for continuing the moratorium. He was shocked when Shoney's agreed. For the next three months, Goldstein and Warren actually drew paychecks from the company they were suing. It was the first money Warren had made in two years. He put it into an account to cover future costs of the litigation.

Len Roberts, meanwhile, who had a business law degree from DePaul and was a member of the Illinois Bar, knew he had to find out what was behind the discrimination charges and the extent of the corporation's exposure. To do that he began calling all the top Shoney's executives into his office, one by one, for private conversations. He even went outside the company to talk to the former CEO, Dave Wachtel. "I had to find out, number one, what did they know, what were they going to say, and if they were deposed were they going to lie or were they going to tell the truth," Roberts said. "You can't just ask them that [in a deposition], you have to find out what they know beforehand. Then you have to make a determination if they're going to tell the truth, which they should under oath. And if they're going to tell the truth under oath, and they know all this information, the conclusion is that this case has to be settled."

What he learned, he said, went beyond his worst-case scenario—about the company, and about Ray Danner. "Much of the plaintiffs' record was very truthful," he concluded. "Confirmed by the senior officers who'd been around for years through the whole thing." The executives he spoke to, Roberts said, also convinced him of something else that pressed on him the importance of trying to settle the lawsuit quickly: "They were not going to lie. For whatever reasons—whether they have good values, or whether they don't understand the criminal justice system, or whatever, I just felt like these folks weren't going to lie."

At the same time Roberts was hearing from company officials about the discriminatory policies, he was also getting an earful from some of the companies that had done business for years with Shoney's. "These old-time suppliers would come around and it would be the same-old same-old," Roberts said. "They'd say, 'God-damnit, the niggers are going to get this company. Thank God you're on board.' I can assure you they had no blacks—or African Americans—in their employ." Many of those suppliers, Roberts discovered, were friends of Danner and some of the older members of the board of directors.

"I'd say, 'If you're going to supply this company you're going to act like it's 1990, not 1950,'" Roberts said. "Did the board members object to that? Oh yeah, with a passion. They had a real problem with that."

Roberts eventually came to the conclusion that at least some of the responsibility for the company's employment practices belonged to the board of directors. "They had certain board members who had no idea—Dan Maddox and Wallace Rasmussen, these were guys like Ray Danner, seventy, eighty years old in the South—and they absolutely never understood this case," Roberts said. "They really didn't understand that Ray Danner did anything that was wrong."

In addition to a series of disconcerting encounters with company officials, suppliers, and board members, Roberts also said he had a number of meetings, many of them in private, with Ray Danner himself, who still had a hand in Shoney's affairs as senior chairman of the board, a position he had returned to even after lining his pockets in the 1988 recapitalization. He found Danner to be "a perfect gentleman." He also said Danner was "a person of absolute denial."

"Quite frankly, around me he acted just the opposite of what I had heard about him," Roberts said. "By the time I came around he acted as if he had marched with Martin Luther King."

Roberts said he concluded, however, that, "Ray Danner was a throwback to the forties or fifties. He had a strong philosophy that blacks weren't good for business."

"The best thing you could say about Ray Danner is you didn't know if it was racially motivated or if it was consumer motivated," he said. "He hired blacks, but he kept them in the back. . . . Maybe he wasn't racially discriminatory, so to speak, in the pure sense, but he was such a strong consumer marketer—really a kind of consumer-driven individual—that [he believed] blacks in the front of a restaurant would not be acceptable to his customers.

"That's what could have been the motivation for the racial prejudice he had. The way it was executed, he would go around very visibly, very vocally, without ever worrying about being brought to trial, without worrying ever about breaking laws. He just went around telling people—in open meetings, without ever writing anything down—what he thought about the niggers: that niggers didn't belong in his restaurants, that he didn't want any nigger serving as a waiter or a waitress, that he didn't want any nigger-lovers. That kind of stuff. There were meetings that never got into the court record. . . . There would be Saturday morning meetings at Shoney's headquarters they called the 'Nigger Meetings' to talk about the niggers."

Those meetings and Danner's other public declarations about race had ended before Roberts joined the company, he said, but the effects remained. "By and large I felt that this was a very guilt-ridden culture," Roberts said. "They felt very bad about the kinds of things that they had participated in, the meetings they had participated in, the sorts of policies they had executed out that were highly charged racially discriminatory policies."

Not that Roberts felt that way about all company officials. Gary Spoleta, corporate president, chief operating officer, and Danner's long-time lieutenant, soon left the company, his departure sweetened by the franchise rights to New Mexico.

Roberts said he knew within his first two or three months that the company would have to settle the lawsuit. Attorney Steve Tallent was telling him the company's contingent liability was half a billion dollars or more, he said, which was in fact what the plaintiffs would later demand in an amended version of their complaint. And the company's chief negotiator, Jim Neal, had made it clear that he thought Shoney's should offer the plaintiffs $100 million— that in fact they would *have* to offer that much to settle the lawsuit, Roberts said. Because Shoney's was still so deep in debt from the 1988 recapitalization, though, and because Ray Danner had been named specifically as a defendant in the suit, Roberts decided that Danner was going to have to pay a good portion of any settlement out of his own pocket.

"I actually believe that if I asked the board to settle this case for whatever they were asking—I believe I could have settled with the company's money," Roberts said. "The board was prepared to settle this case for a very sizeable amount of money, company funds, but it would have put the company in a very precarious position from a debt standpoint.

"That was why I ultimately went after Ray Danner," Roberts continued. "The company was in debt, and he had just cashed out [$140 million]. That was a key factor in the whole thing that made me go after Ray Danner to pay to settle the lawsuit. To protect the shareholders who had nothing to do with this lawsuit. . . . For the company to settle for $200 million would probably have put it into bankruptcy. That kind of thing was my goal from day one—to try to figure out how to get Ray Danner to come back with some of the money we had paid out and to participate substantially in the settlement.

"[Danner and I] would have private meetings together, with the knowledge of certain board members, and I would tell [him] that this was the best thing for him. I would get very personal with him. I would say, 'Ray, you worked very hard your whole life. I don't want to get into whether what you did was right or wrong, or whether it was consumer-driven and so forth. But if we go to court with this one you're going to be destroyed and the company will be destroyed, and I believe it's going to end up costing us hundreds of millions of dollars.' It was very important that I showed Ray Danner what the potential exposure in this case might be."

Roberts got his first opportunity to settle the case in March 1990, when he and Steve Tallent flew to Oakland to meet with Warren, Goldstein, and Guy Saperstein. The plaintiffs had come down to $250 million in addition to the injunctive relief, that is, their proposed court-enforced affirmative action plan, plus a clearly articulated agreement that the corporation would end its discriminatory practices and that the plaintiffs' counsel would monitor the company to ensure compliance. Roberts was carrying Shoney's counteroffer to the California meeting.

Ironically, Tommy Warren, changing planes in Atlanta, was booked on the same flight as Roberts and Tallent, though they were in first-class and he was flying coach. Warren paused on his way back, though, to introduce himself to Roberts and to say hello to Tallent. Shoney's lawyers had already cautioned Roberts not to talk to the plaintiffs' attorneys, but once the plane was in the air Shoney's new CEO decided, over Tallent's renewed objections, to find Warren and suggest the two of them move to seats in an empty section near the back of the plane. He wanted to get to know Warren, Roberts said, and he wanted Warren to know something about him so that they could hopefully develop a level of personal trust for the upcoming negotiations.

Roberts first told Warren the story of his Chicago upbringing, making sure to stress both his liberal credentials and his street-tough background. His father, a draftsman, had been involved in a Chicago-area group that was committed to peaceful integration of their once all-white neighborhood, Roberts said, and he remembered having "Jew Nigger-lover" spray-painted on their house as a result. As a school-patrol boy he had protected black kids from angry whites at their newly integrated school, and he often got into fights with bullies who tried to harass him and his brothers for being Jewish.

Roberts moved the conversation on from there. "I told Tommy I appreciated his passion for civil rights and his passion for what happened or what may have happened wrong [at Shoney's]," he said. "I wasn't around. He wasn't around. I was sure there was money in this thing, that there was opportunity for lawyers. I recognized that, he recognized that. I was just pleading with him: 'If you truly have a passion for this then let's passionately settle this matter so this company can serve as a model.' This was fairly naive of me, I suspect. I'm sure I came off as extremely naive. But so be it. I wasn't debating what needed to happen to this company. In fact I welcomed them to be involved with it. We'd pay them. Let's not get this thing wrapped up in a large class-action lawsuit, which was nothing as far as I was concerned but a way to get lawyers rich."

Over the next two days in Oakland, Roberts and Tallent made their pitch: that any large settlement could bankrupt the company, that Roberts was personally committed to addressing the discriminatory policies of the past, that they would be moving ahead with affirmative action regardless of the lawsuit. "I think they bought into the belief that the injunctive relief was going to be in place," Roberts said. "I think we trusted each other over that. I thought that was already in place. I thought with that part of it we had a meeting of the minds. I think where we didn't have a meeting of the minds was over the money part of it."

The "money part" came on Roberts's last day in Oakland in a theatrically staged offer. First, Steve Tallent arrived alone at Goldstein's office. Len Roberts was downstairs sitting in a taxi, Tallent told the plaintiffs' attorneys. He would be up in a minute to make the company's last offer—take it or leave it—the amount of which Tallent claimed even *he* didn't know.

Warren, Goldstein, and Saperstein apparently weren't in the mood for theater, though, and Roberts's arrival, and his proposal, fell flat. The offer actually went down from the one in December, which had been $32 million. Now, Roberts confirmed to the author, it was $20 million, plus $5 million to be donated to a black nonprofit organization of the plaintiffs' choice and another $5 million for one selected by Shoney's.

The plaintiffs' attorneys weren't impressed. There was no need to bankrupt the company, they said; payments to the plaintiffs could be made over time. As for the amount offered, $32 million had been insufficient and $20 million was even less so to settle the claims of their class members, who could conceivably number as many as one hundred thousand. On top of that, they argued, Shoney's couldn't expect to get off without significant punitive damages, given the egregiously willful nature of the discrimination over the past thirty years. Moreover, Warren and Goldstein told Roberts—prophetically, as it turned out—it would be irresponsible of them to make some sort of gentlemen's agreement today, as Roberts suggested, because there was no guarantee that he would still be around tomorrow to make certain it was carried out.

Roberts said he responded angrily. "It wasn't a game that I was playing," he said. "I was being absolutely honest and believed if the plaintiffs were unreasonable about this thing, as I told them, I would make this a personal battle. It would no longer be Shoney's,

it would be me. . . . From this day forth it was going to cost more
and more money. It was going to get nastier and nastier and nastier. It was going to get bloodier and bloodier and bloodier.

"I made the statement early on, I said if the company is going to
commit suicide it's not going to be because of some San Francisco
law firm, it's going to be because the judge is going to tell us. We're
not going to go broke trying to settle this. The kind of money they
wanted us to settle for we just couldn't afford."

    Warren and Goldstein stood their ground. Roberts returned to
Nashville to make good on his threat. And to ensure that that was
the case, Roberts said, one of his first moves was to designate
Butch Powell as the undisputed lead counsel for the defense. "I
was prepared to do a street battle and really wanted a person who
could fight that battle, and I thought just from my initial impression of the thing that Butch Powell would put out." Roberts added,
"This was going to be a gutter fight—and it was."

    And he continued, "I sat here encouraging that kind of fight, all
the time saying that, first of all, the company has to get on with
the equitable part of the thing—no problem. It needs to be done
anyway. But I knew then that this case had to be settled for a sizeable amount of money in order to satisfy the class and satisfy the
attorneys, and I had to figure out a way to get Ray Danner to pay
for this lawsuit."

    As might be expected, plaintiffs' counsel saw things a little differently. Barry Goldstein's summary of the Oakland meeting was
succinct: "Len Roberts tried to resolve the case early with his
charisma." Later he elaborated. "I think I was really disappointed
when Roberts came out here. We had basically waited three
months since December and they hadn't moved." Goldstein said
he took Roberts at his word that they were in for a "battle in the
gutters." "It was clear that Shoney's wasn't ready to settle at that
point," he said. "It wasn't totally unexpected really, given what we
were seeking—a nationwide class before a Reagan-appointed
judge in Pensacola. We could understand that the company might
want to take that shot.

    "Given the amount of revenue that we were seeking, can you
say that it was unintelligent on their part not to resolve the case
earlier? I think that they could make a legal argument that what

they were doing made some sense, just as far as, 'Let's try to beat these guys at the class-action stage, let's try to drive them out of the box with putting enormous resources against them, let's attack the named plaintiffs, let's attack the lawyers, let's make it very uncomfortable for them, and we can settle the case for a lot less.' And that's their strategy.

"Now if you look at it from the point of view that they should have said, 'We have a very serious problem here, let's correct it as soon as we can, let's just sit down and change the practices of this company, and let's just end this thing,' well, that would have been another strategy they could have taken."

On April 9, 1990, almost two years to the day after Henry Elliott was fired from the Marianna Captain D's, Judge Vinson lifted his stay order. The moratorium—and the settlement negotiations— ended. The litigation, which seemed to have receded for the past several months, had actually been gathering in on itself all that time, swelling with new evidence, new motions, and revised complaints, all of which now broke with a kind of tsunami force.

A few weeks into this new phase of the litigation, though, a personal tragedy struck. Len Roberts's oldest daughter was run down from behind by a drunk driver blasting through a fraternity parking lot at the University of Georgia in Athens. Twenty-year-old Dawn Roberts was thrown onto the hood of the car, and her head smashed through the windshield, extensively lacerating her face and causing massive brain injury. Her pelvis was shattered, her jaw fractured, and her left leg crushed. She finally fell onto the asphalt, but the driver careened on through the parking lot and down the road to his fraternity house. Too drunk to realize what he had done, he went into his room and crawled into bed.

Len Roberts was in Atlanta that weekend with his wife, Laurie, and their other two daughters (they hadn't sold their house yet to move to Nashville). When the phone rang he was there to answer. It was one of Dawn's friends, too hysterical to speak. The friend passed the phone to a doctor who said Len and Laurie Roberts should drive to Athens immediately. There had been an accident. Their daughter Dawn wouldn't survive the night.

Miraculously, Dawn Roberts lived, though she spent weeks in a
coma on full life support, a brain shunt surgically implanted to
relieve fluid pressure that threatened to damage her even more.
When she finally emerged from the coma, she would spend several
more months in hospitals, for operations on her face and her leg
and her pelvis, for more neurosurgery to have a steel plate inserted
where her skull couldn't properly heal, then for physical and mental therapy so she could learn to speak again, and sit up, and feed
herself.

What that meant for her father was that for much of the next
year he led a divided life, his weekends in Atlanta taking care of
his family, his weekdays in Nashville running Shoney's, growing
the business, promoting his "commitment to diversity," pressur-
ing Ray Danner to pay for the lawsuit and make it go away.

It was a punishing regimen, but one Roberts didn't have any
choice about following. By October 1990, with the cost of saving
Dawn's life far exceeding the ceiling in Shoney's insurance plan,
Roberts had paid out nearly a quarter of a million dollars of his
own money to cover medical expenses. "Dawn's lifelong medical
care will run into millions of dollars," he wrote in a letter that year
to an Athens, Georgia, probation officer. "The crushing burden of
my battered child, coupled with the staggering cost of medical
care, has taken its toll on myself and my family."

TWELVE

66 The Inexorable Zero 99

When Barry Goldstein left the NAACP Legal Defense Fund in the summer of 1989 to work on employment discrimination cases with Guy Saperstein's firm, the Washington, D.C., *Legal Times* wrote a story about it. The headline was "Bad Timing."

The reason: the Reagan-stocked Supreme Court had just handed down several major decisions that would have a debilitating effect on civil rights plaintiffs and their ability to bring and win discrimination cases. "Chipping Away at Civil Rights" was *Time* magazine's headline for a cover story on the rulings. By the time the Shoney's moratorium ended in April 1990, those decisions had already radically altered the civil rights landscape—less like chipping, though, and more like the aftermath of a legal neutron bomb: the laws were still standing, but there wasn't much life left inside.

Earlier, in the spring of 1989, Goldstein had received a rude premonition of what was to come when he argued one of those cases

before the Supreme Court. That case was *Lorance v. AT&T Tech-*
nologies, so apparently obvious in its merits that even the EEOC's
then-general counsel, Charles Shanor, had joined with the plaintiffs. The issue in *Lorance* was whether the time period for filing
Title VII bias charges ran from the date a company, in this case
AT&T Technologies, adopted an allegedly discriminatory senior-
ity system, or from the date on which individuals working for the
company were adversely affected by the system. It seemed clear to
the plaintiffs, and to the EEOC, that it should be the latter, and
during oral arguments before the court Goldstein was allotted
thirty minutes to make that case; he planned to speak for twenty
minutes and give the last ten to Shanor. Well into his argument,
though, when Goldstein glanced up to check the time on the wall
clock behind the justices, Chief Justice William Rehnquist, who
had just asked a question, rebuked him sharply. According to *Legal
Times,* Rehnquist snapped, "Don't look at the clock."

"I'm sorry, sir," Goldstein replied, but Rehnquist continued his
attack.

"You're here to answer questions as well as to talk," the chief
justice said.

Goldstein's optimism vanished. In that moment, he said, he
knew *Lorance* was doomed. And he was right.

The case that had the most profound impact on *Haynes v. Shoney's,* meanwhile, and one of those with the most profound impact on employment discrimination law in general, was another
summer 1989 train wreck in the Supreme Court, *Patterson v. Mc-
Lean Credit Union,* which eviscerated much of Section 1981 of
Title 42 of the U.S. Code, the Reconstruction-era law that prohibited racial discrimination in the formation of contracts. For years,
Section 1981, part of what was originally known as the Civil
Rights Act of 1866, had been broadly interpreted to cover hiring,
promotion, harassment, and termination issues; its pertinent text
read, "(A)ll persons . . . shall have the same rights . . . to make and
enforce contracts . . . as is enjoyed by white persons." Indeed,
Patterson involved the case of a black woman who claimed that
she had been harassed, denied promotion, and finally dismissed
from her job because of her race. Section 1981 was attractive to
civil rights plaintiffs such as those in *Patterson* and in *Haynes v.*

Shoney's because it allowed for punitive damages and jury trials, unlike Title VII of the Civil Rights Act of 1964, which also prohibited employment discrimination but limited damages to back pay and required that trials be held before a judge only.

The Supreme Court's controversial 5-4 split decision in *Patterson*, though, was that the plaintiff's racial harassment, denial of promotion, and unfair dismissal claims, whether they were true or not, weren't valid under Section 1981. The reason, the court said, was that Section 1981 only *really* dealt with the initial formation of contracts; it covered discriminatory refusals to hire, in other words, but nothing else. For the plaintiffs in the Shoney's case, that meant that though they still had some Section 1981 claims of discriminatory refusal to hire, most of their charges no longer fit as a class action under the Supreme Court's new, cripplingly restrictive interpretation of that law.

Justice Harry Blackmun, in one dissenting opinion from that time, expressed the anger and the frustration of many when he wrote, "One wonders whether the majority still believes that race discrimination—or, more accurately, race discrimination against non-whites—is a problem in our society, or even remembers that it was."

Soon after the *Haynes* moratorium ended, to no one's surprise, Shoney's and Robertson Investment, citing *Patterson*, filed motions for summary judgment on the plaintiffs' Section 1981 claims. Warren and Goldstein, meanwhile, had to petition the court to allow them to amend their complaint and file it as a class action under Section 1981 and under Title VII of the Civil Rights Act of 1964. As with literally every motion the plaintiffs filed, Shoney's attorneys immediately opposed it. The plaintiffs still wanted a jury trial, and they still sought punitive damages, but the legal sands that they had originally built their case on had shifted radically. Goldstein predicted that the impact of *Patterson* would go far beyond the Shoney's case. "How many outcomes will be affected is impossible to say, but fewer cases will be brought," he said in an interview with the *New York Times*. "Some smaller number will be won, and that's why fewer will be brought."

Democrats in Congress responded to the 1989 rulings by proposing what became known as the Civil Rights Act of 1990 to put back onto the books, clearly and forcefully, the substance of those laws that the Supreme Court had just reversed. Much of the ensuing debate, though, didn't deal with the need for those legal protections against discrimination in the workplace. Instead, Republicans in Congress, and George Bush in the White House, led the charge that "quotas" were the issue and that somehow, if the new civil rights act were passed into law, the country would find itself drowning in a tide of so-called reverse discrimination. Suddenly, opposition to "quotas" became the central rallying cry in conservative election campaigns across the country, not the least of which were those waged by such hard-right national figures as North Carolina Republican senator Jesse Helms and ex-Klansman David Duke, who was then running for governor of Louisiana.

The quotas Barry Goldstein knew about, though, were far different from the phantoms conjured by conservative politicians and others on the right, and in February 1990, he traveled back to Washington, D.C., to testify before the Senate Labor and Human Resources Committee on the need for the Civil Rights Act of 1990. In his testimony, he joined a number of legal experts who outlined the crippling effects of the Supreme Court's decisions on employment discrimination law the year before.

Ironically, testifying shortly before Goldstein at that same hearing was a Temple University business and economics professor named Paul Andrisani, whom Shoney's had hired on as an expert witness to make their statistical case, to construct a sort of argument-by-the-numbers that there was no real evidence of systemic racial bias in the corporation. Andrisani, who for years had made a second career out of testifying mostly on behalf of corporations in job discrimination cases, staked out the then-fashionable economic position in his testimony before Congress that there was no need for the Civil Rights Act of 1990 because, he and other academic experts had concluded, racial and gender discrimination no longer existed in the workplace. His market logic was fairly straightforward: "Profit motives by employers and the stimulus to lower costs to meet competitive prices make it costly for employers to discriminate against capable blacks or women, even if they preferred to hire and promote only white males," he said. "This is because employers who prefer to hire or promote only white males are to some degree precluded or at least limited from doing so by their competitors who might reap a cost advantage by hiring and promoting cheaper minorities and women." And since companies that went with the cheaper labor of minorities and women could then sell their products more cheaply, he argued, that would then force employers who discriminated to stop doing it unless they were willing to accept a reduction in profits. Which, according to Andrisani, would never happen, or if it did would soon be self-correcting.

Moreover, he said, if there *were* racial and gender disparities in earnings and occupational distributions, which he was willing to concede, these would have to have been caused by legitimate differences between whites and minorities (or between males and females) in "productive skills, qualifications, work experience, and preferences for various types of work"—all resulting from what Andrisani called "societal discrimination" outside the workplace. Either by that, he said, or "discrimination by prior employers." Andrisani went on to make the claim that even statistically significant disparities between whites and minorities in the workforce in a specific geographic area didn't indicate the existence of racial bias because there were too many other variables involved for such "facile generalizations."

His arguments, in other words, were that (1) marketplace pressures had eradicated discrimination, (2) what discrimination there was had nothing to do with *current* employers, and (3) no matter what, you couldn't prove discrimination because there were too many other factors involved.

Andrisani's own statistical case on behalf of Shoney's would later be challenged by the admissions of the two CEOs who ran the company during the lawsuit, by the plaintiffs' statistical findings, and by the hundreds of witnesses who eventually came forward to testify to what they claimed were the company's enduring discriminatory policies. Nonetheless, Andrisani, echoing the by-then familiar refrain before the Senate committee, argued that the Civil Rights Act of 1990 was unnecessary, that it would force employers to adopt quotas for women and minorities, and that it would be bad for business.

Georgia congressman John Lewis, an early activist in the civil

rights movement who was severely beaten during the Freedom
Rides of the 1960s, told the *Washington Post* that listening to
much of the testimony in opposition to the proposed new law gave
him a sense of *déjà vu.* "I feel like I'm watching a twenty-six-year-
old TV rerun," he said. "Today we are hearing those same tired
arguments, that civil rights legislation is bad for business, that it
would result in chaos, that the stars would fall out of the sky in
Texas, in Alabama, in Georgia. But the stars didn't fall from the
sky in 1964 with the passage of the Civil Rights Act. The stars
didn't fall from the sky with the Fair Housing Act. And the stars
aren't going to fall from the sky with the passage of the Civil
Rights Act of 1990."

The House and Senate passed the measure later that year, but
then-President Bush, bowing to conservative and business pressures, vetoed the act, denouncing it, predictably, as a "quota bill."

As soon as the *Haynes* moratorium ended, Tommy Warren and
Barry Goldstein found themselves dodging a barrage of motions
filed by Shoney's attorneys, who were obviously emboldened by
the changes in the civil rights landscape. Len Roberts, the company's new CEO, had warned that "attorneys' fees wouldn't be a
problem" if Shoney's returned to the litigation, and he was apparently serious. Even without Roberts's warning, though, that
extreme litigation pressure was not unexpected, according to
Goldstein.

"Shoney's was the largest race-discrimination employment case
ever brought," he said. "We were seeking the most widespread and
significant remedy in any case that had ever been brought. Shoney's responded in kind. Shoney's put an enormous amount of resources into the defense. I believe, according to the Securities and
Exchange Commission, they listed that they had spent over $12
million on the defense. Of course that just covers their lawyers
and the various forms of support they had in the defense, such as
their experts. That money does not include the very significant
executive time, time that their CEO, Len Roberts, put in [and that]
their personnel department put in.

"They also, I think, took a gamble in their defense. The first
strategy they had was putting in the enormous resources that they

put in with the four law firms, [hoping] that they could get us to give up, to be in a position so we couldn't keep up, and either make a mistake before the judge that would hurt the case significantly, or that we just wouldn't think we had the resources to continue to litigate this multistate case involving thousands of class members in Pensacola, Florida.

"On many of their motions they tried to put pressure on us by seeking sanctions, to see if the judge would bite on any of those motions. They tried to make challenges to the techniques that we used to investigate the case, who we talked to. They tried to raise ethical questions, even to the extent that they took Tommy Warren's deposition for an entire day.

"In an employment discrimination case, I had never seen a strategy as aggressive as Shoney's used, where they tried to attack a lawyer the way that they did. But again, it goes back to what I said in the beginning. This was a very big, high-stakes litigation. You have to put in context Shoney's strategy. This was a case that very seriously affected the company, and a lot of lawyers would refer to this as a 'Bet the Company' type of case. . . . There are very few civil rights cases that have been brought with sufficient resources to make such a widespread challenge to a company that would rise to such a level of importance."

Believing, then, that Shoney's was determined to turn the litigation into a war of attrition, Warren and Goldstein didn't waste any time before going back on the attack themselves, an approach that suited both of their personalities. Throughout the lawsuit, the two men were constantly feeding their competitive appetites through a friendly-but-intense rivalry that ranged from racquetball to basketball, golf, and occasionally handball, though Warren gave up that sport after a stretch of games during which three successive opponents went down with ankle injuries. Both men were offensive players, on the court and in the courtroom.

They had put the company on notice during the moratorium that they had a number of new witnesses, including high-ranking former executives, lining up to testify. Now it was time to put those witnesses on the record.

In a supplement to the plaintiffs' Motion for Summary Judg-

ment and in an amended version of the request for class certification, the new witnesses described a corporation where they alleged there was no affirmative action plan before the class-action
suit was filed; where franchises were awarded as business favors;
where there was no job posting, formal application process, or objective criteria for promotions; where racial slurs and limits on the
"right" number of blacks were common; where executives researched and discussed racial demographics when determining lo-
cations for company stores and franchises; where officials charged
with discrimination were rarely, if ever, punished; and where the
decision makers were white.

Much of the evidence pointed to Ray Danner, although it didn't
stop there. Eighty-four black current and former workers and
twenty-three white former employees, ranging from store-level
workers to a former CEO, were now officially entered into the
court record with allegations against two members of Shoney's
board of directors—Danner and Gary Spoleta—eight corporate officers, fifteen current and former division directors, and dozens of
area supervisors and restaurant managers charged with carrying
out the discriminatory policies handed down from above. And
there was more to come.

Don Hitchcock, a Shoney's manager in Nashville, was one of
the new witnesses. He testified that Ray Danner once chewed him
out when he spotted some blacks loitering in front of Hitchcock's
store. "Can you get the goddamn niggers off the front of the building?" Danner purportedly said. "If you can't I'll run the black sons-
of-bitches over." Tim Wilson, who had also run a Shoney's restaurant, said he heard a similar story when he worked as assistant to
a manager named Ron Newby. "There were two black people sitting on a curb next to the driveway," Wilson testified. "Danner
told Ron Newby, the manager, to get the 'niggers' out of the driveway. When Newby didn't get them to move, Danner said, 'I will do
it myself,' and he went outside and tried to run the black people
over with his car."

Thomas Buckner, former director of personnel for the Lee's Famous Recipe division, testified that Danner often told him the
company's discriminatory policy made good business sense.
"Danner would say that no one would want to eat at a restaurant

where 'a bunch of niggers' were working," Buckner said. Wayne Browning, a Shoney's vice president from 1975 to 1983, alleged that everyone in the corporation knew Ray Danner's laws: "Blacks were not qualified to run a store. Blacks were not qualified to run a kitchen of a store. Blacks should not be employed in any position where they would be seen by customers." During a meeting several months later with one of Shoney's lawyers, however, Browning would qualify his remarks, saying that though everyone in the company was aware of Danner's laws, he didn't know any who had actually followed them.

Other witnesses stood by their statements to Warren and Goldstein. Karyn Hudson-Brown, former director of marketing and administration in Shoney's specialty restaurant division, and one of the first high-level executives to contact Warren after the suit was filed, testified that Danner gave her specific instructions about race and employment: "We were not supposed to have blacks in the front of the house. . . . At the Fifth Quarter we were not supposed to have them in what is called 'direct service' to the customer. In other words it was okay, you know, to have a certain amount in the back because the customer couldn't really see into the back of the house that much, the back of the house being the kitchen."

"You have to understand," she added, "that from day one that's the way you were trained, that was the Shoney's Way."

At Monday morning meetings with vice presidents and some division directors, according to Hudson-Brown, Danner often told racist jokes and discussed the number of blacks at different stores and in different areas. There were never any minorities at these meetings because there were none in executive positions in the corporation, she said; until 1987, she testified, only one black ever reached a management level as high as division director. Hudson-Brown also echoed what Len Roberts said he discovered soon after he joined the company. "In the main executive offices in Nashville where several hundred employees worked, there were virtually no blacks," she said.

Hudson-Brown later said in an interview that if she were ever to write a book about her own experiences at Shoney's she would title it *Bulletproof*, because that was how she and other executives saw themselves: as invincible, above the law, cashing in on the highly lucrative and expanding Shoney's business. The money was good and the power intoxicating, and it was theirs, she said, as long as they did things the way Ray Danner wanted them done.

That became increasingly difficult, though, especially in those moments when Hudson-Brown was able to step out of the swirling rush of her job and see what was happening around her. In a deposition taken in 1992, she recalled one of those moments. "I was mad about the way a job had been done," she testified, "and I turned around and I said something had been 'nigger-rigged.'" Hudson-Brown was in a Shoney's specialty restaurant at the time and didn't realize until after she had spoken that a black busboy, "a kid," was standing nearby and had heard every word.

"I wanted to just die of humiliation," she said.

For Hudson-Brown, coming out about what she said she had been part of at Shoney's seemed to be a cathartic experience, what Tommy Warren called "a cleansing of the soul." "She had to do a lot of soul-searching to come to grips with who she was," he said. Years later, after the lawsuit, Hudson-Brown sent Warren a Christmas card; in it she wrote, "You gave me the courage to do the right thing."

All of the new testimony entered into the court record by the plaintiffs after the moratorium appeared to be strong. The most powerful, though, came from yet another high-ranking Shoney's ex-official, the former CEO, Dave Wachtel, who had begun as a busboy in Danner's first restaurant in 1959. Wachtel, after being forced out of Shoney's in 1981, had since started an upscale family restaurant chain called O'Charley's, and the corporation was quick to attack his testimony, claiming that he was an angry rival trying to hurt the competition. Wachtel's testimony was damning nonetheless, widely quoted in newspaper accounts of the lawsuit. "Everyone with whom he came in contact at Shoney's knew of Danner's racist beliefs," he said, "and because of that they were expected to and did carry out the policies that discriminated against blacks in employment."

According to Wachtel, Danner's alleged racial attitudes weren't simply consumer-driven, as others, such as Mitch Boyd, later claimed. "Ray Danner often voiced his support of the Ku Klux Klan," Wachtel testified. "I specifically recall on one occasion Ray Danner being extremely impressed with things that had been said by a KKK Grand Dragon. I recall Danner telling me after having heard the Grand Dragon, 'Those guys are really right concerning segregation, separation of the races, and sending blacks back to Africa.'" In his deposition Wachtel testified that Danner talked privately with him about offering to match his senior officials' possible contributions to the Klan.

Like Hudson-Brown, Wachtel also testified that Danner regularly brought up the subject of race at the Monday morning division meetings in Nashville. "I can recall Danner telling me a thousand times that we should keep the number of blacks in management positions at Shoney's as low as possible," he said.

According to the plaintiffs' attorneys, the personnel statistics bore this out. The disparities could be seen most emphatically in the Shoney's division, they said, where prior to the lawsuit only 1.8 percent of the store managers were black. Out of 441 employees at the supervisory or supervisory-trainee level, only seven, or 1.6 percent, were black. Out of 68 division directors, a position at the low end of out-of-store management, only one was black. And at the highest levels of all corporate management, at the end of 1989, the year *Haynes v. Shoney's, Inc.* was filed, there were no blacks at all—the "inexorable zero." Instead, more than 75 percent of all black workers in the Shoney's division held jobs in three low-paid, non-customer-contact positions: busperson/dishwasher, cook/prep person, and breakfast-bar attendant.

Danner himself, in answers to the plaintiffs' interrogatories, said that at times he had used the word "nigger," but only when he was angry about conditions in his restaurants, he said. He also made this admission: "When a store was underperforming, I have on occasion given my opinion that a possible problem area was that the specific store in question had too many black employees working in it as compared to the racial mix of the geographical area served by the store."

Though Danner didn't know it when he wrote his answers to the plaintiffs' interrogatories, his admission fit hand in glove with another critical piece of evidence Warren and Goldstein had already obtained. That evidence, they believed, was their smoking gun, what they referred to as "the Wankat Letter." This was a three-page letter from Ray Danner to a Jacksonville, Florida, Captain D's franchise owner named Al Wankat written on December 17, 1980. In it, Danner seemed to compare the racial composition of the workers at one of Wankat's stores which he had recently inspected to those in several other fast-food operations in the area.

At Wankat's Dunn Road Captain D's, Danner had written, there weren't enough ashtrays on the tables, the thermostat was set too high, only one employee was wearing a hat, and, at opening time, there were "four total people on duty (black female manager, black cook, two black counter girls)." Danner wrote that he then visited other nearby restaurants "to check price competition and caliber of in-store staff." With him on this tour was the co-owner of the franchise, Danner's then-son-in-law, William Wilson. The letter continued: "Long Johns had two neat looking males with blue vest, one appeared to be approximately thirty, the other twenty-six, two neat appearing white counter girls; prices generally lower than ours. Quincy's—approximately fifteen employees, one black. Burger King—approximately eighteen employees, no black. McDonald's—eighteen to twenty-two employees, no black. Big Mac—$1.10; Quarter Pounder $.99. Wendy's—ten to twelve employees, no black."

Danner's explanation later for why he listed the race of employees at the various restaurants, and why he thought it important to note the absence of blacks at some of the stores, was that he was trying to create a "word picture."

The Wankat Letter had come from a former Captain D's area supervisor named Phyllis Blower, who had contacted Tommy Warren after the lawsuit was filed to tell him what had happened at her stores. She had since left Captain D's, but had kept a copy of the letter. In a 1991 deposition she testified that after Danner's visit, and after his letter, which he had also copied and sent to four top corporate executives, she and Wankat received a call from Danner's son-in-law William Wilson demanding to know how they could have let their store get so "black-staffed" and why they put up with Elaine Danceler, the black store manager. "Mr. Wilson went on to indicate that Ray was upset about that, that they had gone to different establishments up and down the road and how they had seen that we didn't have to settle for black, that all these units had *X* amount of numbers of whites and no blacks, or this huge amount of number of whites and only one or two blacks, that they were able to get young, white, male managers functioning in the same, you know, direct competition as what we were.

"Basically at that point I was given the order by Bill Wilson to terminate Elaine Danceler," an order Blower said she never followed. "I was told in no uncertain terms to get the store lightened up, and that simply meant get rid of blacks, insert whites, and do it as legally as we could, which was shorten hours so the people would get frustrated and quit because they were only getting two hours on a schedule. It was a very unpleasant phone call. You were told what to do. You knew it was job critical. At that point when the phone call was over, you felt about an inch tall."

The plaintiffs' evidence of massive discrimination at Shoney's in hiring, firing, and promotion would eventually come to fill two hundred boxes of records, implicating 36 senior executives, 104 mid-level supervisers, and 70 restaurant managers, 210 in all. In response, Shoney's would eventually line up approximately forty former officials in addition to the dozens of current executives who filed affidavits saying neither Danner nor the company had followed, or ordered them to follow, discriminatory policies in hiring and promotion decisions.

"There was never any companywide policy of discrimination in hiring, or any quotas, or anything else," Danner himself said. "I can never remember an incident where I would have told anyone to fire blacks." Jim Arnett, president of the Shoney's division, also said he knew of no corporate policy to limit employment opportunities for blacks. George Neal, the personnel director for Captain D's, defended Danner. "I have never heard Ray Danner express any opinion on the racial mix of the staff in any store," he said. "The Captain D's division did not have a policy or practice of discriminating against blacks in hiring, promotion, termination, pay or other employment matters." Gary Spoleta attacked the motives of witnesses such as Wachtel. "Mr. Wachtel is a bitter competitor of Shoney's and apparently harbors great resentment to-

wards Shoney's and Ray Danner which I can only attribute to
Mr. Wachtel's discharge in 1982," he said.

Some of Shoney's own witnesses may have proved less than helpful, however. Don Christian, regional vice president for Captain D's franchise operations, in describing what he said was Danner's intense demeanor when he got upset, said, "His face got about as red as your tie, and he would get excited, some hollering."

"Some cursing?" he was asked in his deposition.

"On occasion."

"Would he yell?"

"On occasion."

"Would he grab people?"

"I have never seen him do it."

In his deposition, Christian also gave the following testimony, which the plaintiffs used to make their case against Shoney's and Danner:

Q: Did Mr. Danner ever tell you that it was important to limit the number of black managers?

A: That it was important to limit them, no.

Q: Or to limit the number of black managers?

A: No, not to limit them, no.

Q: Did he ever say anything about the race of managers to you?

A: Occasionally, yes.

Q: What would Mr. Danner say about the race of managers to you, on occasion?

A: Sometimes he would comment on having a black manager in a specific location.

Q: What would he say about having a black manager in a specific location?

A: That maybe a black manager would do better.

Q: Why is that? Would he give a reason?

A: Because of the clientele.

Q: Would that be because the majority of the clientele was black?

A: Possibly.

Q: Did he ever say that?

A: Yes, I guess he did.

Q: Have you ever heard stores referred to as "nigger stores" by any Shoney's supervisors, or managers, or officers?

A: No. . . .

Q: Did Mr. Danner ever tell you that it would be good to have more white employees in particular stores because of the clientele?

A: Yes.

Q: Did he say that on occasion?

A: On occasion.

Q: Would that be because the clientele was predominantly white?

A: Yes.

After the plaintiffs' attorneys finished their questions, Danner's attorney asked Christian what he would do after Danner said "he thought it might be a good idea to have more white employees in a store."

"Nothing," Chistian replied.

"You heard it, and you carried on your duties, and did not do anything about it, is that correct?" the attorney asked.

"That's correct," Christian responded.

On April 30, 1990, Warren and Goldstein submitted a motion seeking permission from Judge Vinson to file an amended complaint on expanded grounds to include Title VII of the Civil Rights Act of 1964. It would take several months, until January 1991, before the judge finally ruled on their motion, and then only after they added eight more named plaintiffs, bringing the total to seventeen on the complaint. For the first time, though, the plaintiffs spelled out on the court record what they were seeking should their case go to trial. It was considerably more than they had been willing to settle for during the moratorium.

As before, they wanted class certification and a jury trial; a declaratory judgment stating that Shoney's employment practices were illegal; an injunction against all further racial discrimination and retaliation; and an affirmative action program to eliminate the continuing effects of those discriminatory and retaliatory practices. They also wanted $530 million: $350 million in back pay, $100 million in punitive damages from Shoney's, and $80 million in punitive damages from Ray Danner. Finally, there were the matters of compensatory damages against Shoney's; back pay, compensatory, and punitive damages against Charlie Robertson, Roger Danner, and Robertson Investment Company; and, of course, attorneys' fees, all to be determined later.

If Shoney's wasn't going to settle, the plaintiffs wanted to take their case to court.

THIRTEEN

" A God-Made Man
and a Self-Made Success "

As the case moved into the summer of 1990, Tommy Warren needed help. A few law students still put in part-time hours taking declarations from prospective witnesses—the sharpest of these was Mary Ellen Martin, who after passing the Bar stayed on as an attorney—but most of those hired in spring 1989 to handle the hotline had long since gone. A law clerk named Steve Mitchell had worked full-time for several months organizing a computer system for recording, indexing, and cross-referencing witnesses and their charges; after he quit, though, Warren and his legal secretary, Lynn Harvey (whose salary was being paid by Warren's wife and her small firm), were left to handle virtually all the discovery work out of the Tallahassee office by themselves.

Barry Goldstein could call on a number of junior attorneys in Guy Saperstein's office to do legal research and help write briefs. Warren, though, needed someone else on site, so once the mora-

torium was over and the next wave of motions broke, he started
looking around town for another lawyer. What he soon discovered
was that few were interested in practicing civil rights law, especially in the aftermath of the 1989 Supreme Court rulings and the
anticipated failure of the Civil Rights Act of 1990 to make it past
the president's veto. Those who might still be sympathetic to
employment discrimination work from an ideological standpoint
also had to clear another hurdle which Warren and Goldstein were
constantly facing in the Shoney's case: the threat of ethical and
procedural challenges and the possibility of sanctions, a potential
liability that few were willing to take on.

Several job candidates came and went before a mutual friend finally put Warren in touch with a young attorney named Sam
Smith, who was then an associate at one of the top firms in Tallahassee. Their first meeting, at Warren's office, lasted half an hour.
Smith, who had lived on a commune, done organic farming, re-
paired Volkswagens, worked as a carpenter, and taken an active
interest in environmental issues, said he liked Warren right away
and instinctively preferred the shorts-and-sandals atmosphere of
Warren's office to the three-piece world of his current firm.

Their second meeting took place over lunch at a Shoney's. Before they arrived, Warren made the same racial predictions he had
made in Fernandina Beach when he and Goldstein were finalizing
their agreement with Guy Saperstein; once again, all the predictions came true: white manager, hostess, and waitresses; black
busboys, salad-bar attendants, and cooks. Smith was impressed,
and he was drawn to the challenges and the political implications
of the Shoney's case.

Warren found plenty that impressed him about Smith as well:
second in his law school class, an editor on the law review, a year
past the Bar but already tagged for success by a top firm. Smith
even wore an earring. Warren offered him the job.

Smith was tempted at first and was ready to sign on, but then
came the warnings. An attorney friend cautioned him about the
contingent liability for plaintiffs' lawyers. One of Smith's brothers
asked if he knew about Warren's drug-conspiracy bust. A senior
partner at his firm reminded Smith that he would be giving up a
prominent, secure—and lucrative—future if he took the risk of

going off with a one-case firm like Warren's. To convince Smith to stay, the partner gave him what was intended to be a choice assignment: representing boat manufacturers before the Florida Cabinet to get a limited exemption to speed restrictions for testing boats in manatee-protected waters. The Florida manatee, facing extinction largely because so many had been maimed and killed by boat propellers, had long been a *cause célèbre* among the defenders of Florida wildlife. Now Smith, who still had deep sympathies with the environmental movement, found himself making a case that he knew would hurt that cause.

He won the exemption for the speedboat manufacturers, much to the delight of his firm. The next day he quit his job, hung up his three-piece suit, and went to work for Warren.

Smith's first assignment in August 1990 was to digest more than forty hours of reading material that Warren had prepared to bring him up to speed in the case. Even at that, Smith said he had difficulty comprehending the "largeness" of the litigation until several months later when he, Warren, Goldstein, and Tony Lawson, a young lawyer from Goldstein's office, sat down at a hearing before Judge Vinson and found themselves facing a virtual army of Shoney's attorneys. Smith and Tony Lawson, who was African American, born in the Bay Area, and a Harvard Law School graduate, would work as a team for much of the next two years, conducting dozens of trial depositions around the country and spending weeks together in Nashville digging through literally millions of documents in Shoney's files, making copies of several hundred thousand, once Judge Vinson finally ruled on the complex legal disputes over the nature of the corporate material that had to be opened to the plaintiffs.

Among their discoveries:

A handwritten note from an unidentified manager: "If you hire another nigger I'll fire you"—though Shoney's executives said they had found that manager and terminated him.

A memo from a Shoney's division director concerning "Ten Ways We Most Abuse Employees." One of those ways: "prejudice."

A list of dozens of possible attendees at a corporate-wide personnel development conference in 1989, none of them black. A Shoney's executive later acknowledged that there had never been any blacks at any of these conferences during the several years they were held.

Another copy of the Wankat Letter, from the file of Shoney's vice president for personnel.

A memo from then-Shoney's president Gary Spoleta to personnel director Benny Ball: "Benny, please take the research info we have and let's communicate it to all our top restaurant leaders to get a commitment to how fast we can eliminate male help from our dining rooms." The memo was included in the court record as an exhibit in Ball's deposition. Ball said in that deposition that he had never ordered any male workers fired in the Specialty Division restaurants, but that he and Spoleta had been concerned about customers' anxieties during the "AIDS scare."

A speech by a corporate vice president to SHOPAC, a political action committee formed by Shoney's executives, about the group's objective: "To position ourselves so that no governmental unit at any level can interfere with the successful operation of our stores. Should interference occur, it [should] be stopped at the earliest stage."

Another division director's response to the ways Shoney's workers are most abused: "When an employee exercises rights of fair treatment and acts through chain of command, severe repercussions occur."

Also included in the mountain of evidence that Smith and Lawson pored through—after still more legal battles—was all Ray Danner's correspondence, both inside and outside the company, dating back to the early years of the business. It was that correspondence, plus reams of newspaper and magazine articles, divorce documents, tax returns, interviews, and other corporate papers, that brought the plaintiffs' image of Ray Danner into focus.

Born December 5, 1924, Raymond Louis Danner spent the first part of his life in a one-bedroom apartment on the second floor of his uncle's grocery store in Louisville. His mother sewed; his father, a German immigrant named Gustave Adolph Danner, was a paperhanger. Danner once told a reporter that the "passion" for golf he developed as an adult stemmed from the fact that he never had an opportunity to play games when he was a boy because he was always forced to work to help support his family—though he did manage to find enough time when he was young to learn the saxophone and clarinet.

Mitch Boyd, the former Shoney's CEO, says Danner's hard-charging drive to succeed started early: "He was a scrappy young entrepreneurial kind of guy. His father was a paperhanger and painter and alcoholic. His mother raised him. His father wasn't around very much, and he lived in a very very poor community in Louisville, a lot of blacks in the community. He was of German background, apparently second generation German, and he was a paperboy. And he was determined that he was going to get himself out of that."

Dave Wachtel, another former CEO, said in a deposition that Danner's racial attitudes were formed during that time. "I wasn't there, but I suspect from the stories he told me about it, it was probably a lower-class neighborhood, lower-income neighborhood, and [he] had associated with blacks. As a result he had developed a dislike for black people and was very vocal in this as he ran the company, and as he gave us instructions as to who we should hire and who we should not hire, where they should work and where they should not work. So his reputation was one of a person who did not like black people."

Boyd said Danner had black customers on his newspaper delivery route whom he resented. The way Boyd saw it, though, that resentment wasn't racist; Danner just said he had difficulty collecting money from black people. The way Danner dealt with that problem, according to Boyd, proved that his attitude wasn't "a matter of black and white," but rather showed how he could "manipulate you for his own purposes."

"As he told me, one of the most difficult things in the black community was to collect," Boyd recalled, "so he said he figured out a way to do it, and it really worked. He would wait until Sunday morning and he'd go around with the funnies and he'd take the funnies out and he'd put them on the outside of the Sunday paper, and come up to the door and tell them that he needs to collect. And he said 90 percent of the time when they saw the funnies they wanted to read those and they wanted to see that paper, but that was the most important part of the paper to them so they'd pay him. And he would collect an awful lot more than if he waited until Tuesday or Wednesday or some other time of the week to go around and collect. A real results-oriented kind of guy."

In a television interview years later for a Vanderbilt University business program, Danner seemed to be talking about himself from that early time in a segment called "The Will To Win": "I guess there are some people who have it inborn. They may be the lucky ones, if it is inborn. You know, take the child at play, you can see this coming on early. It's the little kids who—they want to win, you know, they're, whatever it is, if they're playing a simple game, they want to win. If they don't win they're unhappy; they're downright sometimes so disappointed that they are depressed. So winning isn't something that happens occasionally. It becomes a way of life."

Danner was sixteen when his father died, and in his official biography, included in the literature for a charitable trust he formed in the late 1980s, he was soon holding down three jobs, delivering groceries, pumping gas, and delivering papers, all while attending DuPont Manual High School. He eventually left school, caught on at Louisville Tool and Dye, and began performing on his saxophone with bands at local dances and clubs. That lasted until he joined the Army Air Corps late in World War II; he was still in navigation training, and still stationed in the States, when the fighting ended. Afterward, he went back to Louisville, married his first wife, Juanita, with whom he had four children, and bought an A&P grocery store. His aunt loaned him three hundred dollars to help get started, and years later, after Shoney's went public, Danner said he gave her three hundred shares of Shoney's stock, a gift he repeated annually. He also sold houses for a while but hated it. A story he has told about himself from that time concerned a prospective buyer who complained that the gutters on a house needed repair. Yeah, Danner said he responded, and the roof leaks, too.

From the grocery store, Danner moved on through a succession of businesses in Kentucky and Tennessee, including bowling alleys, drive-in theaters, real estate operations, and gas stations. The Shoney's opportunity arrived in 1958 when Danner was thirty-three. He had accumulated enough money by then from buying, improving, and selling businesses that he was able to start his first

restaurant in Madison, Tennessee, without financing or a mortgage and with $150,000 in working capital. The years that fol-
lowed continued to be a workaholic time for Danner and for Juanita, who friends said worked side-by-side with him to operate the
stores. Old Shoney's hands still speak in awe of what they refer to
as Danner's "work ethic," his constant, hands-on presence at the
middle Tennessee restaurants, his exacting standards, and his fury
whenever things didn't go precisely as he ordered. It was a heady
time, though, for Danner and for the young, white, working-class
executives who got rich along with him as the company grew
wildly during the 1960s and 1970s and then into the 1980s, spreading like kudzu through the South and the Midwest.

In 1988, after Danner reaped more than $140 million in the Sho-
ney's recapitalization scheme, he formed his Danner Foundation
with $13 million of that money, a family trust through which he
began making charitable donations to local schools, churches, and
other nonprofit organizations. In 1989, the first full year that the
philanthropy was in operation—and the year the Shoney's lawsuit
was filed—the recipient list included a handful of African American groups. The next year black schools and organizations domi-
nated the list: Fayetteville State University, North Carolina Central, Edward Waters College, Meharry Medical College, Fisk
University, Tennessee State, the NAACP, the Southern Christian
Leadership Conference.

   Danner, who in a 1992 deposition acknowledged that there were
no minority schools, groups, or causes included in the list of organizations to which he had donated money in the six years prior
to the lawsuit, became a ubiquitous presence at minority fund-
raisers at the end of the 1980s, according to former *Nashville Tennessean* publisher John Siegenthaler. "My first reaction [to the
charges against Danner] was, it just couldn't be true," Siegenthaler
said. "I would have to say everybody in town noted subsequent to
that, whatever his attitude before, it changed radically. He became
very sensitive. If you'd go to these events in the black community
he would be there."

   In one instance, Danner showed up at a program honoring a
black state senator where the featured speaker was Julius Cham-

bers, the executive director of the NAACP Legal Defense and Educational Fund, the organization that was then helping bring the discrimination suit against Danner and Shoney's. Afterward, Danner sent a "Dear Julius" letter to Chambers saying how much he admired "the accomplishments you have made as director of the NAACP Legal Defense and Educationl [*sic*] Fund."

Danner's advisers during this time were Bob Brown of B&C Public Relations, to whom Danner had copied the Chambers letter, and another black conservative named Francis Guess, who had held cabinet positions under former Tennessee governor Lamar Alexander and who had also been appointed by the Republican administration to the U.S. Civil Rights Commission. Danner hired Guess to serve as executive director of the Danner Foundation, and as executive vice president for the Danner Company, an investment firm that was soon bankrolling a variety of business ventures ranging from car dealerships to the Hollywood movie *Bat 21* to a line of African American hair-care products to toxic-waste disposal.

With tens of millions in ready capital, the Danner Company seemed to be everywhere almost overnight. Carol Condon, the Nashville paralegal who had worked extensively with Tommy Warren taking statements from Shoney's witnesses during the first year and a half of the lawsuit, found that out after she moved to Jackson, Mississippi, in 1990 to take a job at a law firm there. Francis Guess showed up one day to talk to the firm's partners about representing the Danner Company in its toxic-waste venture, she said, and when the firm hosted a dinner for other representatives of the Danner Company, someone proposed a toast "To Ray Danner's money." Condon said she soon moved on to another firm.

The Danner Foundation brochure, with its recipient list and application procedure, also carries the two-page, single-spaced biography of Ray Danner. "To understand the values that drive the Danner Foundation is to know Ray Danner," it begins. "The story has been told time and again." What follows is a blow-by-blow account of Danner's every business move, from the three jobs he held down as a Depression-era teenager to the accolades he received for being a nationally recognized CEO at Shoney's. With each new venture, the bio lists the amount of Danner's initial investment, the terms of the financing, and the profit on the sale of the company when Danner decided to move on to bigger things.

Not included in the biography is mention of the death, on June 20, 1974, of Danner's oldest son Michael Ray Danner. Michael, who had just been promoted from manager of a Nashville Shoney's to assistant area supervisor in the newly launched Captain D's division, was the heir apparent to the Shoney's empire, a son as hard-charging as the father. Police reported that Michael lost control of his 1974 Thunderbird late that June night on a Post Road curve in southwest Nashville, skidded 218 feet, then slammed headfirst into a tree. Witnesses said that Michael was trapped inside, though still alive. His wife, who had been following in another car, arrived just as the Thunderbird burst into flames.

Two months later, Ray Danner and his wife separated. When they divorced early the next year, Juanita Danner received a million dollars worth of stocks, $200,000 in alimony payments over ten years, the house, the Cadillac, and ownership of a Shoney's franchise property. Ray Danner was remarried on May 31, 1975, to Judy Boyer. Several years later they had a son of their own.

The Danner biography concludes: "Although Danner met with many obstacles, and lack of opportunity was the norm for the determined Ray Danner, he beat the odds and succeeded. Now, through his many acts of generosity, countless others have an opportunity to pull themselves up by their boot straps. Many refer to him as a 'self-made' man. Others tend to think of him as a God-made man and a self-made success."

FOURTEEN

66 If They Didn't Ask Specifics, I Didn't Give Specifics 99

Most of 1990 was a prelude, a long, contentious buildup to three critical hearings the following year before Judge Vinson. The first of those hearings took place on January 3, 1991, and though there were a dozen issues on the table, the strategy for the plaintiffs remained simple: with 140 sworn statements from anecdotal witnesses, extensive statistical evidence, Danner's own admissions, the Wankat Letter, the inexorable zero—keep the focus on the merits of the case.

And it was here, in oral arguments, that Barry Goldstein shined, laying out the theory of the case, the "vision" that Tommy Warren had seen three years before, and then filling it in with a body of evidence that Reagan-conservative Judge Vinson described as "somewhat overwhelming."

"In a way, the challenge for me was how to sum up the story in a single sentence," Goldstein said. "How to say here was a company that flouted the law and hurt a lot of innocent people, and in doing so exacerbated some of the worst problems in society." Goldstein was able to do that in court, according to his associate Tony Lawson, through meticulous preparation and "a tremendous command of case law." "Barry is very disciplined," Lawson said. "Intellectually he knows his stuff. In those hearings he not only knew all the cases, he could also give full citations, and even name the particular page. Shoney's attorneys were incredulous."

Shoney's game was a more complex one, both offensive and defensive simultaneously. The company had to fight off the plaintiffs' summary judgment motion, their class-certification request, and charges in December that Shoney's attorneys and private investigators had been harassing witnesses. At the same time, Shoney's sought to press a host of counterattacks, like enfilade fire. Among the scattered targets in oral arguments before Judge Vinson: the plaintiffs' Section 1981 claims, their discovery and procedural demands, their continuing violation theory, and a handful of the named plaintiffs themselves. The latter assaults came in the form of individual motions for summary judgment against Dewitt Nelson, Denise Riley, and Buddy Bonsall, although Bonsall, a former Tallahassee Shoney's manager, proved to be too strong a witness and the motion against him was soon dropped. The others, though, were vulnerable to attack.

Riley had claimed that she was passed over for promotion and "constructively discharged" from a Pensacola, Florida, Shoney's—harassed at her job, her hours cut back until she couldn't afford to keep working—because she was black. Shoney's attorneys argued that her claim had come too late. They said she hadn't filed a charge of discrimination with the EEOC within the time allowed under federal law, an administrative step required before bringing a discrimination suit. They also said that she had voluntarily quit her job, which if they could convince the judge was true would undercut her continuing violation claim. She could hardly say that an ongoing practice of discrimination deterred her from reapplying at Shoney's if the company could show she had left the job of her own volition.

Dewitt Nelson had even more problems than Riley. Nelson,

who had worked his way up from cook to night kitchen manager to day kitchen manager at a Tallahassee Shoney's, and then been demoted back to cook, had brought failure-to-promote charges against the company, his claims supported by at least five witnesses. When he was fired a few weeks after filing his original charge of discrimination with the EEOC, he added a retaliation claim as well. Shoney's officials, though, said they had just cause for terminating Nelson: several women he worked with had allegedly complained that he had harassed them, a contention that Ray Danner's attorney, Don Partington, repeated at the January 3 hearing where he warned Judge Vinson, "Your eyes have not had to feast upon the deposition testimony concerning this gentleman's admitted sexual harassment and misconduct in the Shoney's restaurant at which he was employed."

Apparently, though, the judge *had* seen the testimony. That became evident during the debate over Nelson's discrimination claims against the company and the company's charges against Nelson, when Vinson finally interrupted: "I don't have a great deal of sympathy for Mr. Nelson from what I've been reading and hearing both in deposition and other things. I need to go back and look at it, but it sounds to me like Shoney's had adequate cause to terminate Mr. Nelson. Mr. Nelson probably ought to be in jail if these things are true."

But Tommy Warren wasn't ready to concede anything when it became his turn to speak. He acknowledged that a single harassment complaint had been made against Nelson in October 1988 and that he had been reprimanded for it, but Warren also pointed out that it was the only reprimand of any kind Nelson had received during his three and a half years at Shoney's, until after he filed his charge of discrimination with the EEOC in the middle of December 1988. Then, suddenly, his store manager reported a flurry of harassment complaints from female employees. The timing made the charges suspect, Warren said, and the fact that some of the people who Shoney's claimed were witnesses against Nelson later retracted their charges or said they had never made them in the first place, he said, was further evidence that the company had retaliated against the former cook. Also suspect, Warren said, was the fact that two of the top people in the corporation, Butch Powell and Shoney's personnel director, Benny Ball, had traveled to Tallahassee on January 10, 1989, to question Nelson and to approve his firing. Finally, Warren told the court, witnesses had testified that there was discussion among company officials in December 1988 about wanting to get rid of Nelson, not because of any sexual harassment allegations, but because he was black.

In truth, and in hindsight, Nelson was a poor choice as a named plaintiff. Had Warren and Goldstein known how vulnerable he was to charges of harassment, valid or not, it is likely he would not have been included in the original group of nine named plaintiffs. They believed his discrimination claims were legitimate, but defending him against the harassment and assault allegations became an onerous task that consumed far more time and energy than it may have been worth. The way Barry Goldstein saw it, though, they didn't have any choice but to stand by Nelson.

"When somebody puts their name on a case like that and goes to bat to try to sue a large company and is willing to be a class representative, unless that person has something fundamentally wrong with their claim, as the plaintiffs' attorney you've got to support them. I have enormous respect for what Dewitt Nelson did and for what all those plaintiffs did," Goldstein said. "One of the things that we always say to a plaintiff is that if an employer goes after you we'll defend you. We want you to tell us the truth. You tell us what all the problems are, but we're going to defend you. And any judge that I have seen gets very upset if he or she thinks that someone is being retaliated against for using the system. But you have to be willing to defend the plaintiff. That's a no-brainer."

Still, some of the named plaintiffs were obviously weak, and Dewitt Nelson remained the most troublesome. Two years after the lawsuit, he was convicted on an unrelated charge of attempted sexual battery and sentenced to a year in jail. Ironically, though, it was Denise Riley whose discrimination claims the judge ended up severing from the class action, because of the lateness of her filing, while the motion for summary judgment against Nelson was ultimately rejected.

In any event, the overall charge of systemic racism at Shoney's was apparently too strong and the evidence too compelling to be derailed by those individual setbacks, which Goldstein referred to as "peripheral issues." Judge Vinson made that point clear during the January hearing, when he announced that he had decided to grant "conditional" class certification to the plaintiffs. He would allow Warren and Goldstein to revise their complaint, he said, and he instructed them to bring additional named plaintiffs into the suit to more adequately represent the class.

"I don't think there's any question we've got a full-blown Title VII case, and the only question may be what is encompassed in the Section 1981 claims," Vinson said. "The evidence that's been filed in this case is somewhat overwhelming and I think the plaintiffs have certainly established just about all the prerequisites you probably need to in many respects with regard to the liability issue."

Class certification, when it formally came, would mean the case could then go to trial, the last thing most defendants want. It was bad enough to be facing what was potentially the largest class ever certified in a discrimination case, but to have the plaintiffs' charges made aggressively public during trial and reported in the press as witness after witness took the stand to testify—that was another matter entirely. Rather than renewing the effort to seek a settlement, though, Shoney's attorneys and corporate officials kept up what Goldstein, at least, referred to as their "battle around the edges." One aspect of that battle was a clandestine witness whom Shoney's lawyers had flown up from her home in Orlando to sit all day in Judge Vinson's Pensacola courtroom, waiting to hear Tommy Warren speak.

For someone who would later say she didn't want to get involved, Tanya Catani, a young California woman who had followed a series of restaurant jobs to the East Coast, spent an awful lot of time in the thick of *Haynes v. Shoney's*. It was Catani who, as manager of a Tallahassee Shoney's, reported the harassment charges against Dewitt Nelson in December 1988. It was Catani who said she received two threatening phone calls from a man who identified himself as Tommy Warren in April 1989. It was Catani who emerged as Shoney's primary witness against Warren in the company's Emergency Motion for Protective Order and Imposition of

Sanctions in July 1989. And it was Catani whom Shoney's attorneys shepherded into the federal courthouse in Pensacola in January 1991, where she would have blended in with the battalion of company lawyers and executives as just another faceless law clerk or corporate aide if Barry Goldstein's associate, Tony Lawson, hadn't overheard someone say her name shortly before the hearing began.

Lawson immediately told Warren and Goldstein that Catani was in the courtroom, her presence made doubly odd by the fact that Shoney's had brought no other witnesses to testify that day in a hearing essentially scheduled for lawyers to present oral arguments on a variety of disputed motions. The plaintiffs' counsel instructed Lawson and fellow attorney Sam Smith to sit near Catani, and to record whatever she said or did.

What that amounted to for most of the day, while Barry Goldstein spoke on behalf of the plaintiffs, was nothing. Catani sat with the Shoney's people. She went to lunch with the Shoney's people. She returned with the Shoney's people. She waited. Then, at 4:11 P.M.—Smith checked his watch to note the time precisely—Warren finally stood to address the court for the first time. One minute later—a single minute into Warren's oral argument, according to Smith—Catani left the courtroom with a private investigator and one of the Shoney's law clerks. She was driven to the Pensacola airport for her flight back to Orlando, where she had been working for the past two years as manager of a Homestyle Family Buffet Restaurant.

Two months after the hearing, Shoney's filed another declaration from Catani in which she swore that Tommy Warren's voice, which she claimed she had heard in Judge Vinson's courtroom, was the same voice that had purportedly threatened her over the telephone two years earlier. Shoney's then renewed its motion for sanctions against Warren.

Warren had already filed an affidavit of his own saying he had never spoken to Catani and certainly had never, as she alleged, threatened to name her as a defendant in the lawsuit if she didn't agree to testify against Shoney's. At a brief hearing back in 1989, Barry Goldstein had denounced Catani's original affidavit as "fraudulent." "We don't know how it came into existence," he said at that time. "It purports to state that a lawyer identifying himself as Mr. Warren called her. We don't know if some person did that. We don't know anything about it. All we know and what we will put in under penalty of perjury is evidence that Mr. Warren never called Ms. Catani, never spoke to her, never received a call from her. It's a very serious matter and we would cooperate with any inquiry from any source, the FBI or any source that the court thinks appropriate with respect to this particular affidavit."

Now Sam Smith and Tony Lawson also filed affidavits in which they disputed various aspects of Catani's new statement. She claimed that Warren had introduced himself in court as "Tommy Warren," but the hearing transcript showed that Warren never said his own name; it was the judge who had recognized him as "Mr. Warren." She said she had listened to Warren speak for ten or fifteen minutes, but Smith noted that it had only been one. She said that she had left the courtroom between 3:00 and 4:00 P.M., but the plaintiffs' lawyers said, and a time reference in the hearing transcript showed, that Warren had actually spoken later than that. They were small points, admittedly, but the plaintiffs felt they had to take the Catani threat seriously. They hired a voice expert. They had already requested an FBI investigation. They suggested that Judge Vinson bring the U.S. attorney in to examine the allegations against Warren.

In a 1995 interview, Barry Goldstein said he still didn't believe Catani's charges. "There's no way Tommy's lying," he said. "Tommy is as careful as can be, and he's not going to do anything like that. Remember, we were the ones who wanted to get the FBI involved in the case. We wanted to get the U.S. attorney involved in the case. Tommy's situation just got more and more involved. There were a whole bunch of possibilities. Maybe none of the lawyers knew what was going on. Maybe it was coming from somewhere else in the company."

Things only got weirder. During the moratorium, at a March 1990 negotiation session in Washington, D.C., the plaintiffs' attorneys had questioned Benny Ball, Shoney's personnel director, about his possible knowledge of the Catani calls; he denied knowing anything about them. At that same time, though, Butch Powell mentioned that the Shoney's in Tallahassee where Catani worked had received three anonymous "bomb and attack threats" shortly after the calls. Both Warren and Goldstein said that Powell suggested there might be some connection, that whoever phoned in those threats also called Catani and pretended to be Warren.

The calls Catani said she received from the man who identified himself as Warren had come in on April 3 and then April 4, 1989, the day the original class-action complaint was filed in federal court. According to Warren and Goldstein, Powell said the bomb and attack threats came three days later and were made by a group identifying itself as the "Black Liberation Front." The callers threatened not only to bomb the store, but to attack the Tallahassee Shoney's with AK-47s at 10:00 P.M. on the night of April 7 and kill every white person there. Warren subsequently spent hours tracking down police sources and other leads related to the threats, which police said had in fact been reported. Powell, however, then said he had never suggested that the two incidents, the attack threats and the calls to Catani, were related. In their motion to dismiss the ethics charges against Warren, the plaintiffs' attorneys included all the correspondence to and from Shoney's counsel about the bomb and attack threats.

After Tanya Catani's new declaration on March 18, 1991, Shoney's kept the pressure on. They wanted the judge to allow them to depose Warren and force him to give up documents and details about his contacts with Shoney's managers. They wanted an evidentiary hearing. They still wanted sanctions. The judge finally relented, and in an extraordinary decision agreed to the deposition request, though little came of it. Warren repeated the statement he had made in his sworn affidavit, that he had never contacted Catani. Other than that, though, despite Shoney's threats to seek contempt-of-court charges, he refused to divulge any information about his investigation, citing all "work product" as confidential, protected under the attorney-client privilege. Shoney's lawyers also made a point of questioning Warren about his drug conspiracy arrest and his subsequent conviction and incarceration.

In the fall of 1991, the plaintiffs' attorneys got their opportunity to depose Tanya Catani. The assignment went to Laney Feingold, a lawyer from Goldstein's Oakland office, who uncovered a few minor inconsistencies in Catani's statements, but found no smoking gun. "She wasn't that easy to shake from her story," Feingold said, although Catani did seem to stumble over some of the questions provided by the plaintiffs' voice expert. She was certain she recognized Warren's voice at the January 3 hearing as the one she had heard on the telephone two years before, but she said she didn't think she could identify Judge Vinson's voice again, even though he had spoken at length the day she was in his courtroom.

In her deposition Catani essentially fleshed out with more details what she had claimed in her sworn statements: that she had received the two calls from "Tommy Warren" on April 3 and 4, 1989; that after the first call she told her area supervisor but spoke to no one else; that after the second call she again told her area supervisor, who contacted corporate headquarters; that she was alone when both calls came in; that it wasn't until two or three days later that she heard from Shoney's corporate representatives, who said they wanted to come to Tallahassee to speak to her about the calls; that the only times she had heard the voice she said was Tommy Warren's were in those two phone calls and at the January 3, 1991, hearing; that she had never attended any other hearings in the case; and that she had never heard her supervisors use racial slurs.

That deposition took place in Orlando, Florida, on November 11, 1991. Three years later, though, in a series of interviews with the author, Catani told a different story. She now says that Shoney's representatives were present at her restaurant on April 4 at the time of the second call that she allegedly received from Warren. She also says she phoned Warren's office after that alleged call, at the suggestion of one of those representatives, to try to confirm that it had been Warren's voice she had originally heard.

"I called, and said I was Tanya, I think I said Tanya," Catani said. "I think I told them who I was and I wanted to talk to [Warren] and he got on the phone and all he said was 'Hello' and I said 'Is this Tommy Warren?' And he said 'It is Tommy Warren,' and I said that's all I needed and I hung up the phone. I do believe."

Catani, who has remarried and is now Tanya Edwards, also now says she attended a second hearing in the *Haynes* case where she also was able to identify Warren's voice. After being read a statement from her deposition in which she denied that she had ever attended any hearings except for the one on January 3, 1991, she still insisted that she had attended a second hearing where she heard Warren's voice, but she said that the second hearing occurred *after* her November 1991 deposition. Only one other hearing was held after her deposition, however, and the transcript from that hearing makes direct mention of the fact that she was not there.

Finally, Catani now says that racial slurs were often used and discriminatory orders frequently made in the Shoney's restaurants where she worked. "It was a known practice at Shoney's," she says. "Basically, when I first started years before it was a known practice that you knew when certain supervisors came to town you knew not to have a lot of black staff on. You knew things that you shouldn't do if you were going to have a good inspection or you were going to have a bad inspection. . . . Any GM [general manager] that worked for Shoney's at that time, if they worked anywhere in Pensacola, Tally and even Jacksonville, I do believe, had some of it spew over on to them. I believe any GM that worked for the company for more than maybe a six-month timespan had to be in a position to have heard it or know of it and know that if you were going to be successful in that company, what to do and what not to do.

"I think I was way too outspoken for somebody to have said something like that to me. I was very much known in the company for, if I didn't think something was right I was going to give you comeback. And I think [regional vice president] Bill Long and everyone knew that if they had ever told me, 'You have to fire these people because they're black,' I think they know that . . . we would have problems. Because I'm not that type of person.

"But I was in the company of Bill Long many times when he would say, refer to black people as 'niggers.' Yet he would look at my supervisor, who was Ron Larrow, and he'd say, 'You need to speak to Contata'—because he used to call me 'Contata,' I don't know why, because my last name is Catani and I guess he never could get it.

"The way Shoney's was, is, like the the regional VP never really spoke directly to a GM if their division director was in their presence. They would speak to the division director and the division director would speak to you. It was kind of like a power game. And he would say to him things like, 'You need to speak to Contata. She hires too many black people.' But he would use 'niggers' and things of that nature."

Finally, Catani said, "I had gone as far as one time, I put a couple of [black workers] in the employee bathroom, locked the door, and told them please just to stay there."

Asked about the apparent contradictions between her deposition testimony and her account in interviews with the author, Catani said she had answered questions in her deposition "to the best of my knowledge," but that "If they didn't ask specifics, I didn't give specifics."

Shoney's lead counsel, Butch Powell, wouldn't comment on any aspect of Catani's interviews with the author. One of Shoney's other attorneys, Steve Tallent, in a letter to the author, gave the following statement: "The witness Catani was at Mr. Powell's and my insistence interviewed and reinterviewed by lawyers having 'no stake' in the alleged transactions. Only after reconfirmation of her testimony by at least two separate interviews in which Mr. Powell took no part was she maintained as a witness—a witness which the plaintiffs always sought not to have testify. I saw Ms. Catani on one occasion during which she spontaneously reconfirmed her testimony. I will also say that neither Mr. Powell nor I thought that Ms. Catani's testimony was conclusive on the issues involved."

Tommy Warren said that if Catani now told a different story than the one she had given in her deposition, it would be evidence that further undercut the credibility of her original accusations against him. "I know I didn't ever talk to her, and my testimony, given under oath, subject to perjury, is in the record at least two different times," Warren said. "Beyond that I'm not sure what you can make of what she is now saying in light of the history of her statements in the case and in her deposition. I just don't have a clue as to where she's coming from. I don't have a clue as to what really happened at her end."

Perhaps not surprisingly, the Catani story didn't end with her 1995 comments to the author. Months later, after acknowledging that she had had discussions with Butch Powell, she wrote to retract what she had said in one interview with the author (and confirmed in a follow-up interview): "If you are indeed looking for the truth you need to refer to the court documents as they were done at a time when everything was still clear in my mind and are a correct account of what happened. . . . I was an employee at the wrong place and time caught up in a case that was total bull!"

FIFTEEN

“ Why Didn't You Deal with It for the Last Twenty Years? ”

On May 20, 1991, the Equal Employment Opportunity Commission, the agency charged by Congress with enforcing federal fair employment-practice laws, submitted a motion to file a small, fifteen-page legal brief with Judge Vinson in support of the plaintiffs' class certification request in *Haynes v. Shoney's*. The judge summarily rejected the motion for the "Amicus brief" in a one-sentence ruling: "This case already has too much paperwork, and the plaintiffs are adequately represented." In a 1995 interview with the author, Judge Vinson was even more dismissive of the EEOC's motion, stating that anyone attempting to get involved in the litigation at that point, two years after the suit was filed, must have been doing so for "political reasons."

EEOC officials had started making noises about joining the *Haynes* litigation earlier, in spring 1991. When they did, Tommy Warren and Barry Goldstein traveled to Washington to tell those officials that they didn't want the sort of help the EEOC had in mind, not that late in the case. "There are a lot of times when I think it's very effective to have the EEOC intervene," Goldstein said later, choosing his words carefully. "But this was such a rough litigation, and there was such pressure on the parties, that we were very concerned that the EEOC would not be able to keep up and that they would make mistakes, and that [Butch] Powell would jump on it and it would create a sideshow on one of these peripheral issues which we did not want, that would hurt our ability to keep this litigation on track and focused on the merits of the case.

"If I could have picked two or three EEOC lawyers—there are some very good lawyers in the EEOC—to work on it full time, that would have been all right. But if you get good, smart, well-meaning but inexperienced lawyers, they would have been chewed up by the Shoney's defense team, just like the EEOC had been in the past." Goldstein continued. "Of course, we could have said, 'Why didn't you deal with it for the last twenty years? We've taken it on now, and two years into our case you want to get involved? You could have been helpful in some ways, and we appreciate your interest, but as a practical matter right now you can't help.'"

Tommy Warren said the problem ran deeper than that. "The ideal situation in the Shoney's case would have been for the EEOC to have done its job," he said. "To track complaints against the company over the years and measure them against the EEO-1 reports. They should have a system for monitoring charges that raise issues of systemic, overt racism. They should do what Congress created them to do, which is to look at these things from a mountaintop perspective. That's the EEOC's job. If they're not going to do their job, why have it?"

The EEOC chairmen under the last two Republican administrations, Clarence Thomas and Evan Kemp, were "ostriches," Warren said; they were men who for years chose to ignore the evidence laid out in front of them about racism in society, he charged, including the evidence in *Haynes v. Shoney's*. "Their approach has been to say, 'Look, there's a little fire, let's take a fire extinguisher and put it out,' but never mind the huge fire over here blazing," Warren said. "There was an incredible amount of backsliding on civil rights under the Reagan Administration. The message was, 'Hey, it's okay to discriminate. We're not going to do anything about it.'"

One highly placed source in the EEOC acknowledged that there had been problems in the agency: "In that particular timeframe, from private counsel's point of view, there may have been some reservation about the EEOC getting involved for political reasons. There were lots of suspicions about the nature and quality of our work during that period, given the national administration."

Warren's own frustration sprang from his belief that for two and a half years the agency had sat on its hands when it was needed the most. The EEOC had known about the Shoney's case since October 1988, when Warren and Goldstein first contacted the systemic investigations division in Washington, D.C., to advise officials there that they intended to bring the class action. And there had been numerous individual complaints over the years prior to that. The following summer, after the plaintiffs filed their complaint in federal court, they provided the EEOC with copies of sixty-eight individual charges of discrimination, twenty-four of which explicitly named Ray Danner, and they continued to send the EEOC all other relevant documents in the litigation, in addition to dozens of other charges of discrimination as they were taken and sworn.

According to James Finney, who was then director of litigation at the EEOC, "there were a number of people inside the commission who wanted to see us get involved" in the Shoney's case. However, he added, "I don't have the sense that private counsel was necessarily screaming for the EEOC to get into the thing. It's one thing to say it would have been useful or helpful or desirable or whatever it is, and another thing to come in here and say 'We need you.' I never heard that." According to Barry Goldstein, though, the plaintiffs' attorneys did in fact "scream" for the EEOC to get involved, not in the actual litigation, but through a finding of "reasonable cause" after an examination of the evidence. In fact, Goldstein said, they would have welcomed such a finding at any time during the litigation, and he said as much in a letter to the commission's general counsel, which read in part: "An EEOC finding of reasonable cause that Shoney's has engaged in this wide-spread illegality would substantially assist the prosecution of the *Haynes* action."

That letter was written in 1991, after two and a half years of oral requests by the plaintiffs' attorneys for a systemic finding by the commission. They didn't want the EEOC's lawyers coming in late in the case after the grueling work of discovery was done and the bulk of the litigation was over, they said; they wanted the commission to take a long, hard look at their evidence and then tell the court what it meant. "What we wanted was a systemic finding," Goldstein said. "That would have helped us in the class motion because we could have pointed to that as evidence of the common issues of fact and law. If the EEOC found that there was reasonable cause to believe that there was a pervasive system of discrimination emanating from Shoney's Central, that would have been very significant evidence to present to the judge in support of the class motion where you don't have to win on the merits, you just have to show that there are common questions and typical questions."

All along, Warren and Goldstein both said, starting in 1988, they had been clear about what they needed from the commission. They requested copies of all individual race discrimination complaints filed with the EEOC against Shoney's so that they could more thoroughly investigate the case. They contacted at least one EEOC commissioner and urged her to examine the evidence. And they repeatedly asked commission officials to examine the class-action complaint and all the evidence and then conduct a separate investigation of their own on which to base a reasonable cause finding. Aside from the May 1991 Amicus brief, however—essentially a legal argument in support of the plaintiffs' position, a far cry from a systemic cause finding based on a deep examination of the evidence—the EEOC's Washington office took no action. There was no charge from any of the commissioners, no systemic finding of "reasonable cause," no files made available to the plaintiffs' counsel, and no forthright explanation for the EEOC's decisions.

Goldstein said he is reluctant to point a finger at the career employees at the agency for failing to issue a systemic cause finding in the Shoney's case. "It would have been logical for the career people to get approval from the commission," he said. "It may just be that no one at the EEOC wanted to stick out their neck on this thing."

The only significant exception in the EEOC to this apparent pattern of inaction came from the commission's district office in Atlanta, which in 1989 investigated the charges of discrimination brought against Robertson Investment Company and entered a reasonable cause finding in each of a dozen complaints filed by Billie and Henry Elliott and the other former RIC employees from Marianna and Panama City. Even that wasn't enough to compel the Washington office to move against Shoney's, however, in support of the broader, corporate-wide case brought by Warren and Goldstein.

In fact, it was Shoney's itself, not realizing that the EEOC had stonewalled Warren and Goldstein's request, who turned over to the plaintiffs all its own internal files of EEOC complaints made against the company over the then-most recent five-year period: 270 charges of racial discrimination brought by Shoney's employees between 1985 and 1990. The files showed that most of those charges were still open, many had been dismissed, a few settled for amounts of less than $1,000, and only one resulted in an EEOC finding of "reasonable cause." The EEOC had apparently never considered the possibility that all those individual charges against Shoney's from around the country might add up to a "pattern and practice" of systemic, corporate-wide discrimination. The plaintiffs tried to get more records, according to Goldstein, but were unsuccessful. "Although we don't know what charges were filed against Shoney's in the seventies, we have to assume that the discrimination was so overt and outrageous that there must have been a whole bunch of charges filed in the seventies that just got washed away," he said.

Probably the most egregious of the cases, included as evidence in *Haynes,* was also the single one that resulted in a commission finding of reasonable cause. That case, filed by a former prep cook named Harry Thomas, started on May 7, 1987, when Thomas was discharged from a Shoney's in Alexandria, Louisiana, a week after he told his manager he wanted to move up to a higher-level cook's position. He claimed, and the company's employment records later showed, that there were no blacks in store management at that time. The EEOC at first issued a determination of "no cause" but later rescinded it when two other witnesses came forward saying that the area supervisor for Shoney's, Ray Smith, often referred to blacks as "niggers" and "gave orders to the Store Manager and two Kitchen Managers to discharge black employees" two days before Thomas was fired. As the EEOC continued its investigation, more witnesses came forward, ten in all, to point the finger at Smith, saying he was "racially biased." This time around, the EEOC determined that there was reasonable cause to believe Shoney's had acted in a discriminatory manner, and the EEOC's representative in the case insisted that Smith be "disciplined so he no longer has any authority or responsibility involving hiring, firing, or disciplining employees."

The Shoney's attorney who handled the case was Butch Powell, who apparently agreed to the EEOC's terms and even thanked the agency in a letter: "We appreciate your fine work and cooperation in resolving this matter as contemplated by the Act and look forward to working with you again should the need arise." Harry Thomas accepted $1,000 to settle his claim, and he agreed to find another job elsewhere. A month after the settlement, though, Ray Smith, instead of being terminated, removed from his supervisory duties, or disciplined in any way, was transferred from Louisiana to Kansas City, Missouri, where he continued to work as an area supervisor for Shoney's—with a $270 biweekly raise. And that's where the real trouble started.

Several black employees at Kansas City Shoney's stores soon came forward to report what they alleged was a sustained harassment campaign by Ray Smith. Among the allegations: that Smith told one prep cook, Philip Peavy, "Where I come from they call me God," and then informed Peavy that "any good Caucasian could do a job better than [Peavy] could." Peavy alleged that when he complained to his restaurant manager, Smith sprayed him with water. Later, Peavy alleged that Smith broke a water glass, held it to the black worker's throat, and threatened him. Peavy quit and filed discrimination charges against the company. Shoney's officials later acknowledged that reports of the incidents were true.

Two other black workers in Kansas City, Daniel Bailey and Terrell Forte, said Smith frequently referred to blacks as "niggers," and Forte also complained that Smith once threatened him, saying he was going to take a loaf of bread and "shove it up your black ass." Forte later became a named plaintiff in the class action after he filed EEOC charges claiming he was unfairly denied promotions by Smith and other Shoney's managers.

Smith was ultimately removed from his area supervisor's position in Kansas City, after the additional charges were filed against him, but even then Shoney's didn't fire him right away. Instead he was transferred again, to Nashville, where he worked in Shoney's franchise department for eight more months before he was finally terminated, with two weeks of regular pay, two weeks of vacation pay, and an extra $250. The last the plaintiffs' attorneys heard of Smith, he had surfaced at Shoney's yet again, this time working at a restaurant owned by a franchisee in Georgia.

The lack of involvement by the EEOC in the Shoney's case came as little surprise to many observers of the commission during the twelve years from 1980 to 1992, most of that time under the direction of Clarence Thomas, now a U.S. Supreme Court justice. For one thing, Thomas, who ran the commission for eight years, from 1982 to March 1990, made it EEOC policy to deemphasize class cases, stating publicly on numerous occasions that discrimination was an individual act and each allegation should thus be treated on an individual basis. Congressional investigators reported that at one point during the mid-1980s seventy-five workers who had been fired en masse from the same plant in Birmingham, Alabama, marched together into an EEOC district office to file discrimination charges, only to have every single worker's charge taken as an individual complaint and those complaints divided up among several different investigators.

According to former EEOC general counsel Don Livingston, it is literally impossible to determine how many class-type cases were handled by the commission either before or during Thomas's years as chairman, because prior to 1991 there was no definition anywhere in the agency for what constituted a class case. Livingston, who served during the Republican administrations, said,

"This is not going to be all that reassuring to you, but I think generally once the EEOC publishes a number, that becomes *the* number. That's the reality for purposes of research and writing or whatever, but it might not be real. If you ever could get behind it, and you can't, probably, you would find that the number has so many different subjective judgments built into arriving at it that it's not all that reliable."

Whatever the actual class numbers, settlement figures show that individual charges of discrimination received significantly different treatment under Thomas than they had under previous administrations. At the same time resources for systemic investigation and litigation units were being cut. In 1980, the EEOC was settling 32.1 percent of the cases it closed, meaning the complaining party agreed to the resolution of his or her case, whether it involved money, a job, a promotion, or simply an agreement by the employer to end a discriminatory practice. Six years later, that rate had dropped to 13.6 percent. One outside study found that in 1980, 15,328 victims of discrimination received monetary benefits through charges filed with the agency, but in the first half of 1985, only 2,964 received such benefits.

Meanwhile, "no cause" findings during that same period doubled from 28.5 percent to 56.6 percent of all charges brought before the commission.

Pressure to close cases brought other problems into the system. General Accounting Office investigators reported that in some district offices, most notably the one in Birmingham, Alabama, there were wholesale closures of hundreds of cases at the end of the fiscal year, "ostensibly in order to 'pad' the workload statistics," according to a Congressional report. An internal audit of the Chicago district office stated that "cases often appear improperly concluded or written up largely on the statements of respondents," a practice that gave the company or employer against whom a discrimination charge had been made the last word in apparently cursory investigations. At one point Thomas ordered the commission to end the use of "goals and timetables" for hiring women and minorities as a means of resolving cases with businesses that were found to have engaged in discriminatory policies, because, he said, they required those companies to establish unfair quota systems.

An EEOC official in New York likened that directive, which was later rescinded, to "sending soldiers to the field without guns and without bullets."

In a 1992 opinion column in the *Washington Post* defending Thomas's nomination to the Supreme Court, another former EEOC general counsel, Charles Shanor, praised Thomas's work during his eight years on the commission, although Shanor did acknowledge that the class cases brought by the EEOC under the former chairman were "small compared with the 'blockbuster' hiring cases available in earlier years of Title VII enforcement." Shanor continued, "To argue that EEOC chairman Thomas should be faulted even if there were fewer large class actions filed in his term ignores these societal changes. Thomas did not lead the EEOC during the 'bad old days' of the segregated work forces that generated giant hiring class actions. He vigorously fought the battles of the era over which he did preside at EEOC rather than sparring at windmills of the past." One battle of that era that Thomas and the EEOC neglected to fight, though, was *Haynes v. Shoney's,* which turned out to be the biggest in U.S. history, hardly a "windmill of the past." Shanor didn't speak to that litigation in his op ed piece, however, nor did he attempt to explain why the commission for two years under Thomas—and for two more years after Thomas left the agency—declined to make a reasonable cause finding based on the evidence provided by Warren and Goldstein for bringing the suit as a class action.

Still, there was some involvement in the Shoney's case coming out of the EEOC chairman's office—indirectly—though not the sort that the plaintiffs' attorneys envisioned. It took the form of one Armstrong Williams, a young black political protégé of South Carolina Republican senator and longtime segregationist Strom Thurmond. Though he wasn't an attorney himself, Williams had worked in Thomas's office at the EEOC for several years in a vaguely defined position that the *Wall Street Journal* once described as "confidential assistant, image consultant, and traveling companion." He remains one of Thomas's closest friends and advisers. After leaving the commission in 1986, Williams went to work for B&C Public Relations. In July 1990, he formed his own company in Washington, D.C., the Graham-Williams Group, with

Stedman Graham, a prominent figure in the black community (perhaps best known as the fiance of talk-show host Oprah Winfrey). In 1989, while Williams was still at B&C, he was assigned to work with executives at Shoney's, Inc., advising them on how to deal with the EEOC. One internal company memorandum entered into the court record as a deposition exhibit makes reference to an "EEOC Course 101" that Williams conducted for several Shoney's personnel officers. Another memo sent from Shoney's headquarters to EEOC district directors authorized Williams to discuss all charges of discrimination and other commission matters on behalf of Shoney's, Inc.

SIXTEEN

"We Decided to Roll the Dice"

Each of the three 1991 hearings on *Haynes v. Shoney's* had its defining features. On January 3 it was Tanya Catani's clandestine appearance to hear Tommy Warren speak, a bizarre move that cast plaintiffs' attorneys Tony Lawson and Sam Smith in unexpected roles as courtroom detectives. That was also the hearing where Butch Powell brought up Tommy Warren's "criminal convictions" before the judge. Several months later, in mid-September, the judge scheduled a second hearing, this one to resolve a host of discovery motions and to clear the deck for November, when he planned to hear oral arguments on the central issue in the case, the question of class certification. Warren and Goldstein wanted the judge to see that there were real people behind the charges, so at that September hearing they brought the named plaintiffs together for the first and only time in what turned out to be a sort of family reunion among related strangers. Warren called it a "logistical feat," coordinating travel plans with fifteen of the sixteen current and former Shoney's employees whose names were listed on the amended complaint. They came by car, by bus, and by plane, traveling from their homes across the South and the Midwest to spend the night in a cramped Day's Inn, then sit together at the Pensacola, Florida, federal courthouse, waiting to stand and be introduced to Judge Vinson. One of the named plaintiffs, Terrell Forte, even found himself flying to the hearing on the same commercial flight as Ray Danner. To Billie Elliott, those two days were a kind of homecoming, and she would later remember how good it felt to be around so many others who had been through the same things as she and Henry. Carolyn Cobb, a black Shoney's kitchen worker for twenty years who drove down from South Carolina to the hearing, remembered the small details: whom she had lunch with, whom she drove to the airport afterward, and how tightly she clung to her husband for support.

Josephine Haynes, the young black woman who lived in Pensacola and who had been turned down for waitressing jobs at two different Shoney's, said she remembered little about what happened in court but plenty about the people who were there, some of whom she still occasionally heard from, four years later, "like we were pen pals or something." What she also remembered, she said, was Tommy Warren telling her he put her name first on the suit; while most of the others suffered discrimination after they were hired, Shoney's policies had kept her from even making it through the door.

The third hearing that year, on November 20 and 21, 1991, was the most auspicious, starting as it did the day before then-president George Bush signed the Civil Rights Act of 1991, which had won Congressional approval a few weeks earlier after a second year of rancorous national debate over "quotas," but which finally restored most of the legal protections against discrimination that the Supreme Court had jettisoned back in 1989. Of course, that turned into yet another battleground for the attorneys in *Haynes v. Shoney's*. Because the new Civil Rights Act was favorable to their case, Warren and Goldstein argued that it should apply retroactively. Shoney's attorneys naturally disagreed, and after prolonged arguments over the next several months, they convinced the judge to rule against the plaintiffs. Warren and Goldstein were forced to continue pressing their case under the limitations brought by the 1989 Supreme Court decisions.

Even with that dramatic national backdrop, however, what struck Barry Goldstein at the November class certification hearing, and what he would later remember most vividly about the proceedings, was the broad and arbitrary way the judge divided up the limited time he had available. "We had something like seven hours, and Shoney's had five hours, and it was divided among all the parties," Goldstein said. "And you could put on witnesses, or you could put on experts, or you could cross-examine, or you could argue. So we decided to argue. We put on a couple of witnesses, but it was the longest I ever argued. It must have been six hours, or seven hours over two days, going through all the declarations and pointing out all the evidence that we had put in the record."

Shoney's used much of its time on its statistical expert, Paul Andrisani, with his truckload of charts and graphs, including one with blinking red lights that he discussed in the dark after the attorneys asked that the normal courtroom lights be turned off. His argument was that Shoney's overall hiring numbers for minorities were high, which he said was inconsistent with any alleged policy of systemic discrimination.

Goldstein spent part of his seven hours refuting Andrisani's testimony, pointing out that though it was true there were large numbers of blacks in "back-of-the-house" jobs, they were significantly underrepresented elsewhere. In the process, he apparently scored at least one unexpected point in what became a subtle war of attrition as he spoke at length over the course of the two days. "Towards the end of that, Charlie Robertson was in the men's room with someone else," Goldstein said, "and Sam Smith was in one of the stalls, and Charlie Robertson said to whoever he was with, 'I gotta get out of here. I can't stand to listen to that Goldstein anymore.'"

At the end of the November hearing, Judge Vinson reaffirmed his intention to certify the class, and he scheduled a trial to begin in

February. He also set a firm date to end discovery: January 10, 1992. Those discovery deadlines had come and gone in the past, but this time, with the litigation obviously reaching the boiling point, the attorneys took him seriously, setting off a fierce round of activity in the two months they had left to line up their out-of-state witnesses.

For Sam Smith, Tony Lawson, and some of the other junior attorneys from Goldstein's office and from the NAACP Legal Defense Fund, that meant dozens of trial depositions that had to be taken in cities across the South and Midwest, with very little time to take them in, what they later referred to as "The Traveling Depo Show." So they hit the road: Oklahoma, Texas, Missouri, Virginia, Georgia, Louisiana, and Tennessee. Bad food, lousy hotels, and hostile encounters with Shoney's attorneys. "This was not the kind of case where the lawyers might be adversaries but they're still friends," Lawson said. "There was no collegiality, no fraternizing."

Warren and Goldstein, meanwhile, with preparation help from Sam Smith when he was home in Tallahassee, faced the task of deposing the top corporate officials, focusing primarily on executives in Shoney's personnel department, to lock them into whatever stories they planned to tell so there would be no surprises or recantations when the case went to trial. "What we were doing was basically deposing and gaining admissions from any of the people who could actually defend the practices of Shoney's," said Goldstein. "And we were doing it not just asking open-ended questions, but trying to lock the individuals into their story and into admissions based on documents that we had to carefully plan. Also what we were trying to do was organize these masses and masses of information in a way that we could present it efficiently to a jury, because we didn't want the jury to listen to a lot of uninteresting testimony while we tried to authenticate documents. We wanted it all set to move quickly, and we wanted to try the case in less than three weeks."

They saved the best for last. For four days in a crowded hotel conference room near the Nashville airport, starting January 6, 1992, and ending the day Judge Vinson had designated as the end of discovery, Warren and Goldstein deposed Ray Danner himself.

With painstaking deliberation, they took him through an interminable list of questions based on hundreds of corporate documents and discrimination charges taken from sworn affidavits and depositions. At first Danner was happy to talk about the early years of the company, and he demonstrated a remarkable capacity for remembering names and details of the business from thirty years before. When they got to the allegations of discrimination, though, and repeated stories about Danner's use of racial threats and slurs, he either denied the charges or said he didn't recall.

He said he didn't recall whether a black person had ever attended a Shoney's luncheon staff meeting.

He said he didn't know of any black person who had served as a division director in the Shoney's division.

He said he could not recall more than one black division director in the Captain D's division.

He said he could not recall more than one black division director in the Lee's division.

He said he could not recall any black persons who owned franchises in the Shoney's division prior to 1989.

He said he could recall only one black person who owned a franchise in the Captain D's division prior to 1989, and he couldn't explain why corporate documents showed that the Captain D's Danner said was owned by that one black franchisee was instead listed as a company-owned store.

Asked if he ever told anyone that white customers might not be willing to eat at a restaurant with "too many black employees," Danner said, "Not that I can remember."

Asked if he had ever told the former Montgomery area supervisor Gene Yager, "Have you ever seen a black housing project? If you have, you have seen how blacks don't take care of anything and you would know why they don't make good employees," Danner said, "I cannot recall ever saying anything like that."

Asked if he had ever told Yager that "it's too cloudy" in a restaurant, meaning there were "too many black employees," Danner said, "Mr. Goldstein, I never heard the word cloudy used anywhere other than to the weather until this lawsuit has been involved."

Asked why, in the Wankat Letter, he had identified the race of the workers at the Jacksonville Captain D's, Danner replied, "I was trying to give like a photograph. If you had a video camera so that you could see the exact look and whatever of what the competition was made up of and what this Dunn Road store was like."

Asked why he described the race of the four persons at the Dunn Road store "rather than, for example, their age," Danner said, "I have no comment. I was just trying to put a factual word picture of what we found in each store. If this store had been staffed proper and in good shape, we would have never had a reason to compare our Captain D's with the rest of the competition."

Asked repeatedly why he had listed the race of the employees at several other nearby restaurants and fast-food stores in the Wankat Letter, Danner said over and over that he was attempting to give a "factual word picture."

Asked if he had told the owner of the Jacksonville Captain D's to have the black manager "removed" from the store, Danner said, "No, sir."

Asked if he had ever discussed with former Captain D's executive Thomas Buckner the race of manager trainees that should be hired, Danner said "Not that I can recall."

Asked if he ever discussed with Buckner the race of employees to be hired, Danner said no, and said he barely remembered Buckner.

Asked if he had ever referred to the Lee's Famous Recipe store in a predominantly black area of Nashville as "the nigger store," Danner said no.

Asked if he had ever stated in Thomas Buckner's presence that where there was a predominantly white clientele there should be a predominantly white staff in a restaurant, Danner said, "Not to my recollection."

Asked if he had ever stated in Buckner's presence that people would not want to eat at a restaurant where "a bunch of niggers" were working, Danner said, "I have no recall of ever saying anything like that."

Asked if he had ever stated in Buckner's presence that "if you hire a nigger, you will hire nothing but niggers, and soon the whole store will be niggers," Danner said, "I can't recall ever having made any such statement."

Asked if he ever used the term "nigger" in a conversation with a manager at either of two Lee's restaurants mentioned that were in Nashville, Danner said, "I can't recall using that word. I tried awfully to never use it."

Asked if he had ever told former Shoney's area supervisor Steven Sanders to get rid of an employee "because he was a queer," Danner said, "I do not have a recollection of any such incident."

Asked if he had ever given any instruction to a manager, supervisor, or division director to get rid of an employee "because he was queer," Danner said, "Not to my recollection."

Asked if he had ever told former Lee's area supervisor Jim Usrey that customers were prejudiced and Shoney's needed white employees in stores in white areas and black employees in stores in black areas, Danner said, "I can't recall having such a conversation."

Asked if he had ever told former Lee's store manager Terry Toney, who ran a restaurant located on Charlotte Pike in Nashville, that he needed to have the number of black workers coincide with the "neighborhood ethnic group," Danner said, "I have no recollection of a discussion like that. There were always a lot of blacks working in that store."

Asked if he had told Toney, or any other Charlotte Pike Lee's manager, that "you've got way more blacks than you need," Danner said, "I don't recall anything like that."

Asked if he recalled the Valerie Maze incident (when the black counter worker who worked for Terry Toney at the Charlotte Pike Lee's dropped a chicken order while Danner was in the store) Danner said yes, he remembered apologizing to the customer whose order had been dropped. Asked if he had discussed the incident with Toney in the cooler of the restaurant, Danner said, "I do not recall that specific incident, no."

Asked if he could recall a conversation with Toney or another Charlotte Pike Lee's manager in which he said, "There's two types of blacks, there's blacks and there's niggers and you've got niggers working for you," Danner said, "I have no recollection of any discussion containing that type of information."

Asked if he had ever referred to blacks as "niggers" in the presence of former Shoney's vice president for purchasing Linus Leppink, Danner said, "I have no recollection of ever discussing anything like that with him."

Asked if he recalled ever referring to blacks as "niggers" in the presence of former Shoney's CEO Dave Wachtel, Danner said,

"No, sir." In an affidavit, Danner had earlier denied a number of

Wachtel's allegations, including the accusation that Danner had once privately discussed with Wachtel matching contributions senior officials might be willing to make to the Ku Klux Klan. He then said in that affidavit, "Mr. Wachtel's other statements about me also are false or are exaggerations of statements I have made when I may have expressed my opinion that if there was no other explanation for an underperforming store the problem could be the employee mix."

Asked if he recalled ever referring to blacks as "niggers" in the presence of former Captain D's executive Wayne Browning, Danner said, "No, sir."

Asked if he had ever referred to blacks as "niggers" around Hudson-Brown, Wachtel, and Browning, Danner said, "I have no recall of ever having did that in the presence of any of them."

Asked if he had ever told Leppink, after inspecting a store Leppink was then managing in the 1970s, that he "had better" fire black employees, Danner said, "I can never remember an incident where I would have told anyone to fire blacks."

Asked if he had instructed Leppink to "clear out" the black employees at a Nashville Shoney's, Danner said, "I can't recall such an incident ever took place."

Asked if he had ever told former Captain D's division director Jerry Garner he had "too many black employees" working in one of his restaurants, Danner said, "I can't recall such an incident ever with Mr. Garner."

Asked if he had ever told Garner that he had too many black people working on the counter at one of his Captain D's, Danner said, "I can't recall such a discussion."

Asked if he had ever stood on a milk carton or box to talk to former Captain D's manager Ken Adams, Danner said, "That's absolutely not true."

Asked if he had ever told Adams he had "too many niggers" on his counter, "and if he didn't fire the niggers, he would be fired," Danner said, "I have never asked anyone to fire blacks, so therefore in my recollection, that never took place."

Asked if he had ever told former Captain D's executive Billy Dean, at a Shoney's convention in Florida in the early 1980s, "that you could remember at prior meetings or conventions where there were no niggers," Danner said, "I can't recall any such incident ever happening."

Asked if he had ever told Captain D's executive Don Christian that he had "too many blacks" at a store in Nashville, Danner said, "We had an incident that I made a suggestion on at that store," and he went on to describe a situation where there were "almost all the black employees working at night and all the white employees working in the daytime." He had checked out the store because there had been numerous complaints about "playing around" on the night shift, Danner said, "So the suggestion was made would the possibility work if we rescheduled some of the people from the nights, who were willing to shift to the day, and some of the day to the night, that by making this mix where we cut down our tendency to play around at the non-busy hours."

Asked again if he had ever used the term "nigger" in the presence of former Specialty Division executive Karyn Hudson-Brown, Danner said "I recall never having used that in her presence. I do not recall ever having used that in her presence."

Asked if he could state "that you are sure that you did not use the term nigger in [Hudson-Brown's] presence," Danner said, "After all these years and all these times, as I previously stated my position on using that word, I cannot recall the times that I might have used it."

In a sworn affidavit, Danner had previously written, "If the term [nigger] was used it was in reference to a very unsatisfactory situation I observed or learned about concerning a particular store." Asked what he meant by that statement, Danner said, "That would be a similar statement to where I say that if I ever used it, I can't say that I didn't but I cannot recall any specific incidences that I did."

Asked why he said he had used "nigger" in reference to an unsatisfactory situation he had observed in a restaurant, Danner said, "I don't know that I did."

Asked why, then, he had made the statement to that effect in his affidavit, Danner said, "I just can't answer that. I just don't know how to answer it."

Asked if he had reviewed his affidavit before signing it, Danner said, "Yes, sir."

Asked if he had ever told Hudson-Brown that she could not hire blacks as managers or manager trainees, Danner said, "I do not have any recall of having such a discussion."

Asked if he had ever heard former Shoney's division president and chief operating operator Gary Spoleta use the word "nigger" while working at Shoney's, Danner said, "I do not recall ever hearing him use that term in my presence."

Asked if he had heard Spoleta ask a division director at a Monday morning meeting, "How many niggers do you have in the kitchen?" after a cost issue had been raised about a particular restaurant, Danner said, "I have no recollection of him ever making that statement."

Asked had he himself ever stated at a Monday morning meeting, "How many niggers do you have? You know if you have too many, they're taking it out the back door," Danner said, "That type of discussion would have never taken place, in my recollection, in any Monday meeting."

Prior to his deposition, in an answer to one of the interrogatories (written questions posed by the plaintiffs' attorneys), Danner had written that "on occasion" he might have said that "a possible problem area" was that "the specific store in question had too many black employees working in it as compared to the racial mix of the geographical area served by the store." In his deposition, Danner was asked why "too many blacks" would be a problem. He answered, "Well, in trying to call on my memory of all the years I was involved with Shoney's, there was never any hiring practices dictated, there was never any company overall policy, there was never any hire whites, do not hire blacks. There was never any directives to fire blacks and hire whites. The only recollection I could have of anything where it would even be discussed, would be in a situation where over a period of time, a store would be considerably underperforming. Underperforming means in sales, which is the big target. And, of course, from sales you drop down to costs, because if you don't have good sales, your costs get escalated. And after repeated evaluations of a store, it seemed to be staffed well, it seemed to have good people in it, and it seemed to have good operational procedures and it seemed to have good service. The shopper's reports were good. In looking for anything to identify why is this unit underperforming, in some cases I would have probably said that this is a neighborhood of predominantly white neighbors and we have a considerable amount of black employees and this might be a problem."

Danner said he couldn't recall ever giving an opinion to any of his managers that "too many whites in a store" would be a possible problem.

The questions about allegations of discriminatory orders and racial slurs continued. Danner, at one point late in his four-day deposition, said, "Mr. Goldstein, I'm not perfect, but I'm also not a mean guy. I'm a guy who has worked hard for many years, all my life, and I was intent about our operations. Now, if the store was substandard with any of the things that we've identified before that affected customers—quality of food, cleanliness, service times—I would certainly discuss it with whoever the senior manager was. I do not think I was an overbearing, intimidating person at all, but I was certainly one not to avoid the facts of disorder. And it would be discussed, but it would be discussed, as far as my feeling of how I did it, intently but with dignity."

Later, Barry Goldstein said he was satisfied with the deposition. "When you get lots of evidence of discrimination and you've got the guy who can contradict it or explain it but he just says, 'I don't recall,' then where's their defense?" he said. "Like Danner in his deposition. We had all these incidents in which there was evidence of him making some racial slur or committing some direct discrimination, and sometimes he'd admit doing things, and in some cases he'd say, 'I never did that.' Well, my God, if you have some outrageous example of conduct by somebody saying 'Get rid of those black folks,' using racial slurs, and somebody says 'I don't recall doing that,' or 'I don't think I ever did that' or something, that sort of implies to the person listening that [the speaker] might have done it.

"If I said to someone that you went into a restaurant and yelled at a bunch of black people, calling them niggers and telling them to get out of the store, and you said 'I don't recall ever doing that'— if a person didn't do that they'd say 'That is outrageous, don't you ever say I did that, of course I never did that.' So the fact that he said 'I don't recall doing it,' then we have a couple of witnesses saying he did it—where's their defense? Especially when he ad-

mits doing other things that are comparable. 'I don't recall'—
that's a pretty weak statement."

Discovery ended, but the months went by and there was no trial.
Too many questions were still open about the exact definition of
the class, as it turned out, and the judge had to rule on the two-
and-a-half-year-old motions for summary judgment, as well as on
the applicability of the new Civil Rights Act of 1991.

The delay gave Shoney's a chance to reconsider its case. It also
gave the CEO, Len Roberts, a chance to work on Ray Danner some
more to convince him to pay up so the company could settle. As
had been the case for the past two years, though, he said those
talks were inconclusive. Since coming to Shoney's, Roberts had
been successful in paying off a significant amount of the recapitalization debt, in pushing a series of highly visible affirmative-
action initiatives, and in growing the company through an aggressive franchise program. His daughter Dawn had survived the
hit-and-run accident and was home and responding well to therapy. But the lawsuit had plagued him all that time, and he was
ready to do just about anything to make it go away.

Back in October, between the two fall hearings, he had even
tried a little divide-and-conquer. Thinking Barry Goldstein was
the most sympathetic of the plaintiffs' attorneys, Roberts convinced him to fly to Chicago so the two of them could meet alone
in an airport conference room. (They had chosen Chicago, Goldstein said later, because it was "mutually inconvenient.") Roberts
flew up on the corporate plane from Nashville. His offer, though,
was even lower than before: $20 million to settle the claims
against the corporation. Back in March 1990, the money behind
the settlement offer would have come from Danner's bank account, Roberts said, but this time he was dealing strictly with the
corporation's money, and it was all Shoney's could afford. But
Goldstein wasn't buying. He called Warren as soon as he flew back
to Oakland, and the two men agreed that neither would meet
alone with Shoney's attorneys or officials. From then on it would
be both or nothing.

In May 1992, as the parties continued to wait for the judge's
long-delayed rulings on class certification, the summary judgment

motions, and the Civil Rights Act, Shoney's attorneys contacted Warren and Goldstein again, and invited them to a lawyer's office in Pensacola, and then to Butch Powell's beach house on the Gulf of Mexico. Look, they told the plaintiffs' attorneys, Judge Vinson could give you what you want in the class certification, or he could chop your class down to nothing. He already indicated that he's going to cut Lee's and the Specialty Division and the commissary out of the class definition, and with the exception of Robertson Investment Company, you've already agreed yourselves to drop the franchises from the suit. Why wait and take a gamble? They offered to settle for $65 million.

Warren and Goldstein, though, turned down the offer. "We decided to roll the dice," Warren said.

On June 3, 1992, Tommy Warren sat down in his Tallahassee office to go through the day's mail. In it was a fat envelope from the federal court in Pensacola with Judge Vinson's return address. He started reading Vinson's summary of the case, quickly realized what was coming, and flipped through the pages until he found the judge's order in the back. Then he called Barry Goldstein in California to give him the news: Judge Vinson had just certified the largest class of discrimination plaintiffs in U.S. history. Unless Shoney's made a significant settlement offer, and soon, they were going to trial.

The class Judge Vinson had approved was "90 percent of what we were hoping," Warren said later. It consisted of all black store-level employees in company-owned Shoney's and Captain D's restaurants who had valid discrimination claims between February 4, 1988, and April 19, 1991, the cut-off dates based on the earliest and latest charges filed by the named plaintiffs. The proposed class of white plaintiffs, managers who had suffered retaliation because they wouldn't carry out the discriminatory policies, was denied certification because it failed to meet the numerosity requirement by not including enough whites to constitute a class; the Robertson Investment Company employees were also dropped, because the judge ruled that the plaintiffs hadn't established strongly enough that there was direct corporate control over the franchise operations. Shoney's had won around the edges—the judge also axed most of the Section 1981 claims—but with tens of thousands

of putative class members certified, and Ray Danner's own motion for summary judgment rejected, Shoney's had clearly lost the war.

Ironically, among those severed from *Haynes v. Shoney's* in the judge's rulings were Billie and Henry Elliott, who had started everything. Warren told them not to worry, though, and with the judge's approval he immediately filed a separate action against Robertson Investment Company on behalf of the Elliotts, their former assistant manager, Lester Thomas, and the other plaintiffs dropped from the *Haynes* class who had worked for Robertson Investment.

Before concluding his class certification ruling, Judge Vinson included one last note of warning. "It is entirely proper for the trial court to consider the ethical conduct of plaintiffs' counsel in deciding whether to grant class certification," he wrote. "However, as a preliminary matter, I decline to inject yet another highly controversial issue into this already prolonged and complicated action. However, I again stress the seriousness of the defendants' allegations, and I assure the parties that these concerns will not go unaddressed prior to final judgment in this case."

Robertson Investment Company settled first, on October 15, 1992: $437,500 divided among dozens of Marianna and Panama City claimants, including the Elliotts; an equal amount for the attorneys. Shoney's, though, with Ray Danner still refusing to contribute, dragged its heels. July, August, September . . . this time it looked as if the case really would go to trial, and *that*, if only from a business standpoint, was the last thing Len Roberts wanted or believed the company could survive. The holdup, as he saw it, was Danner's Nashville supporters on the board of directors: every time Roberts thought he had Danner nailed down on a settlement plan, they advised against it and everything fell apart.

So in early fall 1992, Roberts called a secret meeting of the four non-Nashville members of the board, plus the two other corporate officers who held a vote. They gathered in Atlanta. "The bottom line of the meeting," Roberts said, "was to all come together and basically say that Ray Danner is not going to settle, we can't get the cooperation from Dan Maddox and Wallace Rasmussen, who were back-pedaling, poisoning the well, trying to make the company come up with more money than I thought at the time was reasonable. They weren't being responsible. Terrible, terrible, terrible, terrible." The participants at the Atlanta meeting agreed that the company would propose a separate settlement agreement with the plaintiffs, according to Roberts, "with the understanding that we would hand over all the evidence and then they could pursue Ray Danner independently."

"That was the play," he said. "It was high-drama, behind-the scenes stuff."

Two others at the meeting, one of whom was Shoney's founder Alex Schoenbaum, confirmed Roberts' account. "That meeting in Atlanta was the turning point of the whole settlement case," Schoenbaum said. "There were four board members at that, and it was something that just had to be done. Hell, it was running everybody crazy. So they asked [Danner] to do it, or else. They had to do it, there wasn't any end to the thing."

Schoenbaum said Gary Brown, Shoney's corporate counsel, delivered the ultimatum to Danner. Roberts said word leaked out about the meeting before it could happen, so he took it on himself to confront Danner's main supporters, Maddox and Rasmussen. "They got wind of the board meeting and the agenda—how they got wind of it, who knows?—but that was the play," Roberts said. "And I said 'With or without the meeting, Dan, you and Wally have forty-eight hours to bring Ray Danner to the table to get this settlement done or this company is going to go down the tubes and I'm not going to be part of it. You've got forty-eight hours or else I'm going to settle it.' And we had the votes."

The total cost of the Shoney's settlement was $132.5 million, which was the plaintiffs' final compromise figure—the largest ever in a racial discrimination case. Ray Danner, in what was supposed to be an anonymous stock donation, paid $67 million. He has consistently refused to comment on his participation.

Tommy Warren, who spent four and a half years of his life fighting Danner and Shoney's, said that aspect of the settlement, while surprising, made sense. "Think about it. You're Ray Danner, you're seventy years old, are you going to let this case go to trial

where you have to sit in court day after day while witness after
witness testifies about how racist you were going back over the
last thirty years of your life with this company? And of course all
this is going to be in the Nashville papers, the *Banner* and the *Ten-*
nessean. Is this how you want to go out? And it's going to take
years, it's going to drag on forever with the trials and the appeals.
You're going to look at what it'll cost you, instead, as a percentage
of your overall worth, and say, 'Maybe $67 million isn't so bad to
make all this go away.'"

Nothing like it had ever happened before, Warren said. "This is
unprecedented in the history of civil rights law for the former CEO
of a major corporation, the principal shareholder, to be forced to
pay half of the cost of a multimillion dollar settlement out of his
own pocket. It's just incredible. I'd say Len Roberts did one amazing job getting Ray Danner to do that."

The final terms of the consent decree guaranteeing the settlement were hammered out during the last week in October 1992,
capped by an all-night negotiation session in Nashville starting at
11:00 A.M. on November 1 and ending the following afternoon.
The attorneys hit an impasse at 3:00 A.M.; the bargaining tool
used by the plaintiffs to get the negotiations back on track was
that if they finished the next day they could then announce the
agreement on November 3, an attractive date for Shoney's because
it meant news of the record settlement would be buried under
front-page coverage of the 1992 presidential election.

Which, in fact, is what happened.

SEVENTEEN

66 If I Had It to Do Over Again, I Would Do the Same Thing 99

Twenty-eight thousand, nine hundred and ninety-four claims were submitted in the Shoney's settlement, which in the end, at Warren and Goldstein's insistence, was expanded beyond the scope of the certified class to include all the Shoney's divisions, though none of the franchise stores, and to cover the period from 1985 through November 3, 1992. Based on a complex formula approved by Judge Vinson to determine the validity of those claims and the amount due each legitimate claimant, 20,909 people ultimately received money from the $105 million settlement pool. The plaintiffs' attorneys spent nearly $2 million to notify those claimants about the settlement, an effort that the judge said was unmatched by any he had ever seen in a class-action case.

Approximately $5 million from the settlement pool was designated for a special class of claimants, those who had been witnesses and named plaintiffs in the case; $10 million was earmarked for black former job applicants; and the bulk of the settlement, $90 million, went to incumbent black employees. The primary considerations for incumbent employees in determining the amount due were length of employment and proof of specific incidents of promotion denial, racial harassment, retaliation, or illegal termination. In the case of job applicants, the date and number of applications filed were the key factors. The average settlement for the 18,565 qualified incumbents who submitted claims was $4,850, based on the formula approved by Judge Vinson; the average for the 2,344 qualified applicants was $4,300. Any money left over once the settlement is complete, after Shoney's final payment in 1998, will be divided among five organizations: the United Negro College Fund, the Southern Poverty Law Center, the Lawyer's Committee for Civil Rights under Law, the Washington Lawyer's Committee for Civil Rights under Law, and Inroads, a group that works to increase management opportunities for minorities.

Warren, Goldstein, and the other plaintiffs' attorneys received $20 million for their four and a half years of work. Shoney's also agreed to pay them $5.5 million more over the next ten years to help implement the federal court-ordered consent decree and to serve as outside monitors of the company's affirmative action plan.

In the final section of the consent decree, Judge Vinson wrote, "These amounts reflect the importance of the case, the high quality of representation, the undesirability of the case, the exceptional results obtained, including the size of the monetary award, the expenditure of time and resources, and the delay in payment of any compensation." He never again addressed the ethics charges brought against Warren, except in an interview with the author three years later in which he dismissed them as "collateral issues."

The settlement was bittersweet for Len Roberts. On the eve of the December 1992 Shoney's board meeting, he was forced out of the company for reasons that were never publicly disclosed. Alex Schoenbaum claimed the board thought Roberts was wrecking the company by over-franchising and that he was spending too much time promoting himself when he should have been in the stores. Some company officials complained to the *Wall Street Journal* that Roberts was too aggressive in pushing affirmative action, and when he extended the program to include Shoney's suppliers, his enemies outnumbered his friends. Whatever the board's reasons, Roberts accepted the approximately $3 million Shoney's offered and took his family on a cruise to Mexico. A year and a half later the Tandy Corporation offered him a job as president of Radio Shack in Fort Worth, Texas, where he now lives with his wife and youngest daughter. His oldest daughter, Dawn, still faces more surgery five years after she was run down by a drunk driver, but she has finished college and now works and has her own apartment in Dallas.

Butch Powell continues to practice law in Birmingham, Alabama, but he no longer serves as Shoney's labor counsel. He refused to be interviewed about his work on *Haynes v. Shoney's* and wouldn't respond to an extensive list of written questions. Roberts and Steve Tallent both contacted the author on his behalf, however. Roberts praised Powell's work, saying he had been a "competent" lawyer for Shoney's. Tallent, in a brief letter, wrote, "As for tactics, Mr. Powell in deed [*sic*] throughout my involvement in the case proved to be a restraining influence on both the client and the lawyers." And he also wrote, "In my professional opinion, the Shoney's lawsuit would never have settled without Mr. Powell's involvement."

The only official comment on the lawsuit for this account by the Shoney's corporation—which agreed to the settlement on the condition that it wouldn't have to admit any guilt, a standard clause in most settlement agreements—was a June 5, 1995, letter from Betty Marshall, an African American brought in by Len Roberts as vice president for corporate and community affairs. The company's "track record" since the lawsuit was filed shows Shoney's "commitment to diversity," Marshall wrote. "Since 1989, the number of black employees in management has increased from 14.5 percent to 22 percent. During that same time period, the number of black hourly employees has risen from 27.5 percent of our total work force to 32 percent." Marshall also noted an increase in Shoney's business with minority-owned companies and the rising number of minority-owned franchises.

Tommy Warren was quick to praise Shoney's compliance with the affirmative action plan in the consent decree and said the company's hiring record looks even better through 1994 when compared to 1988, the year before the lawsuit was filed. "They've continued heading in the right direction," he said recently. "It's very encouraging how they've continued to improve. And if you track Shoney's numbers over time since the lawsuit you'll see that there hasn't been any backsliding."

The most dramatic jump in minority employment has been in the Shoney's division, according to Warren, which is the corporation's largest. In 1988 only 1.8 percent of the Shoney's restaurant managers were black; in 1995 that figure was 12 percent. Assistant managers at company-owned Shoney's restaurants have risen from 5 percent to 21 percent; dining room supervisors from 3 percent to 13 percent; and servers from 7.6 percent to more than 18 percent. Similar trends are apparent in all the other divisions as well, including Captain D's, where the percentage of black managers rose from 9.5 in 1988 to 22.4 in 1995.

Corporate management at Shoney's, Inc. was unstable for several years, however, and the company's stock value dropped significantly, falling by more than half in 1994 alone. Partly as a result, the company announced in January 1995 that it was selling off its Lee's Famous Recipe, Shoney's Inns, and Specialty divisions, keeping only the Captain D's and Shoney's restaurants. In the spring of 1995, though, the board of directors announced that it was bringing in a new management team, the second since Len Roberts' departure. That team, headed by Stephen Lynn, former chairman and CEO of the Sonic Corp., an Oklahoma-based hamburger-restaurant chain, has continued the turnaround in the corporation, both financially and in hiring, promotion, and business opportunities for minorities. Many of the upper-level managers in place during the Danner years and accused in the lawsuit of carrying out the discriminatory practices have since left the company.

A front-page story in the *Wall Street Journal* on April 6, 1996, chronicled more of the changes since 1989: eighty-three more black dining room supervisors; two black vice presidents; an African American woman on the board of directors; thirteen black-owned franchises; and $17 million annually in goods and services from minority-owned companies. The company and the SCLC also say that the voluntary covenant between the two, twice renewed since the original agreement in 1989, has helped funnel more than $194 million overall into minority-owned businesses and organizations and into black employees' salaries.

"This is the kind of turnaround that we like to see," Warren told a *Journal* reporter. "I've been in this business for twenty years and I've seen lots of whitewashes. This is real. Black people know this is a company where they can get ahead."

In 1993, not long after the case settled, Paul and Jan Suggs, the area supervisors who had fired Billie and Henry Elliott from the Marianna Captain D's back in 1988, bought out Charlie Robertson's half of Robertson Investment Company, which they now run with Ray Danner's son Roger as an absentee partner. Charlie Robertson wasn't out of the Shoney's family long, however. He currently owns and operates Captain D's franchises in Tallahassee.

Ray Danner resigned from the board of directors of Shoney's in spring 1993. He agreed at that time to sell his remaining shares back to the company—10.4 percent of all Shoney's stock—severing once and for all his connection to the business he had built. When stock prices began dropping shortly after that, however, Shoney's refused to meet his asking price. Danner subsequently held a press conference to denounce the board and announce that he would probably never eat at a Shoney's restaurant again. He still lives in Nashville, where he has developed an investment empire through his Danner Company worth hundreds of millions of dollars, and he is still one of the wealthiest men in America.

In spring 1995, with the company in the midst of its latest executive turnover, Danner mounted a comeback bid, offering to return as CEO and chairman of the board for $1 a year until he turned the business around. When the board failed to respond to the offer, which had been widely reported in the industry press (including a long article in the *Wall Street Journal*), Danner withdrew his bid and went back home.

Barry Goldstein is now the managing partner of Saperstein, Goldstein, Demchak and Baller in Oakland, California, and continues to bring employment-discrimination cases. An article in *Business Week* recently branded his firm "The SWAT Team of Bias Litigation." He coaches little league baseball for his four children.

Tommy Warren and his wife had their fourth child, Nick, on December 30, 1992, though they deny they were trying to keep up with the Goldsteins. In July 1995, Warren, Goldstein, Sam Smith, and Charles Burr, one of the attorneys who helped represent Shoney's in the *Haynes* litigation, filed another major class-action complaint in a gender-bias case against the Publix grocery store chain, the largest private employer in the state of Florida. That case won class certification in early 1996 and settled in January 1997 for $81,500,000. Much of Warren's time since *Haynes*, however, has been spent volunteering in his children's classrooms and working on community projects in Tallahassee city schools with heavy concentrations of students from low-income families.

Billie Elliott drove a bus for four years at Sunland, a state facility for the mentally handicapped, until a back injury prevented her from working. Henry Elliott bought a bread truck and is now an independent contractor, driving a commercial route for a Marianna bakery. They received approximately $175,000 as their share of the Shoney's and Robertson Investment Company settlements, enough to build a house where their trailer once stood, a couple of miles south of town and a rock's throw away from the Chipola River, though they recently decided to sell the house and move half an hour south to the Gulf Coast.

"If I had it to do over again, I would do the same thing," Billie Elliott told a local reporter shortly after the case ended. "I think it's made me stronger. I will not sit back and watch people do me and other people wrong. If you know what's right, you've got to keep plugging away. . . . I'm so happy that a lot of people were justified by what we did. I feel like if more people would stand up to people like this, a lot of people wouldn't be done the way we were. And there's a whole lot more places around here where the same things happen."

In December 1994, as Warren's Tallahassee law office was busy mailing out settlement checks, he received a letter, handwritten and not very legible, from one of the 21,000 claimants, whom he had never met. The woman's share of the settlement was around $900. "Dear Mr. T. A. Warren," the woman wrote. "You'll said if I don't here from you to write. So I [am] letting you know that my name and address still the same. . . . No one never did anything like this for me. Hay, it's hard out here in this world. I wish that it was more people in the world like you. You have great heart. May God bleast you all."

NOTES ON SOURCES

Chapter 1

The chapter title is taken from a sworn declaration in *Haynes* by a former Shoney's manager, David Pulliam.

Ray Danner was listed as the 266th richest man in America by *Forbes* magazine during the mid-1980s, a ranking that was reported prominently by both Nashville newspapers, the *Banner* and the *Tennessean*. The account of the "fish incident" is taken from Jerry Garner's deposition and sworn declaration in *Haynes* cited in the plaintiffs' July 25, 1989, Motion for Summary Judgment on the Issue of Liability. Garner repeated that account in a 1995 interview with the author. Danner in his own *Haynes* deposition confirmed the visit to Murphy's restaurant and the discovery of the underweight fish, but he denied the rest of Garner's account. Another former Shoney's executive, Barbara Cragg, testified in her deposition about a fish incident at company headquarters similar to the one described by Garner but without the racial slurs. The incident described by Garner is discussed further in chapter 10.

Information about the number of Shoney's, Inc. restaurants and the amount of business is taken from the corporation's annual reports. Shoney's ranking as the second-largest family restaurant chain in the country was reported in the trade publication *Nation's Restaurant News*.

Danner was referred to as "our great leader" in corporate literature, attached as exhibits to Danner's deposition in *Haynes*, by former Shoney's president Gary Spoleta. Other sources on Danner, the history of the company, and *Haynes v. Shoney's* are the *American Bar Association Journal*, *Time* magazine, the *New York Times*, the *Wall Street Journal*, *Business Week*, the *Wall Street Transcript*, the *National Law Journal*, the *Nashville Tennessean*, the *Nashville Banner*, *Louisville Business First*, and a two-page biography included in a brochure produced by the Danner Foundation entitled "Danner Foundation Recipients: A Representative Listing."

The summary of the *Haynes* case is based on the plaintiffs' original and amended complaints. A number of witnesses testified about the use of racial slurs and color-coding applications in the company, and those charges are summarized in the plaintiffs' May 15, 1992, Pre-Trial Stipulation and Exhibits, and Proposed Findings of Fact. Danner's purported threat to run over blacks is taken from the Don Hitchcock deposition, the

Klan allegation is taken from the Dave Wachtel deposition, and the report of Ray Danner's "laws" is taken from the Wayne Browning deposition in *Haynes*. Former Shoney's CEO Leonard Roberts described the litigation as growing "bloodier" in a 1994 interview with the author.

Plaintiffs' attorneys Tommy Warren, Barry Goldstein, and Sam Smith all discussed the failures of the EEOC in dealing with Shoney's in interviews with the author. The original SCLC covenant with Shoney's has been widely reported, most recently in a 1996 *Wall Street Journal* article that reviewed the history of the agreement since it was first signed in 1989. A summary, with supporting documents, of the plaintiffs' charges about the company's failure to fulfill the terms of the covenant is included in several pleadings, including the Pre-Trial Stipulation and Proposed Findings of Fact.

Richard Epstein, in his book *Forbidden Grounds*, has been one of the most forceful in making the case against employment discrimination laws.

Chapter 2

The chapter title is taken from Billie Elliott's deposition in *Haynes*.

Information about Warren's background is taken from interviews with the author, various newspaper accounts, conversations with other attorneys in Tallahassee, and Warren's deposition in *Haynes*. Information about the circumstances of the first meeting between Warren and the Elliotts is taken from interviews with each by the author. The summary of the Elliotts' accusations and all specific references to and quotes concerning their charges are taken from their depositions in *Haynes*. Information on their background is taken from interviews with the author and from their deposition testimony. Some details about the Danners' inspection of the Marianna store are taken from the Elliotts' interview with the author. Sources for this chapter also include the author's interviews with Barry Goldstein and deposition testimony in *Haynes* from Julia Hunter, Deborah Bell, Kim Gilmore, Donna Mongoven, Lester Thomas, Madeline Herring, and Roger Danner. As noted, Paul and Jan Suggs and Charles Robertson denied the charges against them in affidavits; all three, in individual interviews with the author, refused to discuss specific allegations in the case.

Chapter 3

The chapter title is taken from deposition testimony in *Haynes* by Leonard Charles Williams.

Information on Warren's early experiences in Marianna is taken from
the author's interviews with Warren and the Elliotts. Background information on the Elliotts included in this chapter is taken from interviews
with them together and separately by the author. Information on Marianna and Jackson County is taken from a variety of sources: visits by the
author, interviews with current and former residents, deposition testimony from the Marianna witnesses in *Haynes,* Chamber of Commerce
literature, accounts in the *Jackson County Floridan,* and books by histo-
rians Jerrell Shofner and James McGovern. The allegations about discriminatory practices at Robertson Investment Company are taken from
deposition testimony, charges of discrimination, affidavits, and sworn
declarations in *Haynes* by Lester Thomas, Stephanie Cooper, Madeline
Herring, Gwendolyn Smith, Angela Sorey, Debora Newton, Maxine
White, Tracie Holley, Donna Mongoven, Kim Gilmore, Glen McClain,
Mike Oglesby, John Corley, Mike Haisten, Kim Barbero, and Leonard
Charles Williams. Barry Goldstein's comments were made in a 1995 interview with the author. Roger Danner did not respond to the author's
interview requests but did deny the charges against him in a deposition.

Chapter 4

The chapter title is taken from Dave Wachtel's deposition in *Haynes.*

Warren's 1993 comments about the case were reported in an article in
the *St. Petersburg Times.* Other comments about the early stages of the
investigation and Warren's initial contacts with Goldstein come from the
author's interviews with Warren and Goldstein. Background on the LDF
is taken from Jack Greenberg's book *Crusaders in the Courts* and from
the author's interviews with Goldstein. Characterization of the civil-
rights climate at the end of the 1980s and the early 1990s is based on a
number of newspaper and magazine reports; sources include *Nation's
Business, Commentary,* the *New Republic,* the *New York Times,* the
Washington Post, the *National Law Journal,* and the *Atlantic Monthly.*
Warren, Goldstein, and Len Roberts confirmed the account of Shoney's
paying the plaintiffs' attorney's fees during the latter stages of the litigation moratorium in 1990.

The account of the founding of Shoney's and its early growth and development is based on numerous newspaper and magazine reports; sources
include *Time, Business Week,* the *New York Times,* the *Nashville Tennessean,* the *Nashville Banner,* the *Wall Street Journal,* the *Wall Street
Transcript, Restaurant Business,* and *Nation's Restaurant News.* Other
sources include Danner's biography in the Danner Foundation brochure

"Danner Foundation Recipients: A Representative Listing"; the author's interviews with Alex Schoenbaum, Mitch Boyd, Dave Wachtel, Karyn Hudson-Brown, and Linus Leppink; Danner's deposition testimony in *Haynes*, with exhibits including the "Shoney's, Inc. Values" memo; and *Haynes* depositions given by Karyn Hudson-Brown, John Oglesby, Barbara Cragg, and Dave Wachtel.

Chapter 5

The chapter title is taken from the author's interview with Thomas Warren.

The account of the Elliotts' struggles to find work is taken from their depositions in *Haynes* and from interviews with the author. All direct quotes and references to discrimination at Robertson Investment are taken from the Elliotts' depositions. The accounts from Smith, Cooper, Herring, Bell, Hunter, Thomas, and Corley are taken from their depositions in *Haynes*. Corley's allegations about Charles Robertson are taken from Corley's deposition. Other sources for that account were the author's interviews with Thomas Warren, FBI agent Paul Maxwell, and Charles Robertson.

The EEOC cause findings were entered into the *Haynes* court record on June 29, 1990, as a supplement to the plaintiffs' Opposition to Robertson Investment's Motion for Summary Judgment and in support of the plaintiffs' own Motion for Summary Judgment. Robertson Investment officials denied the charges against the company in RIC's May 18, 1990, Statement of Material Facts as to Which There Are Genuine Issues to be Tried with Respect to Plaintiffs' Motion for Summary Judgment.

Warren's and Goldstein's accounts of the early meetings with Robertson Investment's attorneys and with Shoney's attorney Butch Powell are taken from interviews with the author. Powell, in a letter to the author, refused to be interviewed about the case for this account and did not respond to an extensive list of written questions concerning his role in the litigation.

Chapter 6

The chapter title is taken from Brenda Johnston's deposition testimony in *Johnson v. Long*.

Accounts of the early stages of the investigation beyond Robertson Investment Company are taken from the author's interviews with Warren,

Goldstein, attorney Pat O'Rourke, and paralegal Carol Condon. The "key
witness" cited in deposition testimony from *Haynes* purportedly quoting
former Shoney's president Gary Spoleta about the *Johnson v. Long* settlement is Eugene Yager.
    The account of the events in *Johnson v. Long* is based on the depositions
and sworn declarations in that case from Sharon Johnson, Pat Short, Ellen
Nix, Brenda Johnston, Cathy Shaw, Harrell Shaw, and Eugene Yager, supplemented by the author's interviews with Johnson and her attorney,
Larry Raby, and with Yager's subsequent deposition and affidavits in
Haynes.
    All Eugene Yager's personnel documents, including those indicating the
date of his stock purchase and the official reason for his termination, were
introduced into the *Haynes* court record as exhibits to the deposition he
gave in that case. His comments in this account are taken from that second deposition and from two sworn affidavits attached as exhibits to that
deposition.
    Debra Tompkins's comments are taken from her deposition testimony
in *Haynes.* The account of Shoney's response to the Montgomery case and
Powell's comments concerning Yager is taken from the official transcript
of the January 3, 1991, hearing in *Haynes.*
    The account of Shoney's counsel's contact with Goldstein to "warn"
him about Warren is based on the author's interviews with Goldstein and
Warren. Attorney Steve Tallent did not respond to the author's interview
requests. Attorney Butch Powell refused to discuss the case with the author and did not respond to an extensive list of written questions about
his conduct and role in the litigation, including the contact with Goldstein about Warren.
    The summary of the site-survey of Shoney's, Inc. restaurants is taken
from the final report to the plaintiffs' attorneys by the Commonwealth
Group.

Chapter 7

The chapter title is from former FSU football coach Bill Peterson, quoted
in historian Jim Jones's *FSU One Time!*
    Other chapter sources are the author's interviews with Thomas Warren,
David Ammerman, Esther Warren, Barry Goldstein, Charles Burr, and
Tony Lawson; Jones's *FSU One Time!;* the *St. Petersburg Times*, the
Miami Herald, the *Tallahassee Democrat*, and the *Ft. Lauderdale Sun-
Sentinel's Sunshine* magazine; Warren's deposition in *Haynes;* case

summaries in *U.S. v. Warren* 550 F.2d 219 (5th Cir. 1977), and in *U.S. v. Warren* 578 F.2d 1058 (5th Cir. 1978); and the January 3, 1991, hearing transcript in *Haynes*.

Chapter 8

The chapter title is taken from the author's interview with Warren.

Other chapter sources are the author's interviews with Warren, Pat O'Rourke, Carol Condon, Barry Goldstein, Karyn Hudson-Brown, Jerry Garner, and Linus Leppink; *Haynes* depositions from Terry Toney, Valerie Maze, Jim Bland, Wilma Rudolph, Jim Usrey, and Danny Gibson; the *St. Petersburg Times; Glenn v. General Motors Corp.* 658 F.Supp. 918 (N.D. Ala. 1986), and *Glenn v. General Motors Corp.* 841 F.2d 1567 (11th Cir. 1988). Eugene Grayer agreed to be interviewed by the author in Nashville, but failed to show up for those interview appointments.

Chapter 9

The chapter title is taken from the author's interview with Barry Goldstein.

Other chapter sources include the author's interviews with Thomas Warren and Barry Goldstein and the following pleadings: the plaintiffs' April 5, 1989, Class Action Complaint; the plaintiffs' July 3, 1989, Motion for Class Certification; the November 11 and 12, 1991, Class Certification Hearing Transcript; Shoney's August 14, 1990, Motion for Summary Judgment as to All Claims Asserted by Plaintiff Dewitt Nelson; Shoney's October 3, 1990, Motion for Summary Judgment as to All Claims Asserted by Plaintiff Denise Riley; depositions from Haynes, Nelson, Bonsall, Riley; the plaintiffs' July 25, 1989, Motion for Summary Judgment on the Issue of Liability; Ray Danner's April 27, 1989, Motion to Dismiss; the plaintiffs' April 28, 1989, Request for Barry Goldstein to Appear *Pro Hac Vice*; Shoney's April 27, 1989, Response to the Motion to Admit Barry Goldstein *Pro Hac Vice*; the May 30, 1989, order granting the request for Barry Goldstein to appear *Pro Hac Vice*; Shoney's July 12, 1989, Emergency Motion for Protective Order and for Imposition of Sanctions; Shoney's July 26, 1989, Supplement to the Emergency Motion for Protective Order and Imposition of Sanctions; the plaintiffs' August 8, 1989, Response in Opposition to Shoney's Emergency Motion for Protective Order and for Imposition of Sanctions, and subsequent related pleadings.

The list of racial slurs discovered by Warren in his investigation is drawn from extensive testimony cited in the plaintiffs' May 15, 1992, Pre-

Trial Stipulation and Proposed Findings of Fact. The account of the Denny's suit is taken from reports in the *New York Times Magazine,* the *Washington Post,* and the author's interview with plaintiffs' attorney Mari Mayeda.

Other sources for this chapter are the author's interviews with Mitch Boyd, Alex Schoenbaum, Ron Wooten, and Joseph Lowery; the Ray Danner, Dave Wachtel, Benny Ball, and Mickey Skelton depositions in *Haynes;* news reports from the *Wall Street Journal,* the *Nashville Banner,* and the *Nashville Tennessean;* and the SCLC Covenant with Shoney's, Inc. The "Partnership Agreement" memo, the B&C public relations documents, the Jim Patterson memo concerning EEOC reports, and correspondence concerning the "donated" fax machine were attached as exhibits to the Skelton and Ball depositions.

The account of Spoleta's arrest is taken from copies of the bail receipt, arrest warrant, and expungement order, included as attachments to the plaintiffs' March 20, 1992, Response in Opposition to Shoney's Motion for Protective Order as to Depositions Noticed for March 18–20, 1992, and from the author's interviews with Linus Leppink, who bailed Spoleta out of jail after his arrest, and with former Shoney's CEO Mitch Boyd. Spoleta, in a brief interview with the author, refused to comment on the arrest or on any other aspects of the lawsuit.

Shoney's general counsel Gary Brown, in response to the author's requests for interviews with members of the corporation's board of directors, reported that the board had taken a position that no members would comment on the lawsuit or speak to the author for this account.

Chapter 10

The chapter title is taken from an interview with Thomas Warren, quoting attorney Jim Neal.

Other chapter sources are the author's interviews with Warren, Barry Goldstein, Henry Elliott, Lynn Harvey, Carol Condon, Charles Burr, Elaine Feingold, Judge Roger Vinson, Jerry Garner, Wayne Browning, Gary Brown, Mitch Boyd, Len Roberts, Alex Schoenbaum, Sam Smith, Tony Lawson, and Pat O'Rourke; sworn statement, affidavit, and hearing testimony from Debora Newton, cited in the November 20–21, 1991, Class Certification Hearing transcript; Robertson Investment Company's July 21, 1989, Emergency Motion for Protective Order and Imposition of Sanctions, and subsequent related pleadings; the plaintiffs' July 24, 1989, Motion for Summary Judgment; Shoney's November 15, 1990, Memorandum of Points and Authorities with Supporting Materials in Opposition

to Plaintiffs' Motion for Summary Judgment, and subsequent related
pleadings; the Roger Danner, Jerry Garner, Ray Danner, Don Christian,
Buddy Bonsall, Richard Pennington, and James Larry Marks deposition
transcripts, with exhibits; the *St. Petersburg Times*, the *Wall Street Journal*, the *Nashville Tennessean*, and the *Nashville Banner*.

Mitch Boyd was provided with a copy of his comments for this account
by the author and confirmed their accuracy in a fax to the author and in
follow-up interviews.

Warren and Goldstein, in separate interviews, gave the same account of
the 1990 encounter among the four attorneys—Warren, Goldstein, Tallent, and Powell—in the Nashville hotel bar. As mentioned above, Powell, in a letter to the author, refused to comment on any aspect of the case,
and Tallent did not respond to the author's requests for an interview except in a 1995 letter in which he defended Powell's conduct. Powell did
not respond to a written list of questions from the author which included
questions about the encounter in the Nashville bar.

Chapter 11

The chapter title is taken from an interview with former Shoney's CEO
Len Roberts.

Other sources are the author's interviews with Len Roberts, Laurie
Roberts, Mitch Boyd, Thomas Warren, Barry Goldstein, and Alex Schoenbaum; Len Roberts's October 29, 1990, letter to the Athens, Ga., Probation Office; the *Wall Street Journal*, *Nation's Restaurant News*, *Restaurant Business*, and the *Nashville Banner*. Ray Danner originally agreed,
through his spokesman Francis Guess, to respond to written questions
from the author for this account. After receiving that list, which included
questions concerning the statements made by Len Roberts, Danner's attorney, C. K. McLemore, wrote to the author saying that Danner refused
to respond.

Chapter 12

Sources for this chapter include *Legal Times*, *Time* magazine, *Nation's
Business*, the *New York Times*, the *Washington Post*, *Commentary*, the
New Republic, the *Wall Street Journal*, the *Nashville Tennessean*, the
Nashville Banner, *Congressional Digest*, and *The Supreme Court, Race,
and Civil Rights*; the U.S. House Committee on Education and Labor's
Hearings on the Civil Rights Act of 1990; and the U.S. Senate Committee
on Labor and Human Resources' *Report on the Civil Rights Act of 1990*.

Other sources are the November 20 and 21 Class Certification hearings

in *Haynes;* the authors' interviews with Thomas Warren, Barry Goldstein, Len Roberts, Dave Wachtel, and Karyn Hudson-Brown; Shoney's
June 11, 1990, Motion for Summary Judgment on Section 1981 Claims,
and subsequent related pleadings; Robertson Investment Company's December 20, 1990, Motion for Summary Judgment on Section 1981 Claims,
and subsequent related pleadings; the plaintiffs' April 30, 1990, Supplemental Memorandum in Support of the Motion for Summary Judgment,
with Statement of Material Facts; the plaintiffs' May 15, 1992, Trial Brief,
Pre-Trial Stipulation and Exhibits, and Proposed Findings of Fact; Shoney's June 11, 1990, Opposition to Class Certification and Request for
Evidentiary Hearing; Shoney's May 15, 1992, Trial Brief and Proposed
Findings of Fact and Conclusions of Law; plaintiffs' Motion for Leave to
File Third Amended Complaint; depositions and/or sworn affidavits from
Jerry Garner, Phyllis Blower, Don Hitchcock, Tim Wilson, Thomas Buck-
ner, Wayne Browning, Karyn Hudson-Brown, Dave Wachtel, Don Chris-
tian, and Ray Danner, with deposition exhibits from Danner including
the Wankat Letter.

Economist Paul Andrisani did not respond to the author's interview requests except indirectly, through former Shoney's labor counsel Butch
Powell, who in a letter said that Andrisani had been employed by the defense counsel in *Haynes* and that "permission has not been granted to
him to discuss with [the author] any aspect of that litigation."

Chapter 13

The chapter title is taken from the Danner Foundation's biography of Ray
Danner.

Chapter sources include the authors' interviews with Warren, Mary
Ellen Martin, Lynn Harvey, Sam Smith, Barry Goldstein, Tony Lawson,
Mitch Boyd, Linus Leppink, Dave Wachtel, John Siegenthaler, and Carol
Condon; deposition testimony, with exhibits, from Benny Ball, Mickey
Skelton, Dave Wachtel, and Ray Danner; Ray Danner letter to Julius
Chambers; *Danner v. Danner;* the *Nashville Tennessean,* the *Nashville
Banner, Business Nashville, Louisville Business First,* and the Danner
Foundation brochure "Danner Foundation Recipients: A Representative
Listing."

Chapter 14

The chapter title is taken from the author's interview with Tanya Catani
Edwards.

Other sources for this chapter include the author's interviews with

Judge Roger Vinson, Barry Goldstein, Tony Lawson, Tommy Warren, Tim Harley, Tanya Catani Edwards, Sam Smith, and Elaine Feingold; the July 6, 1989, January 3, 1991, September 18 and 19, 1991, and November 20 and 21, 1991, hearing transcripts from *Haynes*; Shoney's July 12, 1989, Emergency Motion for Protective Order and for Imposition of Sanctions and subsequent related pleadings; Plaintiffs' August 8, 1989, Response in Opposition to Defendant Shoney's Emergency Motion for Protective Order and for Imposition of Sanctions and subsequent related pleadings; Shoney's June 11, 1990, Motion for Summary Judgment on Section 1981 Claims and subsequent related pleadings; Robertson Investment Company's December 20, 1990, Motion for Summary Judgment on Plaintiffs' Section 1981 Claims with Supporting Memorandum of Law; Shoney's August 14, 1990, Motion for Summary Judgment as to All Claims Asserted by Plaintiff Dewitt Nelson and subsequent related pleadings; Shoney's September 6, 1990, Motion for Summary Judgment as to All Claims Asserted by Plaintiff Buddy Bonsall and subsequent related pleadings; Shoney's October 3, 1990, Motion for Summary Judgment as to All Claims Asserted by Plaintiff Denise Riley and subsequent related pleadings; June 29, 1992, Order regarding Summary Judgment on Title VII and Section 1981 Claims.

Other sources were depositions, with sworn declarations and affidavits, from Thomas Warren and Tanya Catani Edwards; Sam Smith and Tony Lawson affidavits; Steve Tallent's June 5, 1995, letter to the author; and Tanya Catani Edwards's September 8, 1995, letter to the author.

Chapter 15

The chapter title is taken from the author's interview with Thomas Warren.

Sources for this chapter are the author's interviews with Judge Roger Vinson, Barry Goldstein, Thomas Warren, James Finney, and Don Livingston; deposition testimony, with exhibits, from Philip Peavy, Terrell Forte, Mickey Skelton, and Benny Ball; the *Washington Post*, the *Wall Street Journal*, and the *Atlantic Monthly*.

Other sources were the May 20, 1991, Motion of the Equal Employment Opportunity Commission for Leave to File a Brief as Amicus Curiae; the September 4, 1994, Order denying EEOC Motion for Leave to File a Brief as Amicus Curiae; the plaintiffs' June 29, 1990, Supplement by Submission of Twelve EEOC Determinations against Robertson Investment Co. to Plaintiffs' Opposition to Defendants' Motions for Summary Judgment and Motion to Dismiss and in Support of Plaintiffs' Motion for Summary

and Proposed Findings of Fact; U.S. House Committee on Education and
Labor, *Report on the Investigation of Civil Rights Enforcement by the*
Equal Employment Opportunity Commission; U.S. House Committee
on Education and Labor, Subcommittee on Employment Opportunities,
Hearing on Equal Employment Opportunity Commission Policies Re-
garding Goals and Timetables in Litigation Remedies; U.S. General Ac-
counting Office, *Equal Employment Opportunity Commission Closed*
Discrimination Charges without Full Investigation; Equal Employment
Opportunity Commission, "Office of Program Operations Enforcement
Statistics FY 1981–FY 1991"; EEOC, "Office of General Counsel Litigation Statistics FY 1981–FY 1991"; and Barry Goldstein's July 19, 1991,
letter to the EEOC.

Chapter 16

The chapter title is taken from the author's interview with Thomas
Warren.

Sources for this chapter include the author's interviews with Tony Law-
son, Sam Smith, Tanya Catani Edwards, Tommy Warren, Barry Goldstein,
Billie Elliott, Carolyn Cobb, Josephine Haynes, Len Roberts, Charles Burr,
Alex Schoenbaum, Gary Brown; *Haynes* deposition from Ray Danner,
with exhibits; the *Washington Post*, the *Nashville Banner*, the *Nashville*
Tennessean, the *Wall Street Journal*, *Restaurant Business*, and *Nation's*
Restaurant News.

Other sources are the January 3, 1991, September 18 and 19, 1991, and
November 20 and 21, 1991, Hearings in *Haynes;* Shoney's November 27,
1991, Brief on the Nonapplicability of the Civil Rights Act of 1991; Plaintiffs' Motion for the Court to Rule that the Civil Rights Act of 1991 Ap-
plies to this Action; Ray Danner's December 30, 1991, Memorandum of
Law in Opposition to Plaintiffs' Motion for the Court to Rule that the
Civil Rights Act of 1991 Applies to this Action; the March 12, 1992, Order
Approving Prospective Application but Denying Retroactive Application
of the Civil Rights Act of 1991; the June 22, 1991, Order on Class Cer-
tification; the June 29, 1992, Order regarding Summary Judgment on
Title VII and Section 1981 Claims; the July 7, 1992, Order Creating a
Separate Action, *Elliott et al. v. Robertson Investment;* the October 5,
1992, Order Granting Provisional Approval of Consent Decree, *Elliott v.*
Robertson Investment; and the November 3, 1992, Stipulation of Settle-
ment and Order of Provisional Entry of Consent Decree, *Haynes v.*
Shoney's.

Notes on Sources

The chapter title is taken from Billie Elliott's interview with the *Tallahassee Democrat*.

Sources for this chapter are the author's interviews with Thomas Warren, Len Roberts, Barry Goldstein, Alex Schoenbaum, Charles Robertson, Paul Suggs, Billie and Henry Elliott, Sam Smith, and Charles Burr; the *Wall Street Journal*, the *Nashville Tennessean*, the *Nashville Banner*, *Nation's Restaurant News*, *Restaurant Business*, the *Washington Post*, *Business Week*, *Nashville Business*, the *Miami Herald*, the *St. Petersburg Times*, the *Tallahassee Democrat*, and the *Palm Beach Post*; Betty Marshall's June 5, 1995, letter to the author; Stephen Tallent's June 5, 1995, letter to the author; December 17, 1992, Order Approving Consent Decree, *Elliott v. Robertson Investment*; January 25, 1993, Order Approving Consent Decree, *Haynes v. Shoney's*.

SOURCES

Interviews

Ammerman, David. Former Professor of History, Florida State University. Interview with author April 4, 1995.

Boyd, Mitchell. Former CEO, Shoney's, Inc. Interviews with author Feb. 17, May 8, May 14, June 2, 1995.

Brown, Gary. General Counsel, Shoney's, Inc. Interviews with author Feb. 17, May 8, 1995.

Browning, Wayne. Former Vice President of Captain D's, Shoney's, Inc. Interview with author July 1995.

Burr, Charles. Defense Counsel, *Haynes v. Shoney's*. Interview with author March 13, 1995.

Cobb, Carolyn. Named Plaintiff, *Haynes v. Shoney's*. Interview with author May 8, 1995.

Condon, Carol. Paralegal for Plaintiffs' Counsel, *Haynes v. Shoney's*. Interviews with author April 7, April 9, 1995.

Edwards, Tanya Catani. Former Store Manager, Shoney's, Inc. Interviews with author Feb. 2, March 9, 1995.

Edwards, Troy. Former Store Manager, Shoney's, Inc. Interview with author Aug. 14, 1995.

Elliott, Billie. Named Plaintiff, *Haynes v. Shoney's*. Interviews with author May 1991, April 2, 1993, April 21, 1993, Dec. 15, 1993, Dec. 12, 1994, June 27, 1995.

Elliott, Henry. Named Plaintiff, *Haynes v. Shoney's*. Interview with author Dec. 17, 1993.

Feingold, Elaine. Plaintiffs' Counsel, *Haynes v. Shoney's*. Interview with author Jan. 20, 1995.

Finney, James. Director of Systemic Programs, Equal Employment Opportunity Commission. Interview with author May 3, 1995.

Garner, Jerry. Former Division Director, Shoney's, Inc. Interview with author June 8, 1995.

Grant, Billy. History Teacher, Marianna, Fla. Interview with author October 1994.

Goldstein, Barry. Plaintiffs' Counsel, *Haynes v. Shoney's*. Multiple interviews with author 1994–96.

Guess, Francis. Executive Director, Danner Foundation; Executive Vice President, Danner Company. Interview with author Jan. 31, 1995, March 1995.

Harley, Tim. Assistant State's Attorney, Tallahassee, Fla. Interview with author March 1995.

Haynes, Josephine. Named Plaintiff, *Haynes v. Shoney's*. Interview with author June 5, 1995.

Hightower, Donna Mongoven. Named Plaintiff, *Haynes v. Shoney's*. Interview with author March 6, 1995.

Hinson, Mark. Reporter, *Tallahassee Democrat*. Interview with author Oct. 1994.

Hudson-Brown, Karyn. Former Director of Marketing, Specialty Division, Shoney's, Inc. Interview with author Feb. 26, 1995.

Hyde, Dave. Reporter, *Ft. Lauderdale Sun-Sentinel*. Interview with author April 11, 1995.

Johnson, Sharon. Named Plaintiff, *Johnson v. Long*. Interviews with author Oct. 1994, Dec. 12, 1994.

Keel, Beverly. Former Reporter, *Nashville Banner*. Interview with author May 21, 1995.

Lawson, Tony. Plaintiffs' Counsel, *Haynes v. Shoney's*. Interview with author Jan. 19, 1995.

Leppink, Linus. Former Vice President of Purchasing, Shoney's, Inc. Interviews with author April 28, May 3, May 20, 1995.

Livingston, Don. Former General Counsel, Equal Employment Opportunity Commission. Interview with author June 7, 1995.

Lowery, Joseph. Executive Director, Southern Christian Leadership Conference. Interview with author May 17, 1995.

Madison, Isaiah. Former Intern, Southern Christian Leadership Conference. Interview with author June 9, 1995.

Martin, Mary Ellen. Law Clerk/Attorney for Plaintiffs' Counsel, *Haynes v. Shoney's*. Interview with author March 16, 1995.

Mayeda, Mari. Plaintiffs' Counsel, *Ridgeway v. Denny's*. Interview with author Jan. 20, 1995.

Maxwell, Paul. Federal Bureau of Investigation, Panama City, Fla. Interview with author Aug. 15, 1995.

O'Rourke, Pat. Attorney, Nashville, Tenn. Interview with author April 17, 1995.

Peacock, Paul. Former Resident, Marianna, Fla. Interview with author March 16, 1995.

Raby, Larry. Plaintiffs' Counsel, *Johnson v. Long*. Interviews with author Oct. 17, 1994, Jan. 5, 1995.

Roberts, Laurie. Interview with author Jan. 23, 1995.

Roberts, Leonard. Former CEO and Chairman of the Board, Shoney's, Inc.; President, Radio Shack. Interviews with author Oct. 26, Dec. 8, 1994, Jan. 23, May 31, 1995.

Robertson, Charles. Robertson Investment Company. Interview with author March 2, 1995.

Schoenbaum, Alex. Founder and Former Senior Chairman of the Board of Directors, Shoney's, Inc. Interview with author April 25, 1995.

Seigenthaler, John. Former Publisher, *Nashville Tennessean;* Executive Director, The Freedom Forum. Interview with author May 21, 1995.

Smith, Sam. Plaintiffs' Counsel, *Haynes v. Shoney's.* Interview with author March 15, 1995.

Spoleta, Gary. Former Chief Operating Officer and President, Shoney's, Inc. Interview with author March 9, 1995.

Suggs, Paul. Former Captain D's Area Supervisor, Robertson Investment Company. Interview with author June 26, 1995.

Thomas, Sheila. Plaintiffs' Counsel, *Haynes v. Shoney's.* Interview with author Jan. 20, 1995.

Vinson, Roger. U.S. District Judge, Northern District of Florida, Pensacola Division. Interview with author May 8, 1995.

Wachtel, Dave. Former CEO, Shoney's, Inc. CEO, O'Charley's Restaurants. Interview with author May 26, 1995.

Warren, Esther. Interview with author, March 1995.

Warren, Thomas. Plaintiffs' Counsel, *Haynes v. Shoney's.* Multiple interviews with author, 1990–1996.

Wiggins, Bob. Attorney, Birmingham, Ala. Interview with author April 6, 1995.

Wooten, Ron. Corporate Loan Officer, First Union Bank, Charlotte, N.C. Interview with author March 10, 1995.

Correspondence

Boyd, Mitchell. Fax to author, May 8, 1995.

Danner, Raymond L. Letter to Julius L. Chambers, NAACP Legal Defense and Educational Fund, Nov. 7, 1989.

———. Letter to Shoney's, Inc. Board of Directors, March 28, 1995.

———. Letter to Shoney's, Inc. Board of Directors, March 29, 1995.

Edwards, Tanya Catani. Letter to author, Sept. 9, 1995.

Elliott, Billie. Letter to author, Jan. 3, 1994.

Goldstein, Barry. Letter to Donald Livingston, EEOC, July 19, 1991.

Marshall, Betty J. Letter to author, June 5, 1995.

McLemore, C. K. Letter to author, June 14, 1995.

Powell, Charles A. III. Letter to author, Nov. 21, 1994.

———. Letter to author, March 21, 1995

———. Letter to author, June 29, 1995.

———. Letter to Tanya Catani Edwards, copy to the author, July 31, 1995.

Roberts, Leonard. Letter to Jeanne Davis, Athens Probation Office, Oct. 29, 1990.

Tallent, Stephen E. Letter to author, June 5, 1995.

Warren, Thomas. Letter to Barry V. Frederick, June 17, 1992.

———. "The Real FSU Pioneer." Letter to the editor, *Tallahassee Democrat*, 1983.

Watkins, Stephen H., Letter to Ray Danner, Feb. 1, 1995.

———. Letter to Charles Powell, May 24, 1995.

———. Letter to Ray Danner, June 4, 1995.

———. Letter to Stephen E. Tallent, June 10, 1995.

———. Letter to C. K. McLemore, June 16, 1995.

Books, Magazine Articles, News Releases, Reports, Government Documents, Legal Rulings

Anderson, Charles-Edwards. "Shoney's Suit: 'Largest Ever' Bias Suit Brought against Restaurant Chain." *American Bar Association Journal*, August 1989, 18, 20.

Bacon, Donald. "See You In Court: Employee Suits against Employers Are Turning the Workplace into a Legal Combat Zone." *Nation's Business*, July 1989, 17–28.

B&C Associates. "Shoney's, Inc.: A Corporate Image Campaign." High Point, N.C.: B&C Associates, 1989.

Carlino, Bill. "Danner Exits Shoney's, Sells Shares." *Nation's Restaurant News*, March 22, 1993, 1, 66.

———. "Family Chains Wage War in New Territory: Executive Shake-ups, Racial-discrimination Charges Keep Segment up in Arms." *Nation's Restaurant News*, Aug. 2, 1993, 112, 114.

———. "Roberts-Shoney's Divorce Stirs Questions, Debate." *Nation's Restaurant News*, Jan. 4, 1993, 1, 81.

———. "Shoney's Nixes Danner Deal: Market Price Proviso Thwarts Stock Buyback." *Nation's Restaurant News*, July 12, 1993, 1, 57.

Commonwealth Group. "Report of Survey on Racial Staffing Practices of Shoney's Restaurants." May 2, 1991.

Cooper, Ron. "Shoney's Chairman Does Business 'The Danner Way'." *Louisville Business First*, May 25, 1987, 12–13.

Cox, Dale Alan. "Indian War." *Marianna Area Digest*, Winter 1986, 16–19.

"Danner Feasts on Food Franchising." *Business Week*, Oct. 23, 1971, 120.

Danner Foundation. "Danner Foundation Recipients. A Representative Listing." 1991.

Davis, Abraham, and Barbara Luck Graham. *The Supreme Court, Race, and Civil Rights.* Thousand Oaks, Calif.: Sage Publications, 1995.

Eastland, Terry. "Toward a Real Restoration of Civil Rights." *Commentary,* November 1989, 25–29.

Engardio, Pete. "Shoney's: Bursting Out of Its Dixie Boundaries." *Business Week,* April 15, 1985, 124–25.

Epstein, Richard Allen. *Forbidden Grounds: The Case against Employment Discrimination Laws.* Cambridge, Mass.: Harvard University Press, 1992.

Equal Employment Opportunity Commission, Office of Communications and Legislative Affairs. "Office of Program Operations Enforcement Statistics FY1981–FY1991." 1993.

———. "Office of General Counsel Litigation Statistics FY1981–FY1991." 1993.

Ettel, Herb. *Trial Lawyers Doing Public Justice 1993.* Washington, D.C.: Trial Lawyers for Public Justice Foundation, 1994.

Gewirtz, Paul. "Discrimination Endgame: A Civil Rights Summer Primer." *New Republic,* Aug. 12, 1991, 18–23.

Glenn v. General Motors Corp. 658 F. Supp. 918 (N.D.Ala. 1986).

———. 841 F.2d 1567 (11th Cir. 1988).

Greenberg, Jack. *Crusaders in the Courts: How a Dedicated Band of Lawyers Fought for the Civil Rights Revolution.* New York: Basic Books, 1994.

Hayes, Jack. "Leonard H. Roberts: From Humble Beginnings in Chicago to the Executive Suite of Shoney's, Charismatic Chief Executive Fights Hard to Overcome Any Obstacles to Succeed." *Nation's Restaurant News,* Sept. 16, 1991.

Hertzberg, Hendrik. "Wounds of Race." *New Republic,* July 10, 1989, 4, 42.

Hyde, Dave. "End Zone: The Tragic Story of Calvin Patterson, FSU's First Black Football Player." *Ft. Lauderdale Sun-Sentinel, Sunshine: The Magazine of South Florida,* Jan. 1, 1995, 12–17.

Jackson County, Fla. Chamber of Commerce. "Jackson County Demographic Information." September 1992.

———. "General Information." August 1992.

———. "Major Employers in Jackson County, Florida." September 1992.

———. "Marianna's Founding." Undated.

Jones, James P. *F.S.U. One Time! A History of Seminole Football.* Tallahassee, Fla.: Sentry Press, 1973.

Kohn, Howard. "Service with a Sneer: The Denny's Chain Is Paying Millions to Black Customers Discriminated against in Its Restaurants: Was

Racism an Institutional Strategy for Turning Profits?" *New York Times Magazine,* Nov. 6, 1994, 42–47, 58, 78, 81.

Konrad, Walecia. "Shoney's Needs a Recipe for Succession." *Business Week,* Dec. 25, 1989, 52.

Mauro, Tony. "Polls Dictate Juvenile Death Penalty Debate." *Legal Times,* April 3, 1989.

McGovern, James R. *Anatomy of a Lynching: The Killing of Claude Neal.* Baton Rouge: Louisiana State University Press, 1982.

Mitchell, Russell, and Jonathan Ringel. "The SWAT Team of Bias Litigation: Oakland's Saperstein Law Firm Is Leading a New Rush of Employment Discrimination Suits." *Business Week,* Jan. 23, 1995, 88–89.

Naipaul, V. S. *A Turn in the South.* New York: Alfred A. Knopf, 1989.

"Publix Grocery Stores Charged with Discriminating against Women Employees." News release by Saperstein, Goldstein, Demchak & Baller; Thomas A. Warren; and Charles Burr and Sam J. Smith. July 1995.

Phillips, Lyda. "Did Shoney's Make the Right Decision?" *Business Nashville,* July-August 1995, 44–45.

Rains, Patrick, and Lyda Phillips. "You Can't Go Home Again." *Business Nashville,* July-August 1995, 40–43, 45.

"Ray Danner Is Investing in Black Hair-Care Product." *Restaurant Business,* Feb. 10, 1993, 14.

Romeo, Peter. "What Really Happened?" *Restaurant Business,* May 1, 1993, 116–19, 122–23.

Samborn, Randall. "Bias Law Booms." *National Law Journal,* July 27, 1992, 1, 35–37.

Shofner, Jerrell H. *Jackson County, Florida—A History.* Marianna, Fla.: Jackson County Heritage Association, 1985.

Shoney's, Inc. "Ray Danner and Shoney's, Inc. Jointly Announce Agreement for Purchase of Danner's Stock" (news release). March 9, 1993.

———. "Shoney's, Inc. Announces Settlement of Discrimination Lawsuit" (news release). Nov. 3, 1992.

———. *Shoney's, Inc. 1989 Annual Report.* 1990.

———. *Shoney's, Inc. 1990 Annual Report.* 1991.

———. *Shoney's, Inc. 1991 Annual Report.* 1992.

———. *Shoney's, Inc. 1992 Annual Report.* 1993.

———. *Shoney's, Inc. 1993 Annual Report.* 1994.

———. *Shoney's, Inc. 1994 Annual Report.* 1995.

———. *Shoney's, Inc. 1995 Annual Report.* 1996.

"Supreme Court Rulings." *Congressional Digest,* August-September 1990, 201–2, 224.

"Those Brash New Tycoons." *Time*, Sept. 27, 1976, 75.

U.S. General Accounting Office. *Equal Employment Opportunity Commission Closed Discrimination Charges Without Full Investigation: Report to Congressional Requesters.* Washington, D.C.: General Accounting Office, 1987.

U.S. House Committee on Education and Labor. *Report on the Investigation of Civil Rights Enforcement by the Equal Employment Opportunity Commission Based on a Study of Selected District Offices by the Staff of the Committee on Education and Labor.* 99th Congress, 2d session, May 1986.

U.S. House Committee on Education and Labor, Subcommittee on Employment Opportunities. *Equal Employment Opportunity Commission Policies Regarding Goals and Timetables in Litigation Remedies: Hearing Before the Subcommittee on Equal Employment of the Committee on Education and Labor.* 99th Congress, 2d session, March 11, 13 1986.

U.S. House Committee on Education and Labor and the Subcommittee on Civil and Constitutional Rights of the Committee on the Judiciary. *The Civil Rights Act of 1990: Hearings on H.R. 4000.* 101st Congress, 2d sess. 1990.

U.S. Senate Committee on Labor and Human Resources. *The Civil Rights Act of 1990: Report Together With Minority Views.* 101st Congress, 2d sess. 1990.

U.S. v. Warren. 550 F.2d 219 (5th Cir. 1977).

———. 578 F.2d 1058 (5th Cir. 1978).

Williams, Juan. "A Question of Fairness." *The Atlantic Monthly*, February 1987, 71–82.

Newspaper Articles

"A Solid Foundation." Editorial. *Nashville Tennessean*, Dec. 4, 1992.

Amlong, William R. "Ex-Grid Hero's New Foe—The Establishment. The Two Lives of Tommy Warren." *Miami Herald*, Dec. 22, 1975.

"At Shoney's, Details Count." *New York Times*, June 8, 1984.

Baker, Steve. "Shoney's to Restructure: Chain to Cut Back, Focus on Family Restaurants." *Fredericksburg (Va.) Free Lance-Star*, Jan. 17, 1995.

Barciela, Susana. "Eight Florida Women File Discrimination Lawsuit against Publix Stores." *Miami Herald*, July 20, 1995.

———. "Plaintiff: 'I Had Every Intention of Staying.'" *Miami Herald*, Jan. 21, 1996.

————. "Publix Bias Suit Gets OK: Class-Action Status Granted." *Miami Herald*, March 13, 1996.

————. "Women Sue for Discrimination; Publix Says They Chose Their Jobs." *Miami Herald*, Jan. 21, 1996.

Barrett, Paul. "It's Clinton's Town, but Capital Also Eyes Armstrong Williams: A Young Black Republican, He Has Talk Show, Column, Even a Link with Oprah." *Wall Street Journal*, Dec. 29, 1992.

Battle, Bob. "Danner Wins Alger Association Award." *Nashville Banner*, March 18, 1987.

————. "Mitch Boyd Back in Restaurant Business." *Nashville Banner*, May 28, 1992.

———— "Ray Danner, Two Others Form Firm to Manage Portfolios." *Nashville Banner*, June 30, 1988.

————"Self-Made Success Stories Stress Value of Degree." *Nashville Banner*, April 4, 1991.

Baxter, Emme Nelson. "Ex-Labor Chief Joins Danner: Will Continue Involvement in Fulton Government Group." *Nashville Tennessean*, Oct. 28, 1990.

Biskupic, Joan. "How an Era Ended in Civil Rights Law." *Washington Post*, May 24, 1993.

Cadwell, Mike (as told to Fred Girard). "The Class . . . It Became Survival of the Fittest in PE-117." *St. Petersburg Times*, June 10, 1973.

Cannon, Lou. "Women Win $157 Million in Bias Suit: State Farm Insurance Agrees to Record Civil Rights Settlement." *Washington Post*, April 29, 1992.

Carlton, Sue. "Women Accuse Publix of Sex Bias." *St. Petersburg Times*, July 10, 1995.

Cason, Albert. "Danner Selected as One of Ten 'Rags-to-Riches' Executives in Nation." *Nashville Tennessean*, March 13, 1987.

"Company Gets First Black Board Member." *Nashville Banner*, March 21, 1990.

Cronauer, Bill. "The Coach . . . Nothing but Praise From Jones' Ex-Associates." *St. Petersburg Times*, June 10, 1973.

"Danner's Return Bid Boosts Stock." *Nashville Tennessean*, March 31, 1995.

"Danners Saluted at Benefit." *Nashville Tennessean*, Nov. 7, 1992.

de Lisser, Eleena. "Central Figure in Shoney's Bias Suit Seeks to Return as Chairman and Chief." *Wall Street Journal*, March 31, 1995.

————. "Shoney's Taps a Turn-Around Artist, but It's a Long Way Back to Prosperity." *Wall Street Journal*, April 13, 1995.

Duffy, Tom. "Some Players Defend Pre-Spring Program." *St. Petersburg Times*, June 12, 1973.

Duke, Lynne. "Cofounder of Shoney's Quits Following Racial Bias Lawsuit." *Washington Post*, March 12, 1993.

———. "Shoney's Bias Settlement Sends $105 Million Signal." *Washington Post*, Feb. 5, 1993.

Durcanin, Cynthia. "SCLC Signs Affirmative Action Pact with Shoney's: $90 Million Is Pledged in Jobs, Business Deals." *Atlanta Constitution*, Aug. 19, 1989.

Dyckman, Martin. "Lawyers Can Be Heroes Too." *St. Petersburg Times*, April 11, 1993.

Dyckman, Martin, Bill Van Smith, and Bill McGrotha. "The Death of a Football Player." *Miami Herald*, Aug. 20, 1972.

Eastman, Susan. "Reflection by Lawyer Wins Acclaim." *St. Petersburg Times*, July 1, 1993.

Ensley, Gerald. "Later He Paid Desperation's Ultimate Price." *Tallahassee Democrat*, June 2, 1985.

———. "The Pioneers: FSU's First Black Athletes Cleared Paths for Later Heroes, but the Pioneers Recall Constant Pressure and Little Triumph." *Tallahassee Democrat*, June 2, 1985.

Freedberg, Sydney. "Charges of Racial Bias Plague Restaurants: National Chain Denied Blacks Jobs as Waiters, Suit Says." *Miami Herald*, May 28, 1989.

"FSU President Invites NCAA To Investigate." *St. Petersburg Times*. June 13, 1973.

Gaiter, Dorothy J. "Eating Crow: How Shoney's, Belted by a Lawsuit, Found the Path to Diversity." *Wall Street Journal*, April 16, 1996.

Girard, Fred. "Ex-FSU Players Unveil Violations." *St. Petersburg Times*, June 10, 1973.

———. "New Athletic Breed Demands Answers." *St. Petersburg Times*, June 12, 1973.

———. "Players Charge FSU Reneged on Grants." *St. Petersburg Times*, June 11, 1973.

Greenhouse, Linda. "Marshall Says Court's Rulings Imperil Rights." *New York Times*, Sept. 9, 1989.

Gregory, Ed. "Boyd Sees 'Creative' Changes Underway." *Nashville Tennessean*, June 11, 1989.

———. "Co-Founder Mad and He's 'Not Going to Take It Anymore.'" *Nashville Tennessean*, July 1, 1993.

———. "Danner Wants Stock Curbs Eased: Former Chairman Calls for Vote of Shoney's Holders." *Nashville Tennessean*, Sept. 30, 1994.

———. "Danner, Shoney's to Part Company." *Nashville Tennessean*, March 10, 1993.

———. "Insurer Kicks in $10 Million in Discrimination Lawsuit." *Nashville Tennessean*, Nov. 24, 1992.

———. "Shoney's Chief Quits Suddenly: Financial Officer Replaces Roberts." *Nashville Tennessean*, Dec. 18, 1992.

———. Shoney's Row Snubbed by Street." *Nashville Tennessean*, July 1, 1993.

———. "Shoney's Settles Discrimination Suit." *Nashville Tennessean*, Nov. 4, 1992.

———. "Shoney's Showdown Looming." *Nashville Tennessean*, June 30, 1993.

———. "Shoney's Stock Jumps on News of Settlement." *Nashville Tennessean*, Nov. 5, 1992.

Grossman, Laurie. "Shoney's to Buy Holdings Owned by Its Founder: Danner Agrees to Sell Stake of 12 Percent in Transaction Valued at $107 Million." *Wall Street Journal*, March 10, 1993.

Hance, Mary. "Board Ousted CEO at Shoney's: Report." *Nashville Banner*, Dec. 21, 1992.

———. "Danner at Ease as Successor Leads Shoney's." *Nashville Banner*, March 21, 1990.

Harris, Art. "The Man Who Aided Mandela: PR Whiz Bob Brown Melding Money and Civil Rights." *Washington Post*, June 30, 1990.

Hayes, Arthur. "Job-Bias Litigation Wilts under High Court Rulings." *New York Times*, Aug. 22, 1989.

Hill, Retha, and Pierre Thomas. "Plaintiffs Enjoy an Anti-Bias Victory: Secret Service Agents Hope Denny's Multimillion-Dollar Settlement Will Teach Lesson." *Washington Post*, May 25, 1994.

Holewa, Lisa. "EEOC Joins Discrimination Lawsuit against Publix." *Tallahassee Democrat*, Nov. 29, 1995.

Kamen, Al. "Despite Bill's Signing, Fight Has Just Begun: Second Front Opens over Rights Law's Meaning." *Washington Post*, Nov. 22, 1991.

Kaplow, Larry. "Attorney: Job Bias Can Stare You in Face." *Palm Beach Post*, Jan. 16, 1996.

Keel, Beverly. "Another Shoney's Unit Faces Racial Bias Suit." *Nashville Banner*, Nov. 20, 1992.

———. "Shoney's Fights 'Racist' Label: Bias Suit Appears Headed to Trial." *Nashville Banner*, July 16, 1990.

———. "Shoney's Main Course Now Minority Relations." *Nashville Banner*, Nov. 4, 1992.

———. "Shoney's Settlement Cuts $86M in Profits." *Nashville Banner*, Nov. 4, 1992.

———. "Stock Buy Will Ease Shoney's Doubts." *Nashville Banner*, March 10, 1993.

————, and Mary Hance. "New Chief Sees Shoney's as National Chain." *Nashville Banner*, Dec. 22, 1989.

Kemp, Evan. "Rights and Quotas, Theory and Practice." *Washington Post*, Dec. 8, 1992.

Kenworthy, Tom. "Rights Bill Passes House, May Be Nullified by Veto." *Washington Post*, August 4, 1990.

Kuhn, Brad. "Sex-Bias Suit against Publix a Class Action." *Orlando Sentinel*, March 13, 1996.

Leisner, Pat. "Publix Faces Sex-Discrimination Lawsuit. *Tallahassee Democrat*, July 20, 1995.

Martin, Tim. "Chain Raises Danner's Dander as Buyout Deal Falls Through." *Nashville Tennessean*, July 1, 1993.

Martz, Ron. "The Metamorphosis of Tommy Warren." *St. Petersburg Times*, 1975.

Mathews, Jay. "Denny's Says Black Firm Will Own Forty-seven Outlets: Restaurant Chain Responds to Allegations of Racial Bias." *Washington Post*, Nov. 9, 1994.

————. "Denny's Tackles a Stained Image: Fighting Bias Charges, Chairman Forges Links with Rights Leaders." *Washington Post*, Aug. 1, 1993.

McCampbell, Candy. "Franchising Tops Shoney's Growth Menu." *Nashville Tennessean*, 1990.

————. "Shoney's Chief Caters to Customer." *Nashville Tennessean*, Jan. 13, 1991.

McCarthy, Michael, and Glenn Ruffenach. "Shoney's Chief Resigns in Move Surprising Board." *Wall Street Journal*, Dec. 18, 1992.

Patino, José. "Jailhouse Bottom a Shabby Sight." *Jackson County Floridan*, Dec. 12, 1993.

Pratt, James, and Joel Kaplan. "Boner, Shoney's Linkup Dates to Summer of '81." *Nashville Tennessean*, Sept. 29, 1995.

————. "Boner's $50 Could Reap $247,000: Motel-Restaurant Investment; No Liability if Business Fails." *Nashville Tennessean*, Aug. 22, 1985.

————. "Fulton Buys a Shoney's, Leases It Back." *Nashville Tennessean*, 1985.

Pudlow, Jan. "Marianna Couple's Stand Was a Victory for Thousands." *Tallahassee Democrat*, Feb. 7, 1993.

Pulley, Brett. "Strained Family: Culture of Racial Bias at Shoney's Underlies Chairman's Departure: Officer Was Ousted as He Strove Diligently to Alter Restaurant Chain's Ways." *Wall Street Journal*, Dec. 21, 1992.

"Ray Danner One of Richest Men in U.S." *Nashville Banner*, Oct. 15, 1985.

Rothfeld, Charles. "Rulings on Job Bias: Chilling Effect on Lawsuits." *New York Times*, Oct. 27, 1989.

Shanor, Charles A. "Thomas's Record at the EEOC." *Washington Post,* Sept. 9, 1991.

Schiffman, James. "DWG Vice Chairman Resigns in Dispute with Posner in Latest Blow to Company." *Wall Street Journal,* Sept. 6, 1989.

Schulze, Cathy. "Shoney's Must Act in Maturity, Chairman Says." *Nashville Banner,* March 8, 1988.

Sherburne, Robert. "Two Pictures of Shoney's Ray Danner." *Nashville Tennessean,* Nov. 29, 1992.

"Shoney's, Ex-CEO in Bias-Charge Flap." *USA Today,* Dec. 22,1992.

Spencer, Anne. "People Live in Homes in Dire Need of Repair." *Jackson County Floridan,* Dec. 12, 1993.

Straight, Cathy. "A Family Approach to Fitness: Father, Son Work It All Out at Club." *Nashville Tennessean,* March 19, 1991.

Thomas, Pierre. "Denny's to Settle Bias Suit: $45 Million Awarded in Class-Action Suits in Maryland, California." *Washington Post,* May 24, 1994.

"Three Tennesseans Listed among Richest in U.S." *Nashville Tennessean,* Oct. 11, 1988.

Tierney, Mike. "Shively: Quit with Injury, Loses Scholarship." *St. Petersburg Times,* June 11, 1973.

Torpy, Bill. "Lawsuit Alleges Bias by Shoney's Local Franchisee: Employee Applications Coded to Identify Blacks, Attorneys Say." *Atlanta Journal and Constitution,* Nov. 17, 1990.

"TWST Names Danner Best Chief Executive Restaurant Industry." *The Wall Street Transcript,* Feb. 18, 1985.

West, Phil. "Shoney's Chief Credits Hard Work." *Nashville Banner,* 1991.

Whitley, Bob. "Chicken Wire Worst of All, Verble Says." *St. Petersburg Times,* June 11, 1973 (reprinted from the *Charlotte Observer,* June 10, 1973).

Williams, Armstrong. "Say It Loud, I'm Right-Wing and Proud." *Washington Post,* Aug. 20, 1995.

Wood, Thomas. "Ambition Serves Up Success: New Shoney's CEO Has Come a Long Way." *Nashville Tennessean,* April 16, 1995.

———. Co-Founder Cool to Danner Bid: Shoney's No. 1 Institutional Owner Is, Too." *Nashville Tennessean,* April 6, 1995.

———. "Danner Insists He's Needed: Franchise Group Agrees." *Nashville Tennessean,* April 1, 1995.

———. "Danner Pulls Offer to Return to Shoney's." *Nashville Tennessean,* April 7, 1995.

———. "Sonic Chairman Chosen as New Shoney's CEO." *Nashville Tennessean,* April 12, 1995.

———. "Shoney's Pick Helps Stock Price." *Nashville Tennessean*,
April 13, 1995.

———. "Wanted: CEO Job at Shoney's: Danner Seeks Former Position for
$1 a year." *Nashville Tennessean*, March 30, 1995.

Wozniak, Lara. "California Suit Gave Women 'a Big Whip.'" *St. Petersburg Times*, March 24, 1996.

———. "Publix Team Brash, yet Reserved." *St. Petersburg Times*, March 24, 1996.

———. "Lawyers Travel Different Paths." *St. Petersburg Times*, March 24, 1996.

———. "A Law Firm's Commitment to a Cause: A California Law Firm Gains a National Reputation by Suing Companies for Discrimination— and Winning. Its Latest Target: Publix Super Markets." *St. Petersburg Times*, March 24, 1996.

Legal Documents

Danner v. Danner. Circuit Court of Davidson County, Tenn. No. 76346.
   Pleadings and Orders
     Petition for Absolute Divorce. Nov. 6, 1974.
     Answer and Cross Bill. Nov. 18, 1974.
     Answer to Cross Bill. Nov. 22, 1974.
     Order. Jan. 29, 1975.
     Certificate of Divorce or Annulment. Feb. 3, 1975.
   Depositions
     Danner, Mrs. Raymond. Jan. 28, 1975, Nashville, Tenn.
     Dunn, Barbara. Jan. 28, 1975, Nashville, Tenn.
     Wilson, Donna Danner. Jan. 28, 1975, Nashville, Tenn.
     Wilson, Gail Danner. Jan. 28, 1975, Nashville, Tenn.

Johnson v. Long. U.S. District Court for the Middle District of Alabama, Northern Division. Civil Action 85-H-1183-N.
   Pleadings and Orders
     Complaint. Oct. 1, 1985.
     Consent Decree and Order. Dec. 26, 1985.
     Stipulation for Entry and Final Judgment Decree, and Writ of Injunction. Dec. 26, 1985.
   Depositions
     Johnson, Sharon. Nov. 11, 1985, Montgomery, Ala.
     Johnston, Brenda. Dec. 12, 1985, Montgomery, Ala.
     Shaw, Harrell. Dec. 9, 1985, Montgomery, Ala.

Shaw, Cathy. Nov. 22, 1985, Montgomery, Ala.

Short, Patricia. Nov. 26, 1985, Montgomery, Ala.

Yager, Eugene. Dec. 9, 1985, Montgomery, Ala.

Shores v. Publix Super Markets Inc. U. S. District Court, Middle District of Florida, Tampa Division. 95-1162-CIV-T-25E.

Pleadings and Orders

First Amended Complaint: Injunctive Relief Sought and Demand for Jury Trial. Oct. 11, 1995.

Order on Plaintiffs' Motion for Class Certification. March 12, 1996.

Haynes v. Shoney's. U.S. District Court, Northern District of Florida, Pensacola Division. PCA-89-30093-RV.

Pleadings and Orders (organized chronologically by date filed)

April 5, 1989. Plaintiffs' Class Action Complaint.

April 27, 1989. Defendant Raymond Danner's Motion to Dismiss Plaintiffs' Complaint.

April 27, 1989. Defendant Raymond Danner's Memorandum of Law in Support of His Motion to Dismiss the Plaintiffs' Complaint Due to Lack of *In Personam* Jurisdiction and Insufficiency of Service of Process.

April 28, 1989. Defendant Shoney's, Inc. Response to Motion to Admit Barry Goldstein *Pro Hac Vice.*

April 28, 1989. Plaintiffs' Request for Barry Goldstein to Appear *Pro Hac Vice.*

May 16, 1989. Plaintiffs' First Amended Complaint.

May 16, 1989. Plaintiffs' Response in Opposition to Defendant Danner's Motion to Dismiss Plaintiffs' Complaint Due to Lack of *In Personam* Jurisdiction.

May 30, 1989. Plaintiffs' Motion to Compel Defendants Shoney's, Inc. and Ray Danner to Preserve and Maintain Records.

May 30, 1989. Order Granting Request for Barry Goldstein to Appear *Pro Hac Vice.*

May 30, 1989. Order Denying Motion to Dismiss Plaintiffs' Complaint.

June 1, 1989. Defendant Robertson Investment Co.'s Answer to First Amended Complaint.

June 1, 1989. Defendant Raymond Danner's Answer to First Amended Complaint.

June 7, 1989. Defendant Shoney's Answer and Affirmative Defense to Amended Complaint.

July 3, 1989. Plaintiffs' Motion for Class Certification.

July 6, 1989. Transcript of Hearing.

July 12, 1989. Defendant Shoney's Emergency Motion for Protective Order and for Imposition of Sanctions.

July 14, 1989. Defendant Raymond Danner's Memorandum in Opposition to Plaintiffs' Motion for Class Certification.

July 14, 1989. Defendant Raymond Danner's Motion for Summary Judgment.

July 14, 1989. Defendant Raymond Danner's Memorandum as to Issues in the Case and in Support of His Motion for Summary Judgment.

July 17, 1989. Defendant Robertson Investment Co.'s Statement of Material Facts.

July 21, 1989. Defendant Robertson Investment Co.'s Motion for Protective Order and for Imposition of Sanctions with Memorandum of Law.

July 25, 1989. Plaintiffs' Motion for Summary Judgment on the Issue of Liability.

July 25, 1989. Plaintiffs' Memorandum in Support of Motion for Summary Judgment, with Ninety-Three Exhibits attached.

July 26, 1989. Defendant Shoney's, Inc.'s Supplement to Emergency Motion for Protective Order and for Imposition of Sanctions.

July 31, 1989. Defendant Robertson Investment Co.'s Motion for Partial Summary Judgment with Supporting Memorandum of Law.

Aug. 8, 1989. Plaintiffs' Response in Opposition to Defendant Shoney's, Inc.'s Emergency Motion for Protective Order and for Imposition of Sanctions.

Aug. 8, 1989. Plaintiffs' Response in Opposition to Robertson Investment Co.'s Motion for Protective Order and for Imposition of Sanctions.

Aug. 9, 1989. Supplement to Plaintiffs' Memorandum of Law in Support of Plaintiffs' Motion for Class Certification.

Aug. 21, 1989. Stipulation and Joint Motion for Stay of Proceedings during Pendency of Settlement Negotiations.

Sept. 8, 1989. Plaintiffs' Second Amended Complaint.

April 30, 1990. Plaintiffs' Supplemental Memorandum in Support of Motion for Summary Judgment on the Issue of Liability.

April 30, 1990. Plaintiffs' Statement of Material Facts Not in Dispute with Respect to Plaintiffs' Motion for Summary Judgment on the Issue of Liability.

April 30, 1990. Plaintiffs' Second Supplement to and Amendment of their Motion for Class Certification.

April 30, 1990. Order, Consented Motion to Defer Consideration of and Ruling on Emergency Motion of Defendant Shoney's for Protective Order and for Sanctions.

May 14, 1990. Plaintiffs' Motion in Opposition to Defendant Raymond Danner's Motion for Summary Judgment.

May 15, 1990. Plaintiffs' Emergency Motion for Protective Order and to Quash Subpoenas.

May 18, 1990. Defendant Robertson Investment Co.'s Statement of Material Facts as to Which There are Genuine Issues to be Tried with Respect to Plaintiffs' Motion for Summary Judgment.

May 21, 1990. Defendant Raymond Danner's Response to Plaintiffs' Statement of Material Facts Relative to the Entry of Summary Judgment against Raymond Danner.

May 29, 1990. Defendant Shoney's, Inc.'s Reply to Plaintiffs' Response in Opposition to Defendant Shoney's, Inc.'s Emergency Motion for Protective Order and for Imposition of Sanctions.

June 6, 1990. Plaintiffs' Supplement and Response to Shoney's Reply regarding Shoney's Emergency Motion for Protective Order and Imposition of Sanctions and Plantiffs' Response to Shoney's Request for an Evidentiary Hearing.

June 11, 1990. Defendant Shoney's Motion for Summary Judgment on Section 1981 Claims.

June 11, 1990. Defendant Shoney's Brief in Support of Its Motion for Summary Judgment on Section 1981 Claims.

June 11, 1990. Defendant Shoney's Opposition to Class Certification and Request for Evidentiary Hearing.

June 18, 1990. Defendant Shoney's Reply to Plaintiffs' Supplement and Response to Shoney's Reply Regarding Shoney's Emergency Motion for Protective Order and Imposition of Sanctions and Plaintiffs' Response to Shoney's Request for an Evidentiary Hearing.

June 29, 1990. Plaintiffs' Supplement by Submission of Twelve EEOC Determinations Against Robertson Investment Co. to Plaintiffs' Opposition to Defendants' Motions for Summary Judgment and Motion to Dismiss and in Support of Plaintiffs' Motion for Summary Judgment.

July 7, 1990. Plaintiffs' Opposition to Shoney's Summary Judgment Motion.

July 27, 1990. Defendant Shoney's Reply to the Plaintiffs' Opposition to Shoney's Motion for Summary Judgment on Section 1981 Claims.

Aug. 14, 1990. Defendant Shoney's Motion for Summary Judgment as to All Claims Asserted by Plaintiff Dewitt Michael Nelson.

Aug. 27, 1990. Plaintiffs' Reply to Defendants' Opposition to Motion for Class Certification.

Aug. 27, 1990. Plaintiffs' Supplement by Submission of a Letter Written by Defendant R. L. Danner in Support of Plaintiffs' Motion for Summary Judgment on the Issue of Liability and in Support of Plaintiffs' Briefs in Opposition to Shoney's Motion for Summary Judgment.

Sept. 5, 1990. Plaintiffs' Emergency Motion to Enforce the Court's Aug. 18, 1989, Order and Plaintiffs' Petition for Order to Show Cause Why Defendant Shoney's, Inc. Should not be Held in Contempt for Violation of the Court's Order.

Sept. 6, 1990. Defendant Shoney's Motion for Summary Judgment as to All Claims Asserted by Plaintiff Buddy Lee Bonsall.

Sept. 6, 1990. Defendant Shoney's Brief in Support of Motion for Summary Judgment as to the Title VII Claims of Buddy Lee Bonsall.

Sept. 27, 1990. Plaintiffs' Brief in Opposition to Shoney's Motion for Summary Judgment as to the Title VII Claims of Plaintiff Dewitt Nelson.

Sept. 27, 1990. Plaintiffs' Response to Shoney's Statement of Facts Filed in Support of Shoney's Motion for Summary Judgment regarding the Title VII Claims of Plaintiff Dewitt Nelson.

Oct. 3, 1990. Defendant Shoney's Motion for Summary Judgment as to All Claims Asserted by Plaintiff Denise Riley.

Oct. 12, 1990. Plaintiffs' Brief in Opposition to Shoney's Motion for Summary Judgment as to the Title VII Claims of Plaintiff Buddy Bonsall.

Oct. 12, 1990. Plaintiffs' Response to Shoney's Statement of Facts Filed in Support of Shoney's Motion for Summary Judgment Re: the Title VII Claims of Plaintiff Buddy Bonsall.

Oct. 22, 1990. Plaintiffs' Response to Shoney's Statement of Facts Filed in Support of Shoney's Motion for Summary Judgment Re: the Title VII Claims of Plaintiff Denise Riley.

Oct. 22, 1990. Plaintiffs' Brief in Opposition to Shoney's Motion for Summary Judgment as to the Title VII Claims of Plaintiff Denise Riley.

Nov. 15, 1990. Defendant Shoney's Memorandum of Points and Authorities in Opposition to Plaintiffs' Motion for Summary Judgment.

Nov. 15, 1990. Defendant Shoney's Notice of Filing of Materials in Support of Defendant Shoney's Memorandum of Points and

Authorities in Opposition to Plaintiffs' Motion for Summary Judgment.

Nov. 15, 1990. Plaintiffs' Sur-Reply to Defendants Shoney's and Raymond Danner's Responses to Plaintiffs' Class Certification Reply.

Dec. 17, 1990. Plaintiffs' Reply to Defendant Shoney's Memorandum of Points and Authorities in Opposition to Plaintiffs' Motion for Summary Judgment.

Dec. 20, 1990. Defendant Robertson Investment's Motion for Summary Judgment on Plaintiffs' Section 1981 Claims, with Supporting Memorandum of Law.

Dec. 21, 1990. Plaintiffs' Supplemental Brief in Opposition to Defendants Shoney's and Raymond Danner's Motions for Summary Judgment on the Plaintiffs' Section 1981 Claims.

Dec. 21, 1990. Defendant Raymond Danner's Notice of Filing of Affidavits of Mary Fiddler, Lou Wright, and Vernon Edens.

Dec. 26, 1990. Plaintiffs' Emergency Motion to Strike Defendant Shoney's Replies to Plaintiffs' Opposition to Shoney's Motions for Summary Judgment as to the Title VII Claims of Plaintiffs Nelson and Riley.

Dec. 31, 1990. Plaintiffs' Emergency Motion to Exclude Evidence Because of Shoney's Improper Conduct and to Bar Such Conduct in the Future.

Dec. 31, 1990. Plaintiffs' Memorandum in Support of Plaintiffs' Emergency Motion to Exclude Evidence Because of Shoney's Improper Conduct and to Bar Such Conduct in the Future.

Jan. 3, 1991. Defendant Shoney's Response to Plaintiffs' Emergency Motion to Exclude Evidence Because of Shoney's Improper Conduct and to Bar Such Conduct in the Future.

Jan. 3, 1991. Transcript of Hearing.

Jan. 4, 1991. Order on Hearing of Jan. 3, 1991.

Jan. 11, 1991. Plaintiffs' Reply to Shoney's Response to Plaintiffs' Emergency Motion to Exclude Evidence Because of Shoney's Improper Conduct and to Bar Such Conduct in the Future.

Jan. 15, 1991. Order Denying Emergency Motion to Exclude Evidence Because of Shoney's Improper Conduct and to Bar Such Conduct in the Future, with Memorandum.

Feb. 8, 1991. Plaintiffs' Third Amended Complaint.

May 20, 1991. Motion of the Equal Employment Opportunity Commission for Leave to File a Brief as Amicus Curiae.

Aug. 27, 1991. Defendant Shoney's Notice of Filing Declaration in Support of Shoney's Emergency Motion for Protective Order and for Imposition of Sanctions.

Sept. 4, 1991. Order Denying EEOC Motion for Leave to File a Brief as Amicus Curiae.

Sept. 11, 1991. Plaintiffs' Response to Shoney's Notice of Filing Declaration in Support of Shoney's Emergency Motion for Protective Order and for Imposition of Sanctions.

Sept. 18, 1991. Defendant Robertson Investment's Motion to Strike EEOC Determinations, and Memorandum in Support.

Sept. 18 and 19. Transcript of Hearing.

Sept. 26, 1991. Letter from Plaintiffs' Attorney Warren Re: Withdrawal from Representation of Plaintiff Debora Newton.

Sept. 27, 1991. Order on Various Motions, including Denial of Defendants' Emergency Motion for Protective Order and for Imposition of Sanctions.

Sept. 27, 1991. Order for Pretrial Conference and Setting Trial.

Oct. 4, 1991. Plaintiffs' Opposition to Defendant Robertson Investment's Motion to Strike EEOC Determinations.

Nov. 20, 1991. Defendant Shoney's Notice of Filing Deposition of Tanya Lynn Edwards and Original Deposition of Thomas A. Warren in Support of Defendant Shoney's Opposition to Plaintiffs' Motion for Class Certification and Request for Evidentiary Hearing and in Support of Defendants' Emergency Motion for Protective Order and for Imposition of Sanctions.

Nov. 20, 1991. Defendant Shoney's Motion for Civil Contempt and for Sanctions Pursuant to Rule 37 Fed.R.Civ.P.

Nov. 20 and 21, 1991. Transcript of Class Certification Hearing.

Nov. 27, 1991. Defendant Shoney's Brief on the Nonapplicability of the Civil Rights Act of 1991.

Dec. 12, 1991. Plaintiffs' Opposition to Defendant Shoney's Motion for Civil Contempt and for Sanctions Pursuant to Rule 37 Fed.R.Civ.P.

Dec. 16, 1991. Plaintiffs' Motion for the Court to Rule that the Civil Rights Act of 1991 Applies to This Action.

Dec. 16, 1991. Plaintiffs' Response to Shoney's Statement of Facts in Support of Motion for Summary Judgment.

Dec. 16, 1991. Plaintiffs' Opposition to Shoney's Motion for Summary Judgment on Claims of Robertson Investment Plaintiffs.

Dec. 19, 1991. Defendant Shoney's Notice of Non-Abandonment of Issue of Ethical Adequacy of Class Representation.

Dec. 30, 1991. Defendant Raymond Danner's Memorandum of Law in Opposition to Plaintiffs' Motion for the Court to Rule That the Civil Rights Act of 1991 Applies to This Action.

March 12, 1992. Order Approving Prospective Application but Denying Retroactive Application of Civil Rights Act of 1991.

March 20, 1992. Plaintiffs' Response in Opposition to Shoney's Motion for Protective Order as to Depositions Noticed for March 18–20, 1992.

April 8, 1992. Defendant Shoney's Emergency Motion for Protective Order.

April 10, 1992. Plaintiffs' Response to Shoney's Emergency Motion for Protective Order.

May 15, 1992. Plaintiffs' Trial Brief and Legal Argument.

May 15, 1992. Plaintiffs' Pretrial Stipulation and Exhibits.

May 15, 1992. Plaintiffs' Proposed Findings of Fact Re: Defendants' Robertson Investment Co., Roger Danner, and Charles Robertson.

May 15, 1992. Plaintiffs' Proposed Findings of Fact Re: Defendants Shoney's, Inc. and Raymond Danner.

May 15, 1992. Defendant Shoney's Proposed Finding of Fact and Conclusions of Law.

May 15, 1992. Defendant Robertson Investment Co.'s Trial Brief.

May 15, 1992. Defendant Shoney's, Inc.'s Trial Brief.

June 22, 1992. Class Certification Order.

June 29, 1992. Order Regarding Summary Judgment on Section 1981 and Title VII claims.

Oct. 10, 1992. Order Granting Provisional Consent Decree, *Elliott v. Robertson Investment.*

Nov. 3, 1992. Stipulation of Settlement and Order of Provisional Entry of Consent Decree, *Haynes v. Shoney's.*

Dec. 17, 1992. Order Approving Final Consent Decree, *Elliott v. Robertson Investment.*

Jan. 25, 1993. Order Approving Consent Decree, *Haynes v. Shoney's.*

Depositions

Ball, Howard. Oct. 28–31, 1991, Nashville, Tenn.

Barbero, Kim. Nov. 7, 1990, Panama City, Fla.

Bell, Deborah. Nov. 5, 1990, Tallahassee, Fla.

Bland, James. Dec. 12, 1991, Nashville, Tenn.

Blower, Phyllis. June 7, 1991, Memphis, Tenn.

Bonsall, Buddy. June 27, 1989, Tallahassee, Fla.

Browning, Royce. Feb. 3, 1992, Nashville, Tenn.

Christian, Don. Jan. 15, 1991, Nashville, Tenn.

Cobb, Carolyn. March 18, 1991, Nashville, Tenn.

Cochran, Melkannah. March 19, 1991, Nashville, Tenn.

Cooper, Stephanie. Nov. 5, 1990, Tallahassee, Fla.

Corley, John. Nov. 7, 1990, Panama City, Fla.

Cragg, Barbara. Jan. 17, 1991, Nashville, Tenn.

Danner, Raymond. Jan. 7–10, 1992, Nashville, Tenn.

Danner, Roger. March 10, 1992, Panama City, Fla.

Days, Calvin. May 29, 1991, Panama City, Fla.

Dean, Paula. March 26, 1991, Pensacola, Fla.

Edwards, Tanya Lynn (Catani). Nov. 12, 1991, Orlando, Fla.

Elliott, Billie. June 28–29, 1989, Tallahassee, Fla.

Elliott, Henry. June 30, 1989, Tallahassee, Fla.

Forte, Terrell. March 21, 1991, Nashville, Tenn.

Garner, Jerry. Dec. 23, 1991, Irving, Tex.

Gibson, Danny. May 16, 1991, Nashville, Tenn.

Haisten, Mike. Nov. 8, 1990, Panama City, Fla.

Hamilton, Kim (Gilmore). May 29, 1991, Panama City, Fla.

Haynes, Josephine. July 10, 1989, Pensacola, Fla.

Hitchcock, Don. Dec. 11, 1991, Nashville, Tenn.

Hudson-Brown, Karyn. Feb. 5, 1992, Nashville, Tenn.

Hunter, Julia. May 28, 1991, Panama City, Fla.

Herring, Madeline. Nov. 5, 1990, Tallahassee, Fla.

Holley, Tracie. May 28, 1991, Panama City, Fla.

Lepley, Tara. July 29, 1991, Nashville, Tenn.

Leppink, Frank. Dec. 5, 1991, Memphis, Tenn.

Leppink, Linus. Jan. 27, 1992, Nashville, Tenn.

Marks, James Larry. March 12, 1991, Nashville, Tenn.

Maze, Valerie. March 4, 1991, Nashville, Tenn.

McClain, Glenn. Nov. 6, 1990, Tallahassee, Fla.

Miles, Elaine. March 27, 1991, Pensacola, Fla.

Mongoven, Donna. June 26, 1989, Tallahassee, Fla.

Nelson, Dewitt. June 26, 1989, Tallahassee, Fla.

Oglesby, John. May 29, 1991, Panama City, Fla.

Peavy, Phillip. April 27, 1992, Kansas City, Mo.

Pender, John. Jan. 16, 1992, Atlanta, Ga.

Pennington, Richard Charles. Dec. 16, 1991, Hebron, Ky.

Riley, Denise. July 10, 1989, Pensacola, Fla.

Rudolph, Wilma. Dec. 12, 1991, Nashville, Tenn.

Sanders, Steve. Jan. 16, 1991, Nashville, Tenn.

Skelton, Mickey. March 3–5, 1991, May 1–2, 1991, Nashville, Tenn.

Smith, Gwendolyn. Nov. 6, 1990, Tallahassee, Fla.

Spires, Patricia. Nov. 9, 1990, Panama City, Fla.

Thomas, Lester. July 6, 1989, Tallahassee, Fla.

Tompkins, Debra. Nov. 6, 1991, Irving, Tex.

Toney, Terry. Dec. 11, 1991, Nashville, Tenn.

Usrey, James. May 16, 1991, Nashville, Tenn.

Vidrine, Mickey. Dec. 6, 1991, Alexandria, La.

Wachtel, Dave. Feb. 4, 1992, Nashville, Tenn.

Warren, Thomas. Nov. 15, 1991, Tallahassee, Fla.

Williams, Leonard Charles. July 11, 1989, Pensacola, Fla.

Yager, Eugene. Jan. 13, 1992, Montgomery Ala.

INDEX